ORGANIZING AGAINST DEMOCRACY

Organizing Against Democracy investigates some of the most important challenges modern democracies face, filling a distinctive gap in the literature, both empirically and theoretically. Ellinas examines the attempts of three of the most extreme European far right parties to establish roots in local societies, and the responses of democratic actors. He offers a theory of local party development to analyze the many factors affecting the evolution of far right parties at the subnational level.

Using extraordinarily rich data, the author examines the "lives" of local far right party organizations in Greece, Germany and Slovakia, studying thousands of party activities and interviewing dozens of party leaders and functionaries, as well as antifascists. He goes on to explore how and why extreme parties succeed in some local settings, while, in others, they fail.

This book broadens our understanding of right-wing extremism, illuminating the factors limiting its corrosiveness.

ANTONIS A. ELLINAS is Associate Professor of Political Science at the University of Cyprus. He authored *The Media and the Far Right in Western Europe* and co-authored *The European Commission and Bureaucratic Autonomy*, both published by Cambridge University Press.

ORGANIZING AGAINST DEMOCRACY

The Local Organizational Development of Far Right Parties in Greece and Europe

ANTONIS A. ELLINAS

University of Cyprus

CAMBRIDGE
UNIVERSITY PRESS

CAMBRIDGE
UNIVERSITY PRESS

University Printing House, Cambridge CB2 8BS, United Kingdom

One Liberty Plaza, 20th Floor, New York, NY 10006, USA

477 Williamstown Road, Port Melbourne, VIC 3207, Australia

314–321, 3rd Floor, Plot 3, Splendor Forum, Jasola District Centre, New Delhi – 110025, India

79 Anson Road, #06–04/06, Singapore 079906

Cambridge University Press is part of the University of Cambridge.

It furthers the University's mission by disseminating knowledge in the pursuit of education, learning, and research at the highest international levels of excellence.

www.cambridge.org
Information on this title: www.cambridge.org/9781108415149
DOI: 10.1017/9781108227926

First published 2020

Printed in the United Kingdom by TJ International Ltd. Padstow Cornwall

A catalogue record for this publication is available from the British Library.

ISBN 978-1-108-41514-9 Hardback

For Daphne, Irene and Paris

Contents

Figures

Tables

Preface and Acknowledgments

A few days before the killing of an antifascist protester in Charlottesville, Virginia, in August 2017, a resident debated how to confront the neo-Nazi militants who marched through his city. A few days later, he wrote an editorial in the *New York Times* expressing regret that he sat on the fence, promising that next time, he will take a stronger stance against extremism. Facing a similar dilemma, in March 2017, a resident of Saarbrücken, Germany, spent her Saturday morning protesting in front of the city castle against the hosting of the annual conference of the National Democratic Party in her city. Alone at first, the protester thought she was fulfilling her civic duty by quietly holding for hours a small "Never Again" poster in front of the castle. She was later joined by thousands of organized demonstrators whom I observed peacefully protest the presence of the party in their city.

The rise of extremism raises important dilemmas for democratic societies and the purpose of this book is to examine how they resolve them. This book explores how institutional and societal responses to extremist right-wing parties shape their evolution, and, ultimately, their fate, in democratic settings. The different responses to extremism in Charlottesville and Saarbrücken are similar to those of many actors and millions of citizens in different polities and settings. In contested neighborhoods in Leipzig and loud university campuses in California; in the busy streets and colorful squares of Athens and London; in courtrooms in Bratislava and Budapest and legislatures in Berlin and Stockholm, institutional and societal actors are taking action to defend democracy from extremism. Their responses contrast with those of many others, who choose to stay on the sidelines. Institutional or societal inaction might be due to the faith many share in the capacity of democracies to overcome challengers without the need for institutional or societal confrontation. After all, institutional or societal confrontation might seemingly undermine some of the freedoms democratic societies cherish. Inaction might also occur because many do not see extremism as a threat big enough to merit their involvement. Extremism always starts as a marginal phenomenon before it becomes politically important.

The way institutional and societal actors respond to extremism shapes the environments in which extremist groups or parties develop in contemporary democracies. This book systematically traces the evolution of some of these parties by examining how they interact with their national and subnational environments. A large strain of literature on party development tends to underemphasize the importance of these environments. Echoing important and distinct intellectual traditions, this literature largely sees organizational development as an endogenous process driven by the mechanics of organization (Michels 1915) or by the organizational choices political entrepreneurs make (e.g., Kitschelt 2006; Bolleyer 2013). This endogenous dimension of party development is unquestionably important and a considerable amount of the evidence presented in this book highlights the significance of looking inside parties (Berman 1997) to understand how they evolve.

However, the focus on endogenous drivers of party development tends to neglect how environments shape organizations. A long tradition in organizational sociology points to the theoretical limits of this neglect (e.g., Aldrich 2008; Scott 2008). Applied to the type of parties examined here, the emphasis on endogenous aspects of party development overlooks the empirical reality of institutional and societal responses to extremism, implying that they are nearly inconsequential. Moreover, the emphasis on endogenous drivers of political development ascribes a lot more autonomy to extremists to shape their environments than many democracies are willing to afford. Simply put, the neglect of environmental factors suggests that the fate of extremism is sealed by the extremist leaders and functionaries themselves. There is considerable historical evidence pointing to the opposite: that, under certain conditions, even the most troubled democracies can effectively shield themselves from extremism (Capoccia 2005). Rather than denying institutional and societal actors the agency necessary to shape the trajectories of anti-democratic groups, it is best to subject it to social scientific inquiry.

This book brings to the surface a significant amount of new evidence to examine how the interplay of endogenous and environmental factors shapes party developmental outcomes. Theoretically, it seeks to strike a better balance between the endogenous and environmental drivers of party development. Empirically, it takes a very rare look "inside" some of the most extreme far right parties in Europe to understand how these factors affect their development.

The main focus of the empirical analysis is at the subnational level: the book examines how not only national but also subnational extremist right-wing organizations interact with their environments. The focus on the local development of these parties helps highlight the broad array of actors involved in attempts to confront extremism and brings to the surface their varied interactions. The analysis of dozens of interviews with right-wing extremists and their opponents, hundreds of local party organizations and thousands of party activities sheds light on different developmental patterns and distinct outcomes. The data collection for this book started in 2012 and ended in 2018, before the European Parliament and Greek national elections of 2019. Although this book does not focus on electoral results, it provides the necessary tools for analyzing the electoral fortunes and misfortunes of these parties and, more importantly, the interaction between organizational and electoral processes. One major point this book makes is that the fate of extremism cannot easily be foretold by electoral outcomes. After all, all three parties examined here were seemingly relegated to electoral irrelevance before their electoral breakthroughs. This relative indeterminacy might frustrate efforts to come up with neat and parsimonious answers to the questions asked in this book. It might be less frustrating to those who appreciate the complexity of the phenomenon under study and the intricacies of the democratic process.

I unknowingly began this book project in 2012, when the editors of *South European Society and Politics*, Susannah Verney and Anna Bosco, invited me to submit an article on the rise of the Greek Golden Dawn. Since then I have incurred many debts. Throughout the many phases of this project I received considerable institutional help. The basic idea for the book came when I was a visiting fellow at the LSE's Hellenic Observatory in 2015 and the final parts of the book were drafted in 2018 during another visiting fellowship there. The Observatory and its outstanding group of academics and administrators provided an excellent and enjoyable research environment for initiating and finishing the project. A visiting fellowship at the Seeger Center for Hellenic Studies at Princeton University allowed me to return to Princeton and begin drafting the book. The fellowship afforded me long hours in the amazing Firestone Library; and Dimitri Gondicas and a wonderful group of fellows and colleagues offered guidance and support. A Research Fellowship by the Leventis Foundation provided the resources for field trips in Greece, Germany and Slovakia and for research assistance. I am grateful for the Foundation's important support and repeated trust.

This intellectual journey would have been less enjoyable and considerably longer without assistance of excellent colleagues, associates and friends. Jason Lamprianou, my trusted colleague at the University of Cyprus and collaborator in a number of other projects, went out of his way to help me analyze and interpret my data. I am grateful for his patient guidance, inspiring rigor and unwavering support. Dimitris Comodromos helped with the careful coding of thousands of pages of documents and his superb research assistance and critical eye helped improve key parts of the project. Dimitris Psarras, who has been closely monitoring and writing on the Golden Dawn for decades, generously and graciously provided access to his unique archive of party newspapers and magazines as well as other relevant material. This project would have been different without his help. Teresa Avgousti, Julia Hartingerova and Martin Koller helped with the research in Slovakia and Germany. Walter Jung as well as the Landesamt für Verfassungsschutz Sachsen provided useful insights on extremism in Germany. During the many years of research on this project, dozens of other individuals provided precious information, helped identify documents and aided my access to organizations or groups that are not accustomed to welcoming academics. Apart from those mentioned eponymously in the next, I also express my gratitude to those who spoke under the condition of anonymity.

Various universities and centers provided opportunities to present parts of the book: Anáhuac University, the City University of London, the Center for Hellenic Studies at UC San Diego, the Center for Research on Extremism of the University of Oslo, Durham University, the Hellenic Observatory at the LSE, ITAM, the Seeger Center for Hellenic Studies at Princeton and Panteion University. I am grateful to Mark Beissinger, Denise Demetriou, Olga Demetriou, Yael Sandra Siman Druker, Spyros Economides, Kevin Featherstone, Vasiliki Georgiadou, Dimitri Gondicas, Anders Ravik Jupskås, Iosif Kovras, Vassilis Monastiriotis and Stephan Sberro for being wonderful hosts. David Art, Sheri Berman and Giovanni Capoccia deserve special thanks for their constructive criticism and useful feedback, which gave the necessary boost at a critical juncture of the project. As always, Nancy Bermeo generously provided intellectual guidance, precious insights and moral support at different stages in the process. Ezra Suleiman kindly gave valuable guidance and support throughout the many years this book has been in the making. I am also thankful for the useful comments, insights and critiques of Mary Beth Altier, David Art, Uwe Backes, Tim Bale, Marc Berenson, Thomas Christiansen, Elias Dinas, Anastasia Kafe, Thanasis Kampagiannis, Ioannis

Konstantinidis, Jennifer Lieb, Neophytos Loizides, the late Caesar Mavratsas, Jan-Werner Müller, Roula Nezi, Lamprini Rori, Yiannis Papadakis, Kostis Papaioannou, Stavros Tombazos, Nikos Trimikliniotis, Anna Tsiftsoglou, Haridimos Tsoukas, Nikos Vafeas and Nicholas Vrousalis. My home department, the Department of Social and Political Sciences at the University of Cyprus, provided the best working environment an academic can hope for: excellent colleagues, curious students and ample (though never enough) time for research in the spectacular new library.

I am particularly thankful to the editors of *South European Society and Politics*, Susannah Verney and Anna Bosco, and of *Party Politics*, David Farrell and Paul Webb, for the opportunity to publish earlier work on the Golden Dawn.

I am enormously indebted to my editor at Cambridge University Press, Robert Dreesen, for showing genuine interest in the project from its inception, supporting it during its various phases and professionally shepherding it through the review and publication process. His trust has truly energized the project. I am also grateful to Jane Bowbrick, Hillary Ford, Orvil Matthews and Erika Walsh for the smooth and effective production process.

The writing of this book has been admittedly more enjoyable and eventful than the previous ones. I cannot thank Daphne, Irene and Pari enough for making it so.

Nicosia, August 2019

CHAPTER I

Introduction

Late on a Friday night in June 2017 about twenty green T-shirted, camou-
flage-wearing, physically strong males gather at the main train station in
Poprad, one of the biggest towns in the northern Prešov region of Slovakia.
They are ready to embark on the train going eastwards to Kežmarok and
other towns in the nearby Spiš district. Their mission is simple: to enforce
law and order in the train routes passing from Roma-inhabited towns and
deter Roma "trouble-makers." A law passed by the Slovak parliament a few
months earlier prohibits this type of activity but the well-built vigilantes
claim to be simply assembling in the railcars. Their mere presence is enough
to compel a group of incoming Roma passengers to disembark.[1] Train
patrols like the one observed in the route from Poprad to Kežmarok have
been instituted by Kotleba – People's Party Our Slovakia (*Ľudová strana –
Naše Slovensko*, LSNS) as part of its programmatic pledge to address "Gypsy
terror." The twenty activists in Poprad are members of the local party
branch, one of dozens the party set up across Slovakia to penetrate local
societies and gain electoral support. The local functionaries are convinced
that train passengers and, more broadly, local societies will come to appreciate their vigilantism and support the party.

   For decades, parties with a neo-Nazi or neo-fascist outlook and practices
seemed forever relegated to the margins of European electoral politics.
Extremist right-wing parties such as the LSNS seemed unable to put forth
the "winning formula" that allowed more moderate far right parties to
make significant electoral inroads in most European democracies. As a
result, the scholarly literature has mostly treated these parties as fringe
electoral phenomena penalized by voters for their extreme ideas and
militant practices and, consequently, unworthy of much scholarly attention. Systematic examinations of the far right focused, instead, on more
moderate and electorally successful parties. In recent years, though, a

---

[1] Author's observation of train patrols in Poprad, June and July 2017.

number of these really extreme parties have defied scholarly expectations
and made stunning electoral inroads across a number of European countries. Their success has generated new interest not only in the relative
attraction of their non-democratic ideas but also in the controversial
organizational methods they deploy to propagate these ideas and to dominate their respective environments. The purpose of this book is to
systematically examine the organizational efforts of such extremist right-
wing parties and to analyze their attempts to grow roots in democratic
societies.

The very nature of extremist right-wing parties and the way they
practice politics poses a major challenge for modern democracies. Not
surprisingly, institutional and social actors across a number of democratic
settings have come up with different ways to respond to this challenge. At
the institutional level, the organizational efforts of far right parties have
initiated measures by legislative, police and judicial authorities against
them. Legislators have sought to institute responses to the controversial
local presence of such parties, reminiscent of interwar attempts to protect
democracy from extremism (Capoccia 2005). Parliaments have been busy
drafting laws to ban some of these controversial practices, such as food
rationing based on racial criteria or, as in the example above, train patrols
in Roma-inhabited localities. Law enforcers have devised mechanisms to
monitor, contain and prosecute extremist rhetoric and activity. Across a
number of countries, police authorities have developed tools to spot
symbols of neighborhood radicalization and prosecutors have brought
dozens of extremists before justice. And jurists have occasionally advocated
or ruled in favor of curbing freedoms to protect those most affected by
extremism. Some of the judicial measures have targeted the parties themselves and others have aimed at their leaders and functionaries. Beyond this
varied institutional responses, societal actors have also been at the forefront
of efforts to counter the organizational development of far right parties. In
dissimilar local contexts, such as Leipzig in Germany and Patra in Greece,
a wide array of antifascist actors have mobilized to undermine the organizational spread of extremist right-wing parties. Varied in form, frequency
and size, antifascist mobilization has relied on different resources and
employed diverse tactics but similarly focuses on eliminating the local
organizational presence of extremist right-wing parties.

Whereas European states and societies have been paying closer attention
to the organizational efforts of far right parties, the extant literature has
largely treated far right parties as discursive rather than organizational
phenomena. The emphasis on the discursive input of far right parties in

liberal democratic systems helped generate considerable knowledge about the ideological and programmatic profile of these parties; their positioning in the political or issue space; and the factors associated with their electoral performance (e.g. Kitschelt and McGann 1995; Norris 2005; Mudde 2007; Golder 2016; Rydgren 2018). But the emphasis on discursive components of the far right phenomenon has primarily come at the expense of systematically examining their organizational life. Although single or comparative case studies often describe various organizational features of far right parties (e.g., Betz and Immerfall 1998; DeClair 1999; Carter 2005), their organizational development remains one of the least studied areas of this sizable literature. With few exceptions (e.g., Art 2011; Heinisch and Mazzoleni 2016), analyses of organizational features of far right parties usually rely on broad sketches rather than systematic observations of organizational reality. More importantly for the purposes of this book, analyses of far right organizations solely rely on observations of national and central party mechanisms, missing important subnational variation in organizational realities. In part, this is due to the intrinsic difficulty of studying parties that tend to be wary of academic observers. Access to far right parties is generally more difficult than access to most other party families. But the emphasis on the national level is also due to the "whole nation bias" inherent in comparative political analyses (Rokkan 1970: 49).

This book breaks new ground by examining the organizational development of some of the most extreme parties in Europe at the local, rather than the national, level. The systematic analysis of evidence from hundreds of local branches and thousands of local activities demonstrates that even these highly centralized parties display notable subnational variation in how they develop. In some local settings, these really extreme parties have been particularly successful, and in others they have miserably failed. To account for the remarkable differences in local organizational life, this study explicates and then tests an analytical framework for understanding the local organizational development of extremist right-wing parties. It systematically examines how endogenous and environmental factors affect the capacity of these parties to penetrate local societies. The local organizational fate of these parties is partly linked to factors intrinsic to their organization. Extremist right-wing parties are charismatic movement parties, engaging in a dual track of conventional and contentious politics that complicates their capacity to develop well-defined institutions for managing people and resources. These basic organizational characteristics affect how they adjust to environmental

change but also generate environmental responses that tend to complicate their organizational development. The book examines three distinct
sets of environmental factors affecting the local development of extremist
right-wing parties: electoral, institutional and societal. First, the book
shows how electoral dynamics affect variation in local developmental
outcomes. It shows the extent to which extremist right-wing parties
adapt to changing electoral environments. Second, local organizational
development also depends on how institutional actors (e.g. the police,
courts, local governments) respond to attempts by extremist right-wing
parties to penetrate local societies. The contentious and, often, violent
activism of these parties generates militant institutional responses against
them. This book traces the range of institutional responses and, more
importantly, gauges the effects of institutional hostility on the local
trajectories of extremist right-wing parties. Third, local organizational
outcomes are also linked to societal responses to extremism. Many local
branches of extremist right-wing parties face considerable societal hostility and their organizational fate depends on their capacity to respond to
societal mobilization against them. The analysis of thousands of antifascist events undertaken here allows an assessment of how a wide range
of antifascist actors, using different resources and varied tactics, affect the
organizational development of extremist right-wing parties. Overall, the
analysis shows how the interplay of endogenous and environmental
factors affects the local organizational development of extremist right-
wing parties.

   The book develops and tests this analytical framework through the
analysis of the organizational development of all local organizations set
up by one of the most extreme parties in Europe, the Greek Golden
Dawn (GD). It probes the generalizability of the framework by analysing
the local organizational development of two similar parties in different
democratic settings, the National Democratic Party of Germany (*Nationaldemokratische Partei Deutschlands*, NPD) and the Slovak LSNS. The
book relies on the analysis of thousands of events publicized by hundreds
of local party branches in the three countries. It also utilizes insights from
more than one hundred interviews with national and local leaders and
functionaries of the extremist right-wing parties, antifascist groups and
institutional actors. About fifty interviews were conducted with top
leaders and functionaries of the GD in eight locations across the country
and nearly two dozen interviews took place with the top NPD and LSNS
leaders and functionaries, primarily in the Saxony and Prešov regions,
respectively. Leaders and members of antifascist groups were interviewed

in different localities in all three countries. The list of interviewees also includes institutional actors, primarily local authorities but also the police and secret services. In addition, the analysis uses evidence from observations of activities organized by local party branches, including the controversial train patrols of the LSNS mentioned above. Finally, the analysis builds on evidence collected from reading thousands of pages of court, police and other official documents.

Contributions

This book builds on and pushes beyond the voluminous literature on the European far right parties and contributes to the broader literatures on political parties, social movements and militant democracies. As suggested above, the main contribution in the extant literature on far right parties is the systematic examination of their local organizational development. Comparative works on European far right parties sometimes acknowledge links between organizational and discursive elements of the far right phenomenon, recognizing the importance of party organization in explaining their varied electoral outcomes (Kitschelt and McGann 1995; Betz 1998; Lubbers et al. 2002; Carter 2005; Mudde 2007; Art 2008; Ellinas 2010; de Lange and Art 2011). But these works tend to treat organization as an independent variable, associating strong party organizations with long-term electoral success. The few works that use organizational development as a dependent variable (Art 2011; Bolleyer 2013; Bolleyer et al. 2018) demonstrate the importance of understanding how parties evolve. Based on these analyses, neo-Nazi or neo-fascist parties should be organizationally doomed because they are usually run by extremists and lack ties to civil society. Yet, the organizational evolution of extremist right-wing parties provides a much more complicated picture than the one expected by the literature. These parties display notable variation in their capacity to build and grow their organizational infrastructure. This variation is evident across but is most striking within countries, generating a need to better understand how local party organizations develop. In some settings, extremist right-wing parties manage to build organizational strongholds, while in others their attempts to infiltrate local societies flounder. The book seeks to contribute to the burgeoning literature on the far right by taking a rare look inside three of the most extreme European parties to systematically account for variation in their local organizational trajectories.

The examination of the organizational trajectories of extremist right-wing parties is in line with a notable strain in the broader party literature that looks "inside" parties (Berman 1997) for clues on how endogenous and environmental factors shape their trajectories (Webb 2002; van Biezen 2005). Such clues have proved useful in understanding the organizational form, evolution, and, subsequently, the behavior of not only contemporary but also interwar extremist parties (Duverger 1959; Berman 2008). Going beyond this notable strain in the party literature, this book systematically examines the distinct evolution of subnational, rather than national, party organizations and the micro- rather than macro-level processes shaping party development. As recent literature on party organizations acknowledges, the origins of organizational strength constitute an understudied area in the study of political parties (Tavits 2013) and the systematic examination of local organizations helps fill this gap. The specific focus on extremist right-wing parties can also help refine theories that mostly tend to view the state or society as facilitators of party development (Katz and Mair 1995). Unlike cartel parties and like interwar extremists, right-wing extremist parties often have to cope with hostile political environments (Art 2011) that complicate their organizational development. The varied subnational responses of institutional and social actors to local neo-Nazi or neo-fascist organizations can help uncover the micro-dynamics of organizational development in conditions of high environmental uncertainty. The analysis here also helps distinguish between institutional and societal responses to extremism, highlighting the role and relation of each to extremist right-wing mobilization.

Moreover, by focusing on local extremist right-wing party organizations, the book also engages with the social movement literature. Unlike most radical right-wing parties, neo-Nazi or neo-fascist parties are movement parties – a rare breed of organization that seeks to combine institutional and non-institutional, or even violent, forms of political participation. Although the party literature acknowledges this type of organization (Kitschelt 2006), systematic efforts to trace the evolution of this phenomenon across time and space are scarce (e.g., della Porta et al. 2017). More importantly, there is still a sharp conceptual divide that sets apart the study of political parties from that of social movements (McAdam and Tarrow 2010). The analysis of local neo-Nazi or neo-fascist party mobilization can help narrow this divide by showing how the hybrid nature of these parties can help to account for the notable variation in the organizational fate of their subunits. Borrowing from the social movement literature the emphasis on process, rather than outcomes (della Porta 1995; McAdam et al. 2001; Tarrow 2011), and relying on clues from the party activism literature (Huckfeldt and

Sprague 1992; Whiteley and Seyd 1994; Pattie et al. 1995; Gerber and Green 2000; Denver et al. 2004; Fisher et al. 2006; 2016), the book systematically analyzes the unfolding dynamics of neo-Nazi or neo-fascist activism and the organizational processes set in motion by institutional and societal responses to extremist right-wing mobilization. The study of dozens of local extremist right-wing organizations shows how macro-level structural opportunities yield distinct micro-level dynamics and, ultimately, different outcomes. Even in the same polity, institutional actors behave differently toward neo-Nazi or neo-fascist organizational activity and societal actors display varying capacity to counter-mobilize against them.

Finally, the analysis of extremist right-wing organizations provides insights into the workings of militant democracies. The rise of extremist parties is one of the major challenges facing contemporary democracies and yet another signal of a broader democratic decline (e.g. Diamond 2015; Plattner 2015; Bermeo 2016; Bernhard and O' Neill 2018). The examination of institutional responses to this challenge provides insights into what democracies do to defend themselves from those who seek to harm them. Challenges such as the ones posed by non-democratic actors compel democracies to turn militant to defend themselves from perceived threats to regime stability. For historical reasons and due to their very nature, neo-Nazi and neo-fascist parties are among the most usual targets of militant democracy policies. In the past decades European democracies sought to disrupt or disband such organizations, curbing their rights to political expression, participation or assembly (de Witte and Klandermans 2000; Pedahzur 2004; Bale 2007; Downs 2012; Capoccia 2013) in ways reminiscent of interwar attempts to protect democracy (Loewenstein 1937a; 1937b; Capoccia 2005). Democratic defences against neo-Nazism are sometimes controversial, giving rise to important normative questions about the use of such policies (Kirshner 2014). Beyond its normative significance, militant democracy also raises important practical questions about its effectiveness. The systematic analysis of party organizational development offers an opportunity to explore how organizations evolve in a hostile environment. The varied trajectories of subnational organizational units also offer the possibility to understand possible factors affecting organizational resilience in the face of institutional pressure.

Besides these theoretical contributions, the book also brings original empirical evidence to bear on the understanding of the organizational workings of these parties. The violent tactics and extreme ideology of the Golden Dawn have helped generate a budding literature analyzing various dimensions of this phenomenon (Psarras 2012; Dinas et al. 2013; Ellinas 2013; 2015; Fragoudaki 2013; Georgiadou 2013; Hasapopoulos 2013; Vasilopoulou and Halikiopoulou 2015; Lamprianou and Ellinas 2017; Ellinas and Lamprianou 2017; 2018). The book contributes to the evidence produced by these works by systematically collecting, coding and analyzing material published since 1993 in nearly one thousand issues of the party newspaper *Golden Dawn*; collecting, coding and analyzing all antifascist posts published since 2007 on the *Athens Indymedia*; using insights from interviews with nearly all top officials and functionaries of the party, including the party leader, Nikos Michaloliakos, and from many observations of local party activities across the entire country; and relying on evidence from thousands of pages of judicial reports. The long and combative presence of the NPD in German politics and its occasional regional electoral breakthroughs have similarly attracted considerable scholarly attention over the years (Nagle 1970; Stöss 1991; Backes and Mudde 2000; Art 2004; Gnad 2005; Backes 2006; Decker and Miliopoulos 2009; Brandstetter 2013; Backes 2018). The investigation of the NPD case undertaken in this book relies on the systematic collection, coding and analysis of more than 1,400 activities organized by the party since 2000 in Saxony. It also uses data on hundreds of NPD structures set up across Germany since 2001 and insights from a dozen onsite interviews with the party leadership. As do most studies of the NPD, the analysis here uses evidence from thousands of pages of official reports on the party produced by the sixteen regional Offices for the Protection of the Constitution since 2000. The newest of the three parties under study, the LSNS, has also gained some scholarly attention, especially after its regional electoral breakthrough in 2013 (Nociar 2012; Bodnárová and Vicenová 2013; Spáč and Voda 2014; Kluknavská 2015; Kluknavská and Smolík 2016). Whereas most of this work focuses on its history, ideology and electorate, the investigation here focuses on its organizational development in the past few years. It relies on the examination of its regional and local organizational structures, the analysis of 250 reported party activities and interviews with national and local party leaders. Overall, the book systematically analyzes unique organizational data, rare in-depth interviews and voluminous party and official material to trace the local development of the three parties and to make theoretical and empirical contributions to the extant literature on far right parties and the broader literatures on political parties, social movements and militant democracies.

Plan of the Book

Chapter 2 of this book conceptualizes and then classifies extremist right-wing parties, distinguishing them from their radical right-wing cousins and highlighting the importance of going beyond the discursive level to understand what these parties stand for. Chapter 3 develops the analytical framework for understanding the organizational development of political parties in general and extremist right-wing parties in particular. Chapter 4 traces the organizational trajectory of the GD from the 1980s onwards before focusing on its local organizational development. Chapter 5 examines the life of local party organizations, using measures of organizational longevity and activity to demonstrate the remarkable variation in the organizational trajectories of seventy-four local branches set up by the GD over the years.

The next four chapters examine in turn how endogenous, electoral, institutional and societal factors affected the local organizational development of the GD. Each of these four chapters brings together insights from the various literatures mentioned earlier to develop and subsequently test hypotheses for local organizational development. Chapter 6 examines endogenous factors. More specifically it shows how two important features of these parties – their dual track of conventional and contentious politics and their charismatic nature – shape the development of their local organizational network. Chapter 7 examines how electoral outcomes shape the organizational development of extremist right-wing parties. Chapter 8 explores the effect of institutional responses to extremism on the organizational evolution of extremist right-wing party structures and activism. Chapter 9 describes societal responses to extremism by describing the range of actors, resources and tactics involved in antifascist activity; it then assesses the effect of antifascist mobilization on the local organizational development of extremist right-wing parties. Chapter 10 probes the generalizability of the detailed analysis of the Greek case by exploring the organizational development of the NPD and the LSNS – two similar parties in settings very different to that of Greece. The book concludes with a summary of the findings and a consideration of how they help illuminate various scholarly debates on the development of political parties, the nature of movement parties and the effects of militant democratic policies.

CHAPTER 2

Extremist Right-Wing Parties in Europe

Before developing an analytical framework to examine organizational development, it is important to conceptualize and classify extremist right-wing parties. This chapter conceptualizes and classifies these parties by identifying their similarities and differences with radical right-wing parties. It first produces a conceptual framework for identifying the two subgroups of the far right. Borrowing from existing literature on party families, it examines how various criteria such as the ideology, program, electorate, origins and international links of political parties can help distinguish between these two subfamilies. It then adds an important criterion this literature ignores, the type of political action parties undertake. Using this conceptual framework and the various criteria, the chapter then proceeds to the classification of forty-one parties in thirty countries.

Conceptualizing Extremist and Radical Right-Wing Parties

Extremist and radical right-wing parties are subtypes of the broader far right party family. Their juxtaposition requires a consideration of the party family approach in the study of political parties and the various criteria it has employed for identifying similarities parties share. One of the major analytical elements of this approach is the emphasis it places on the ideological congruence of party families (Mair and Mudde 1998). Echoing this emphasis, a number of works demarcate the ideological contours of the far right party family by emphasizing the centrality of nationalism (Eatwell 2000; Hainsworth 2000; Minkenberg 2000; Mudde 2000). Both extremist and radical right-wing parties can be broadly characterized as nationalist parties – a definition that matches the way many of these parties describe themselves – because nationalism is a core component of their ideological platform. Most far right parties identify the *demos* with the *ethnos*, mostly using ethnic criteria to distinguish the in-group from the out-group, be they immigrants or minorities. Far right parties rely on the propagation of the idea of a homogenous nation, highlighting its historical achievements and, often, the historical injustices it has endured. Beyond this commonality, though, there are also some differences in the type of nationalist appeals these parties make (Minkenberg 2015: 29). Extremist right-wing parties adopt more biological or racially marked nationalist claims that bring them closer to the definition of fascism, especially to Nazi racial nationalism (Mann 2004: 13). Radical right-wing parties differ from the extremist subtype in that they make nativist appeals that distinguish between in-groups and out-groups (Mudde 2007) but usually not explicitly on the basis of racial or biological criteria. The ideological differences between the two subtypes are mostly a matter of degree, as they are both exclusionary forms of nationalism targeting non-natives, non-Christians or non-whites and identifying their presence as a major social problem.[1]

In line with their ideology, both party subtypes tend to programmatically converge on appeals against immigration and minorities. Far right parties diverge significantly on other programmatic issues, such as economic or foreign policy, but they are similar in associating many of the problems their respective societies face with the presence of ethnic minorities, be they immigrant or indigenous. Although they might differ in the degree of linguistic vulgarity used when they refer to immigrants or minorities (with the extremists using more inflammatory language), in their respective party systems these parties tend to have the toughest stance on these issues. The programmatic convergence of West European far right parties on the issue of immigration has encouraged a number of scholars to label them anti-immigrant parties (e.g., Fennema 1997; van der Brug et al. 2000; Art 2011). Indeed, party positions on immigration constitute a significant component in factor analyses, hence demonstrating their programmatic congruence (Ennser 2012). In Eastern Europe, where immigration was not, until recently, as important of a political issue, the nationalist ideology of far right parties is programmatically directed against minorities (Mudde 2007; Bustikova 2014). East European far right parties consider these minorities a threat to ethnic homogeneity, internal security and territorial integrity. The presence of indigenous ethnic minorities across states is also the source of irredentist claims alluding to territorial expansionism.

---

[1] It has been argued that the radical right-wing variant of far right parties is not only nationalist or nativist but also populist (Mudde 2007). Extremist right-wing parties might also employ populist style (Aslanidis 2015) or appeals (Mudde 2004) but this is not their most distinctive characteristic (Pappas 2016).

A third major criterion for inclusion in the far right party family examines their electorates. Drawing from the analysis of social cleavages (Lipset and Rokkan 1967), this approach examines the electoral alignment associated with the rise of this party family. The basic idea is that recent decades witnessed a shift in the political preferences of European electorates (Inglehart 1990; Kitschelt 1994; Kriesi et al. 2008), generating opportunities for new entrants into the electoral market. The far right is seen as one of the beneficiaries of these changes, representing a "counter-revolution" (Ignazi 1992) or a reaction to universalistic or postmaterialist values. Far right parties are thought to draw support from constituencies holding communitarian, identitarian, traditionalist or authoritarian values (Kitschelt and McGann 1995; Ignazi 2003; Bornschier 2010). Evidence regarding voter demand for far right parties has largely come from the analysis of attitudinal, demographic and contextual variables. At the individual level, far right voters are thought to share various attitudinal predispositions and demographic characteristics. At the aggregate level, these predispositions along with various contextual factors, such as immigration and unemployment, are thought to generate support for these parties. Most of the individual-level evidence regarding political demand for far right parties comes from already successful and relatively large parties, for which there are hundreds of respondents in major international surveys such as the European Social Survey or the World Values Survey. Much less is known about the electorates of smaller parties, especially during the period before their major electoral breakthroughs. Party size makes it harder to use the attitudinal or demographic characteristics of party electorates as criteria for distinguishing between extremist and radical right-wing parties.

The origins of political parties in historical conflicts offer more analytical leverage than party electorates when it comes to distinguishing between extremist and radical right-wing parties. Extremist right-wing parties are rooted in past conflicts and display some continuity with the past (Klandermans and Mayer 2006). This continuity is sometimes evident by the involvement of party founders or leaders in past wars or previous regimes – by what they did during that era – or by their association with or advocacy of the ancien régime. The continuity with the past is sometimes at a more symbolic level, through the use of signs, outfits or paraphernalia that communicate a link with the past. Rootedness in past conflicts is also signaled by the way these parties go about remembering the past as well as by the range of events they choose to commemorate. Extremist and radical right-wing parties differ on the degree of ideological or programmatic investment they have with the past. Extremist right-wing parties make much more of the past in their ideological platforms and programmatic statements than their radical right-wing counterparts. That being said, whereas extremist parties tend to explicitly acknowledge their historical rootedness, as they grow bigger, they seek to distance themselves from the past or disguise it. This is precisely what some of the most successful radical right-wing parties have done in the past decades, changing their profile and becoming more acceptable. This is not surprising: as parties grow bigger and as electoral considerations get to trump the desire for explicit historical continuity, any perceived association with a discredited past becomes a liability that parties want to get rid of. Some of the successful radical right-wing parties have loosened their ties with the neo-fascist or neo-Nazi milieu and have minimized the use of controversial symbols. Exactly because parties change, the static dimension of the party origins approach limits its utility as a criterion for defining the familial bonds between parties. Further limitations come from the observed diversity in the origins of radical right-wing parties. Whereas some radical right-wing parties seek to cut their ties with people, symbols and events of the past, others have never been rooted in the extremist movements of the past. These are new parties formed by political entrepreneurs without any investment in past conflicts or existing parties that adopt radical political repertoires to capitalize on electoral opportunities. On a number of occasions, the latter are parties of "parliamentary origin" (Duverger 1959), founded by individuals or groups that were members or parliamentarians of established mainstream parties. Their inclusion in this party family is largely based on the ideological and programmatic criteria analyzed earlier rather than on their historical continuity with extremist movements and parties. Parties rooted in the past – of "extra-parliamentary" origin, in Duvergerian terms – can change from extremist to radical but the transformation might take years.

Apart from their ideology, program, electorate and origin, the international affiliations of far right parties have might also be useful in distinguishing subtypes between them. This criterion has not received as much traction in scholarly works on the far right, and more broadly, it has been discounted as an indication of familial bonds between political parties (Mair and Mudde 1998). Although the growing significance of the European Parliament has enhanced the political clout and cemented the coherence of European political groups (Hix et al. 2007), this cannot be said of the far right, which failed to form a political group for decades. The various transnational links that have long existed between some of these parties

(Mammone 2015) did not acquire solid organizational form. In the European Parliament, some radical right-wing parties joined other political groups, like the Europe of Freedom and Democracy or were not members of any group (Ennser 2012). All this changed in 2015, when thirty-eight members of the European Parliament from eight countries formed the Europe of Nations and Freedom (ENF). The group includes some of the most electorally successful far right parties, belying well-founded expectations that their exclusivist ideologies inherently hamper transnational collaboration. A number of other parties, though, are not included in this group. Some belong to the European Conservatives and Reformists Group (ECR) and to the Europe for Freedom and Direct Democracy (EFD). A number of extremist right-wing parties remain unattached to any political group. As with some of the other criteria, the different transnational links far right parties have points to the diversity characterizing this party family. Rather than discarding the transnational links criterion altogether, it is probably more fruitful to consider it as a good reminder of this diversity.

Examining What Parties Do

Existing criteria for identifying party families mostly focus on what parties are, paying scant attention to what they do (Mair and Mudde 1998). Focusing on their ideology, program, electorates, origins or links is undoubtedly important for understanding political parties. But it is also necessary to appreciate what parties do to send ideological cues, disseminate party programs, signal their origins, connect with electorates and attract international partners. When party activists march in military uniforms in the city center or ride on motorcycles in immigrant neighborhoods they make statements about who they are, what their party stands for and how they want to link to society. The broader literature on political parties acknowledges the importance of party activism and there is a significant body of works demonstrating its importance for electoral outcomes (Huckfeldt and Sprague 1992; Whiteley and Seyd 1992; 1994; Gerber and Green 2000). The more specific literature on far right parties has made considerable inroads in understanding the profile of party activists and their role in party organizational development (Kandermans and Mayer 2006; Goodwin 2010; Art 2011). But while they both focus on party activists, neither systematically considers how this activism affects what parties stand for.

This omission is not as important for understanding liberal, conservative or, even, modern socialist parties that do not invest as much in political action. But it is particularly important for understanding other types of parties. For example, the analysis of ecological parties cannot be understood in isolation from the propensity these parties have for undertaking, participating or encouraging political activism. The formative experiences of political parties are important (see Chapter 3). Because ecological parties grew out of the social movements of the 1960s and 1970s, their political profile is largely built in the street protests they launched against the established political order. An ecological party that never sets foot on the street and never takes part in some form of social protest is hard to conceive of as being green. The same can be said of radical left parties (March 2011), many of which, again, grew out of social movements or as parts of various movement alliances, networks and structures (Kriesi 2015). Even after their long and sometimes torturous and fractious path to political power, these parties have not entirely deserted their movement identities. Especially when in opposition, they are involved in all sorts of political action seeking to challenge political authority not only in legislative chambers, but more importantly, on the street. The range of political action parties take varies considerably depending on their origins, ideologies and programs. The few remaining communist orthodox parties, for example, are more likely to be involved in worker strikes than in ecological protests. It is hence important to understand the nature of political action and the kind of cues it gives about what the party is.

The concept of "movement parties" Kitschelt (2006) and della Porta et al. (2017) use to describe hybrids of parties and movements rightly acknowledges the importance of political action for understanding what parties are. The movement component of the concept comes down to contentious action – to the resort to street politics and disruptive activities outside the institutional arena of politics. Although political *praxis* is not the only characteristic of movement parties, it is a key element that distinguishes them from more conventional political parties. "In terms of external political practice, movement parties attempt a dual track by combining activities within the arenas of formal democratic competition with extra-institutional mobilization. One day, legislators of such parties may debate bills in parliamentary committees, but the next day, they participate in disruptive demonstrations or the non-violent occupation of government sites" (Kitschelt 2006: 281). Part of the reason movement parties are rare is exactly because of the difficulty in sustaining this double track of conventional and contentious activism. The organizational set up necessary for each is quite different and, as Chapter 3 analyzes, the two tracks often conflict. For this reason, movement parties are mostly considered as transitory phenomena – a developmental phase political parties desert as they become bigger, gain access to institutional resources and have their demands met. Alternatively, movement parties might be viewed as a form a party takes at a particular point in time, to best capitalize on the political opportunities available in a given context. "Movement party as an ideal type thus refers to a process embedded in time that may not last for long, but it is crucial in revealing significant broader social transformations that other interpretative tools or social science methodologies might not grasp" (della Porta et al. 2017: 24). At times of high tension or political polarization (e.g., the War in Iraq, Heaney and Rojas 2015; the economic crisis, della Porta et al. 2017), the movement component of a party might become more important than the more institutional component.[2] That being said, the abandonment of the movement component is not simply a matter of tactical or strategic choice. Some types of parties can be expected to find it more difficult to abandon the streets and exclusively embrace institutional modes of polit- ical engagement than others. For example, radical left parties can be expected, more or less, to try to stay on the streets and to sponsor political action that is mostly associated with social movements, especially when in opposition.

The incorporation of political action into the analysis of the familial bonds shared between political parties helps to describe radical parties on the left and also on the right of the political spectrum. Kitschelt applies the concept of movement parties to ecological parties and to parties broadly termed as "far right" or "extreme right." Unlike radical left parties, far right parties are not known to originate in social movement activism or to be the vehicles for the coordination of movement networks and alliances. The strong hierarchical elements in the organizational structure of these parties prohibit the type of linkage usually associated with ecological parties or the radical left (Tsakatika and Lisi 2013). Yet, some far right parties are quite active on the streets, using symbolic language and sending action-induced ideological cues that parallel the noisy, disruptive and contentious politics social movements have become associated with. Put simply, some parties of the far right family portray movement elements in the way they practice politics. Nevertheless, this is not a homogeneous party category when it comes to political practice. The application of the movement party con- cept to the entire party family risks ascribing more homogeneity to the

---

[2] Moreover, the size of the movement component can be expected to vary significantly across time, making it difficult to consider size the most reliable gauge of this component.

range of organizational forms making up the far right spectrum than there actually is.

The examination of the political action parties undertake sharpens the distinction between extremist and radical right-wing parties. The emphasis is both on the propensity of these parties to undertake political action usually associated with social movements and also on the nature of the activities undertaken. Extremist right-wing parties are much more likely to organize, participate and encourage street-level activism than their radical right-wing cousins. This is because of differences in resources and ideology. As explicated in Chapter 3, the extremist parties tend to lack the range of financial, communicative or other institutional resources that other parties might have at their disposal. To make up for their resource deficiencies they are more likely to employ labor intensive campaign techniques and spend more time on the streets. Radical right-wing parties are different because they are less reliant on such labor intensive forms of mobilization. This is due to their legislative or entrepreneurial status. Some of these parties began differently but over time, they reached a more mature stage in their development, having passed the threshold of political relevance and having become institutionalized in their party systems. Others were formed from the beginning as entrepreneurial parties, relying on the access of their leaders to communicative or institutional resources. Regardless of how these parties acquired political relevance, their access to resources makes them less reliant on political action.

The difference in the propensity of extremist and radical right-wing parties to undertake political action is also due to the ideological differences mentioned earlier. Extremist parties with neo-fascist or neo-Nazi ideological leanings are more likely to undertake political action because it is an inseparable element of their ideology. As works on fascism point out, political action is fused with this particular ideology and often takes the form of paramilitarism. The ideology, then, has a particular political value for those projecting it but it also translates into a particular organizational form. The idea of political soldiers marching on the streets is intrinsic to this ideology and it affects how they go about practicing politics. As Mann notes, "in no case was a fascist movement merely a 'party'" (Mann 2004: 16). Extremist parties with neo-fascist or neo-Nazi ideological affinity are more likely to be active on the streets than radical right-wing parties because street-level action is part of their ideological emphasis on dominating through the display of might. It is also intrinsic to their complete rejection of the political system and their intention to replace it with a new one. Their outsider status makes extremist right-wing parties more likely to turn to the street than parties wanting to work within the confines of the system to modify it.

Ideology can also help account for differences in the *nature* of the activities undertaken by extremist and radical right-wing parties. Unlike their radical cousins, extremist parties are involved in contentious and often violence-prone political activity that sets them apart from most other party families. For the purposes of this book, contentious political activity means the range of political activity the behavioralist literature deems extra-institutional because it falls outside the normal channels of political participation (Barnes and Kaase 1979; Teorell et al. 2007; Marien et al. 2010; Stolle and Hooghe 2011). Although the boundaries of conventional and contentious action tend to be porous, the distinction is relevant for the analysis of extremist right-wing parties. These parties are different from radical right-wing parties not only because they are much more active on the streets but also because they organize a broader range of activities that often involve aggressive or violent political action. The activities organized by these parties include demonstrations that occasionally take up a violent form and lead to clashes with the police, leftists or antifascists; social activism at the neighborhood or local level; participation in or organization of commemorative events; anti-tax or anti-immigration protests; the occupation of public or private buildings, and so on. Radical right-wing parties tend to avoid such action because the institutional stakes for them are too high. Involvement in this type of action can jeopardize their efforts to gain legitimacy by distancing themselves from violent tactics and can make them more vulnerable to political attacks by their opponents or the media. Even presence on the street can generate counter-action that can undermine their institutional profile.

Overall, then, extremist and radical right-wing parties display similarities and differences across the various criteria explicated above. The familial bonds of these parties are primarily shown by their common nationalist ideologies as well as their programmatic convergence on such issues as immigration and minorities. These similarities explain why these parties are generally treated as members of the same party family. Beyond these similarities, though, there are also important differences, which are particularly instructive in our understanding of the parties examined in this book. Extremist right-wing parties adopt biological or racial nationalist platforms, present some form of continuity with the ancien régime and are not convenient partners for most other parties, including some of the best known nationalist parties in Europe. More importantly, these are usually "movement parties" frequently involved, not only in institutional forms of political participation, but also in unconventional, and sometimes violent, political action. Radical right-wing parties rely on more generic nationalist platforms, distance themselves from the stigmatized past and are included in various transnational political groups in the European Parliament. They are not as active on the streets as their extremist counterparts and are mostly involved in politics through institutional channels.

Classifying Extremist and Radical Right-Wing Parties

The classification of parties to be included in the extremist or radical right-wing party subfamily requires a careful analysis of the various criteria explicated above. Table 2.1 presents a list of parties that can be broadly categorized as belonging to the far right based on the criteria developed above and on recent literature. The list only includes parties that participated in the last national legislative elections for the lower house, hence excluding a number of parties from earlier periods that are now defunct. In this sense, the list of parties constitutes a snapshot of far right parties in the European Union, Norway and Switzerland.

Ideology

Regarding their ideological platform, all parties in Table 2.1 display some form of nationalism but there is considerable variation in the type of nationalist appeals they make. At one end of the nationalist spectrum, there are parties that make mild nationalist appeals, mostly using cultural arguments. At the other end, there are those making extreme nationalist appeals, using language that alludes to biological or racial differences between the ethnic majority and various minorities. As mentioned earlier, these are differences of degree, not kind. They partly signal the particularities of the national context and the developmental phase these parties find themselves in. The particularities of the context include historical legacies, the presence of minorities (e.g., in Eastern Europe), territorial disputes and the form that – mostly ethnic – nationalism has taken in certain countries across time (Minkenberg 2015). Contextual specificities also include the laws in place to prohibit the use of racial rhetoric and language and the legal space available for making explicit references to racial inequality or biological differences. The developmental phase of far right parties also matters (Ellinas 2010). In their earlier stages of development, some of these parties are more willing to risk being stigmatized with appeals reminiscent of interwar ideologies.

Table 2.1 *Indicative list of far right parties, 2016*

Country	Far Right party	Acronym	Founded	Top result, %[a]	Last result, %[a]	Last EP result, %	Seats in EP
Austria	Freedom Party of Austria	FPÖ	1956	26.9 (1999)	20.5 (2013)	19.7	4
	Alliance for the Future of Austria	BZÖ	2005	10.7 (2008)	3.5 (2013)	0.5	0
Belgium	Flemish Interest	VB	(1979)	12 (2007)	3.7 (2014)	4.3	1
	National Front	FN	1985	2.3 (1995)	0.5 (2010)	0	0
Bulgaria	Attack	Ataka	2005	9.4 (2009)	7.3 (2013)	3	0
Croatia	Croatian Party of Rights	HSP	2009	n/a[b]	n/a[b]	n/a[b]	0
Cyprus	National Popular Front	ELAM	2008	1.1 (2011)	3.6 (2016)	2.7	0
Czech Republic	Worker's Party of Social Justice	DSSS	(2003)	1.1 (2010)	0.9 (2013)	0.5	0
Denmark	Danish People's Party	DPP	2005	21.1 (2015)	21.1 (2015)	26.6	4
Estonia	Estonian Independence Party	EIP	1999	0.5 (2003)	0.2 (2015)	1.3	0
	Estonia National Conservative Party	EKRE	2012	8.1 (2015)	8.1 (2015)	4	0
Finland	Finns Party		(1995)	19.1 (2011)	17.7 (2015)	12.9	2
France	National Front	NF	1972	14.9 (1997)	13.6 (2012)	24.9	23
Germany	National Democratic Party of Germany	NPD	1964	4.3 (1969)	1.3 (2013)	1	1
	Republicans	REP	1983	2 (1990)	0.1 (2013)	0.4	0
	Alternative for Germany	AfD	2013	4.7 (2013)	4.7 (2013)	7.1	7
Greece	Golden Dawn	GD	1983	7 (2015)	7 (2015)	9.4	3
	Independent Greeks	IG	2012	10.6 (2012)	3.7 (2015)	3.5	1
Hungary	Jobbik	Jobbik	2003	22.2 (2014)	22.2 (2014)	14.7	3
Italy	Forza Nuova	FN	1997	0.7 (2006)	0.3 (2013)	n/a	n/a[b]
	Casa Pound Italia	CPI	2003	0.1 (2013)	0.1 (2013)	n/a[b]	n/a[b]
	[Lega Nord]	LN	1991	10.8 (1996)	4.1 (2013)	6.2	5

Ireland							
Latvia	National Alliance	NA	2010	16.6 (2014)	16.6 (2014)	14.3	1
Lithuania	Nationalist Union	NU	2011			2	0
Luxembourg							
Malta							
Netherlands	Party for Freedom	PVV	2005	15.5 (2010)	10.1 (2012)	13.3	4
Norway	Progress Party	FrP	1973	22.9 (2009)	16.3 (2013)	n/a	n/a
Poland	[Congress of the New Right]	KNP	2011	1.1. (2011)	0 (2015)	7.2	4
Portugal	National Renovator Party	PNR	2000	0.5 (2015)	0.5 (2015)	0.5	0
Romania	Greater Romania Party	PRM	1991	19.5 (2000)	1.5 (2012)	2.7	0
Slovakia	Slovak National Party	SNS	1989	13.9 (1990)	8.6 (2016)	3.6	0
	People's Party – Our Slovakia	LSNS	2010	8 (2016)	8 (2016)	1.7	0
Slovenia	Slovenian National Party	SNS	1991	10.2 (1991)	2.2 (2014)	4	0
Spain	National Democracy	DN	1995	0.6 (2004)	0 (2015)	0.1	0
	Spanish Falange of the JONS	FE-JONS	1977	0.2 (1986)	0 (2015)	0.1	0
Sweden	Sweden Democrats	SD	1988	12.9 (2014)	12.9 (2014)	9.7	2
Switzerland	Swiss People's Party	SVP	1971	29.4 (2015)	29.4 (2015)	n/a	n/a
United Kingdom	UK Independence Party	UKIP	1993	12.6 (2015)	12.6 (2015)	26.8	24
	British National Party	BNP	1982	1.9 (2010)	0 (2015)	1.1	0

[a] National Legislative Elections, lower house.
[b] in coalition.
The analysis includes all parties that took part in the last national election and partly relies on/updates the list of parties included in Mudde 2007, Pop-Eleches 2010, Bustikova 2014, Minkenberg 2015.
[borderline case] (founded with a different name)

21

The ideological platforms of most far right parties are close to the "master frame" of the French National Front. The French far right party has mostly relied on the ethnopluralist ideas of Nouvelle Droite, recognizing the equality rather than the hierarchy of nations or cultures but highlighting their differences. Along with anti-establishment populism, this basic frame is thought to have helped lift far right parties out of the ideological ghetto that their biological or racist nationalism had condemned them to (Rydgren 2005). The Vlaams Blok, which was banned in 2004 and succeeded by the Vlaams Belang, seems to have relied on these ethnopluralist notion of the Nouvelle Droitte, adopting a "people-nationalism" (Swyngedouw and Ivaldi 2001: 18) or ethnic nationalism (Mudde 2000). An inseparable component of the ethnopluralist master frame is cultural protectionism – the idea that political institutions should embody and protect the cultural traditions of the ethnic majority and that cultural minorities should conform to these traditions. One of the most electorally successful parties, the Danish People's Party, makes such cultural protectionist claims about the need to preserve Danish culture and to prevent Denmark from becoming a multi-ethnic society (Danish People's Party 2002). Similarly, True Finns, the predecessor to the Finns Party, claims that "Finishness is strength" and that "Finishness is a competitive advantage." This nationalist notion is not necessarily exclusivist – the party acknowledges the right of immigrants to exist in Finland on an equal footing, but also stands for a "when in Rome do as the Romans" approach that rejects multi-culturalism (Arter 2010). The cultural elements in the nationalist platforms of far right parties allow them to make appeals to Christian values and to reject anything related to Islam. The Dutch Party for Freedom is the most explicit exponent of Islamophobia, putting forth inflammatory claims about the "Islamification" of Europe by mass migration of Muslims (Vossen 2011). Although the party does not have an ethnic nationalist platform and rejects the anti-Semitism of some far right parties (Mudde 2010), its Islamophobia draws on a similar form of cultural protectionism and exclusionism found elsewhere in Europe. The UK Independence Party (UKIP) is also a somewhat special case in the far right party family because it mostly relies on civic, rather than ethnic, nationalist claims, demanding the reinvigoration of British culture. "UKIP will promote a unifying British culture, open to anyone who wishes to identify with Britain and British values, regardless of their ethnic or religious background" (UKIP 2015: 60). Similarly, the Alternative for Germany uses national symbolism and makes claims for a stronger Germany in the EU but, at least in its earlier official documents, it stopped short of ethnic nationalist claims that the ethnopluralist frame is mostly associated with. "One would be hard pressed to find any statement that is nationalistic in the usual sense of the term in this or in fact in any other part of the manifesto" (Arzheimer 2015).

Despite the electoral success of some parties using this ethnopluralist frame, other far right parties rely on more extreme versions of nationalism. Parties in Eastern Europe such as the Bulgarian Ataka, the Greater Romania Party or the Slovak National Party are sometimes categorized as "extreme nationalist" (Pop-Eleches 2010) or "highly nationalistic" (Bustikova 2015). A number of the far right parties in Eastern Europe are thought to adopt cruder versions of – again, ethnic – nationalism. As Minkenberg (2009) has pointed out, historical legacies are important: patterns of nation-building in Eastern Europe have been different than those in Western Europe. National uprisings against multi-national empires and the resulting borders that include ethnic minorities have helped make nationalism more mainstream, rather than confining it to the far right of the political spectrum. East European far right parties are naturally more extreme, then, than their counterparts in some West European countries, where nationalism bears a stigma of the past. This might help an outsider understand why some of the dominant far right actors in such countries as Bulgaria, Hungary, Romania and Slovakia are thought to belong to the "extremist right" (Minkenberg 2015). The appeals of East European far rightists – mostly their references to national minorities – are often closer to the racist or biological variant of national-ism. This is not always as obvious in their ideological proclamations or programmatic statements as it is in their rhetorical outbursts.

Although historical legacies can go a long way to account for the more extreme version of nationalism in Eastern Europe, a number of West European parties have adopted this version as well. The British National Party, for example, has roots in a tradition of biological nationalism that goes beyond the ethnopluralist master frame adopted by other far right parties in Western Europe. Although the party flirted with cultural instead of racial nationalism in the early 2000s, as part of an effort to widen its electoral appeal, the rhetoric of the party remained rooted in biological arguments about British descent (Goodwin 2011). Among the parties listed in Table 2.1, the Golden Dawn is probably one of the most extreme in terms of its ideology. As the next chapter shows, its version of national-ism comes closer to the National Socialist emphasis on race. A similar version of biological nationalism is also at the ideological core of the NPD and the LSNS (Chapter 10).

Program

Far right parties display notable programmatic variation when it comes to economic or social policy, but are similar in their views on immigrants and minorities, identifying them as a threat to the homogeneous nation they idealize (Minkenberg 1992). In most countries, far right parties have managed to gain ownership of issues related to immigrant or indigenous minorities because they adopt the toughest positions or rhetoric against them. Without any known exceptions, West European far right parties are unequivocally against immigration, demanding toughest regulations against the influx of foreigners, be they economic migrants or asylum seekers. Their claims against immigration combine arguments about economic costs, public security and cultural threats. In France, such arguments were part of the programmatic agenda of the National Front since the 1970s, but it was only in the subsequent decades that such slogans as "France for the French" started gaining political and electoral traction. In Austria anti-immigrant rhetoric started becoming politically relevant in the late 1980s, after the dissolution of the Soviet bloc and, subsequently, the wars in former Yugoslavia led to an influx of migrants. In the 1990s, the Freedom Party managed to establish ownership on the issue by demanding – and forcing mainstream parties to adopt – tougher immigration laws. The Norwegian Progress Party, which started in the 1970s as an anti-tax protest party, discovered the electoral potential of immigration in the 1980s. Whereas in the 1980s its arguments revolved around the economic cost of immigration, in the 1990s the party started using cultural arguments (Hagelund 2003). Similarly, the Swiss People's Party, which was a mainstream center-right party until the late 1980s, turned to identity politics in the 1990s, demanding tougher immigration, asylum and refugee policies. Its arguments were mostly cultural, "based on exclusionary beliefs and fueled by xenophobic sentiments" (Mazzoleni and Skenderovic 2007: 94). The inclusion of the Italian Lega Nord in the far right party family is often based on its similarly xenophobic stance on immigration. A regionalist rather than a nationalist party, and hence lacking the ideological foundations most far right parties share, the Lega Nord sought to capitalize on anti-foreigner sentiment in the late 1990s, strategically incorporating immigration into its anti-establishment and pro-independence program (Albertazzi and McDonnell 2005; Ignazi 2005). Although the stance of the UK Independence Party on immigration has encouraged its inclusion in the far right party family, the partly has mostly shied away from the cultural arguments made by its counterparts in other West European countries. It largely focuses on immigration policy, "the uncontrolled, politically-driven immigration that has been promoted and sustained by Labour and the Conservatives" (UKIP 2015: 10). In some ways the Alternative for Germany is similar to UKIP in advocating a more restrictive immigration policy without fully adopting the nativist claims that usually accompany this position (Arzheimer 2015).

Whereas immigration is the signature issue of West European far right parties, in Eastern Europe this issue has not gained as much political traction. Some East European far right parties mention immigration in their programs or statements (e.g., Auers and Kasekamp 2015: 151) but, until the refugee crisis of the mid-2010s, this was yet to become a core issue. The refugee crisis that prompted the closing of national borders gave more attention to this issue but, for the most part, East European far right parties continue to primarily target indigenous ethnic minorities rather than immigrants. The Hungarian Jobbik, for example, gained notoriety in the mid-2000s for its anti-Roma rhetoric. Its 2010 electoral manifesto devotes a section to "Gipsy issues," warning about the risk that they sink Hungary "into a state of virtual civil war." Jobbik states that it is "simply beyond dispute, that certain specific criminological phenomena are predominantly and overwhelmingly associated with this minority" and asks for the establishment of a special rural Gendarmerie to halt "gipsy crime" (Jobbik 2010: 11–12). The Bulgarian Ataka similarly wants to institute "civic patrols" to curb "immigrant and Roma terror on the streets." In addition to the vulgar language the party uses to refer to ethnic minorities, Ataka wants to ban Turkish-language services on public television. The Slovak National Party also presents radical views on the Roma issue. Slovak far rightists additionally take issue with the presence of a sizable ethnic Hungarian minority. They portray ethnic Hungarians as being disloyal to the state and a threat to territorial integrity of Slovakia. Ethnic Hungarians were also targeted by the Greater Romania Party, along with the Jews and the Roma (Pop-Eleches 2008). In Latvia and Estonia, far right parties concentrate on the rights of their sizable ethnic Russian populations and on foreign relations with Russia. As the next chapter shows, the GD combines the tough programmatic positions against immigration shared by most Western European far right parties with the negative rhetoric against minorities used by similar parties in Eastern Europe. The party uses strong and negative rhetoric not only against immigrants but also against the Muslim minority in Western Thrace and most of Greece's neighbors.

Electorates

Analyses of party electorates provide useful insights into the various patterns of support far right parties attract but cannot offer much analytical leverage in distinguishing between various subfamilies. It is beyond the scope of this chapter to offer a comprehensive review of these analyses. Some general observations can help highlight some of their main findings and explain the limitations of using electorates as a criterion for distinguishing between party subtypes. First, there are two sets of attitudinal predispositions associated with far right voting. The first, mostly found in Western Europe (Allen 2015), relates to the attitudes voters have toward immigrants (van der Brug et al. 2000; 2005; Ivarsflaten 2005; 2008; Rydgren 2008). The second, mostly found in Eastern Europe (see Lubbers and Scheepers 2000; Lubbers et al. 2002 for Western Europe), links far right support with political dissatisfaction (Allen 2015). After two decades of research on far right electorates, there is still limited evidence of economic voting. Second, demographic evidence has shown notable similarities among far right electorates. These similarities are most striking when one examines the gender of far right electorates both in West (Givens 2004; Mudde 2007) and East Europe (Harteveld et al. 2015). The picture is more varied when one focuses on the occupational and age profile of far right electorates (Norris 2005; Bornschier 2010). Third, there are a number of contextual characteristics that tend to be associated with far right support, such as immigration and unemployment. These seem to mostly hold in Western rather than in Eastern Europe, where the context differs (e.g., Jackman and Volpert 1996; Golder 2003; Arzheimer 2009).

Despite their important insights, analyses of party electorates are not well suited for distinguishing between extremist and radical right-wing parties. Cross-country analyses of individual voter attitudes or attributes tend to be based on larger parties, for which there are big enough samples in international or national surveys (e.g., Allen 2015: 5). This leaves out many of the extremist parties across Europe, which are usually smaller in size and for which there are less survey data available. More importantly, national surveys of extremist parties suggest that, in terms of their electorates, these parties are more similar to their radical cousins than one would think. An analysis of the British National Party, for example, shows that its electorate is predominantly male, anxious about immigration and disaffected with mainstream political parties. In this sense, it is very similar to the electorate of some of the most successful radical right-wing parties identified and examined in the literature (Ford and Goodwin 2010).

Another example comes from the analysis of voter support for the Hungarian Jobbik. Again, their electorate is predominantly male, disaffected with democracy and prejudiced against the Roma and the Jews (Karácsony and Róna 2011). The attitudinal profile of Golden Dawn voters is similar: they show high levels of distrust toward political institutions and, more importantly, democracy. They are also negative toward immigration, for both economic and cultural reasons (Lamprianou and Ellinas 2017a). Overall, this quick survey of the electorates of far right parties suggests that voter profiles are not as useful in distinguishing the really extreme from the more moderate far right parties. Extremist right-wing parties seem to draw support from electorates that are similar to those of radical right-wing parties. Although much more research needs to be done to identify the typical far right voter (Mudde 2007), supporters of extremist parties cannot be expected to be very different from those of radical right-wing parties.

Origins

The distinction between extremist and radical right-wing parties partly rests on their origins. A number of radical right-wing parties are of parliamentary origin, set up by people or groups who broke ranks with mainstream parties rather than individuals with the extra-parliamentary profile Duverger described (1959). The most notable example of a radical right-wing party with parliamentary origins is the Dutch Party for Freedom. Geert Wilders, its founder and leader, was a member of parliament with the Liberal Party for six years before leaving it to found his own party (de Lange and Art 2011: 1235). Another example is the party of the Independent Greeks, founded by legislators who defected in 2012 from the conservative New Democracy, after the latter agreed with the second bailout agreement Greece signed with its creditors. The leader of the party, Panos Kammenos, was a member of the ND parliamentary caucus for nearly twenty years before defecting. Other examples include the German Republicans, founded in 1983 by two disgruntled members of the conservative Christian Social Union; the UK Independence Party, founded in 1993 and subsequently led by Nigel Farage who left the Conservative Party in disagreement with its signing of the Maastricht Treaty; and the Alternative for Germany, founded in 2013 by a group that included disaffected long-time members of the Christian Democratic Party (Arzheimer 2015: 540). Some radical right-wing parties were founded as splinter groups from long-existing radical right parties: the Danish People's

Party was founded in 1995 by the long-time legislator of the Progress Party, Pia Kjærsgaard (Widfeldt 2014); and the Alliance for the Future of Austria was founded in 2005 by the former leader and legislator of the Freedom Party, Jörg Haider.

Another set of radical right-wing parties of parliamentary origins have been transformed from existing mainstream parties by adopting a nationalist ideology and anti-immigrant program. This transformation was probably easier for the Freedom Party of Austria, which is rooted in the national-liberal camp of Austria (Bluhm 1973; Katzenstein 1976) and succeeded the Association of Independents, a postwar party that sheltered many former Nazis (Riedlsperger 1978). The party followed a liberal trajectory in the 1970s and joined the Liberal International in 1979 (Luther 2000) before being hijacked by its nationalist faction in the mid-1980s. The Norwegian Progress Party started as an anti-tax protest party before transforming itself into a national populist party, with a strong anti-immigration agenda. The transformation came about in the late 1980s and early 1990s and paid off electoral dividends, turning the party into one of the most successful radical right-wing parties in Europe (Widfeldt 2014: 83–89; see also Jupskås 2016). The most successful member of this party family, the Swiss People's Party, similarly converted from a relatively small-sized conservative party in the 1970s and 1980s to a much larger, radical right-wing party in the 1990s and 2000s. Adopting a platform against the immigration regime and the political establishment, the party managed to gain a second seat in the seven-seat Swiss governing council (Mazzoleni and Skenderovic 2007).

Another subset of far right parties has different origins than the parties described above. The French National Front has clear extra-parliamentary roots. The 1972 founding of the National Front brought together "warriors" of older conflicts (e.g., the Algerian war) under a single political umbrella. It took three decades for the party to partly moderate its political outlook, with the biggest change coming in 2011, after Marine Le Pen succeeded her father to the leadership of the National Front (Shields 2013). The Sweden Democrats followed a similar trajectory, transforming, like its French counterpart, from an extremist to a radical right-wing party. Founded in 1988, the party displayed notable continuity with previous extremist movements. In its early years the party had among its members and supporters a number of fascist or Nazi veterans, some with tenure in interwar extremist parties. Leadership change was critical for transforming the Sweden Democrats into a radical right-wing party (Rydgren 2006: 108–119). After 1995, the new leader of the party, Mikael Jansson, sought to distance the party from its links with Nazism, getting rid of many extremists and recruiting more moderates. The transformation of the party continued into the 2000s, especially after 2005, when Jimmie Åkesson sought to further move the party away from its extremist past, adopting a more moderate ideological platform (Widfeldt 2014: 180–186).

Whereas radical right-wing parties have diverse origins, nearly all extremist right-wing parties remain rooted in earlier historical conflicts or display some continuity with the past. The oldest extremist party, the NPD, never sought to escape the heavy burden of Germany's Nazi past (Chapter 10). The British National Party was founded in 1982 by people who were involved in neo-Nazi or neo-fascist groups and parties in the 1960s and 1970s, especially the National Front and the New National Front. This strong continuity with the past was evident not only in personnel but also in the biological nationalist platform the party inherited from its predecessors. In the next two decades the party failed to transform itself into a more moderate exponent of British nationalism. After 1999, under the new leadership of Nick Griffin, the party made a new effort to get out of the extremist ghetto by recruiting new members, focusing on immigration and changing its street tactics. But, unlike the experience of the Sweden Democrats, the leadership change at the BNP did not succeed in pushing it away from its extremist past (Goodwin 2011). The Greek Golden Dawn and the Spanish Falange of the JONS also display notable continuity with a discredited historical past. As discussed in Chapter 4, the Golden Dawn is the only Greek party commemorating divisive and controversial events that took place during the Greek civil war. Similarly, the Spanish Falange is a direct descendent of the Spanish interwar fascists who thrived under the Franco regime. Although Falangists have been represented by a number of parties in the past decades, the Spanish Falange de JONS is one of the most notable representatives of the ancien régime, still commemorating the anniversary of the deaths of the Falange movement's founder, José Antonio Primo de Rivera, and of General Franco.

Party origins are less useful in distinguishing between extremist and radical right-wing parties in Eastern Europe. The many decades of communist rule disrupted the extremist networks and dismantled the fascist or Nazi groups and parties that operated in a number of these countries during the interwar years. Although historical legacies can go a long way to explain the evolution of right-wing radicalism in Eastern Europe in the past few decades (Minkenberg 2013), the distance from the interwar years has brought about a generational gap that limits the continuity evident elsewhere in terms of human and organizational resources. A number of these parties

have extra-parliamentary origins but unlike their West European counterparts, they do not have direct ties with conflicts of the past. That being said,
some of the symbolism these parties use has generated concerns about their
ties to interwar extremism. Gábor Vona, the leader of Jobbik, for example,
registered the Hungarian Guard, a paramilitary group whose military
marches, army boots, black shirts and Árpád-striped flags have brought
memories of interwar extremism. Similarly, Marian Kotleba, the leader of
Kotleba – People's Party Our Slovakia, is known for his public support of the
Slovak Nazi puppet state and for wearing fascist-looking uniforms reminiscent of that murderous regime (Chapter 10). The Czech Worker's Party of
Social Justice presents interesting similarities to the Slovakian one. The party
is the direct successor to the Worker's Party, outlawed by Czech courts in
2010, for its ties to Nazism and for its extremist views.

Transnational Links

International links can also help distinguish between various types of far
right parties. Although it is beyond the scope of this chapter to provide an
exhaustive description of these links, Table 2.2 provides an overview of
some of the most important transnational associations in which far right
parties are organized. The most notable of these associations are in the
European Parliament. The Europe of Nations and Freedom (ENF)
includes representatives from some of the most successful far right parties
in Europe. Founded in 2015, and co-chaired by Marine Le Pen of the
French National Front and Marcel de Graaf of the Dutch Party for
Freedom, the ENF is dominated by the Front, which has twenty out
of its thirty-eight members. In 2016, the group included parties such as
the Austrian Freedom Party (4 MEPs), the Dutch Party for Freedom
(4 MEPs) and the Vlaams Belang (1 MEP). It also included the borderline
far right cases of the Lega Nord (5 MEPs) and the Polish Congress of the
New Right (2 MEPs) as well as two independent MEPs, one initially
elected with the UK Independence Party and the other with a Romanian
cross-party electoral alliance. The formation of the political group is a
major development for European far right parties, which previously lacked
their own political group and the institutional privileges granted to political groups in the European Parliament.[3] Seven other European far right
parties joined two more moderate political groups, the European

---

[3] European Parliament, Rules of Procedure, Title I, chapter 4, September 2015 [retrieved on March 31,
2016, from http://tinyurl.com/h2knnau].

Table 2.2 *The international links of far right parties, 2016*

Country	Far Right Party	Membership in EP [or other membership]
Austria	Freedom Party of Austria	Europe of Nations and Freedom
	Alliance for the Future of Austria	Not in EP
Belgium	Flemish Interest	Europe of Nations and Freedom
	National Front	Not in EP
Bulgaria	Attack	Not in EP
Croatia	Croatian Party of Rights	Not in EP
Cyprus	National Popular Front	Not in EP
Czech Republic	Worker's Party of Social Justice	Not in EP, Alliance of Peace and Freedom (APF)
Denmark	Danish People's Party	European Conservatives and Reformists
Estonia	Estonian Independence Party	Not in EP
	Estonia National Conservative Party	Not in EP
Finland	Finns Party	European Conservatives and Reformists
France	National Front	Europe of Nations and Freedom
Germany	National Democratic Party of Germany	Not attached members in EP (APF)
	Republicans	Not in EP
	Alternative for Germany	European Conservatives and Reformists
Greece	Golden Dawn	Not attached members in EP (APF)
	Independent Greeks	European Conservatives and Reformists
Hungary	Jobbik	Not attached members in EP
Italy	Forza Nuova	Not in EP (APF)
	Casa Pound Italia	Not in EP
	[Lega Nord]	Europe of Nations and Freedom
Ireland		
Latvia	National Alliance	European Conservatives and Reformists
Lithuania	Nationalist Union	Not in EP
Luxembourg		
Malta		
Netherlands	Party for Freedom	Europe of Nations and Freedom
Norway	Progress Party	Not applicable
Poland	Congress of the New Right	Europe of Nations and Freedom
Portugal	National Renovator Party	Not in EP
Romania	Greater Romania Party	Not in EP
Slovakia	Slovak National Party	Not in EP
	People's Party - Our Slovakia	Not in EP, (APF)
Slovenia	Slovenian National Party	Not in EP
Spain	National Democracy	Not in EP (APF)

Table 2.2 (*cont.*)

Country	Far Right Party	Membership in EP [or other membership]
	Spanish Falange of the JONS	Not in EP
Sweden	Sweden Democrats	Europe for Freedom and Direct Democracy
Switzerland	Swiss People's Party	Not applicable
United Kingdom	[UK Independence Party]	Europe for Freedom and Direct Democracy
	British National Party	Not in EP

The analysis includes all parties that took part in the last elections and partly relies on/ updates the list of parties included in Mudde 2007, Pop-Eleches 2010, Bustikova 2014, Minkenberg 2015.
[borderline case]

Conservatives and Reformists (ECR) and the Europe for Freedom and Direct Democracy (EFD). As an indication of the diversity found in this group, five European far right parties belong to the ECR alongside the British Conservatives and the Polish Law and Justice. These parties tend to have more moderate positions than those belonging to the ENF and try to avoid association with parties such as the French National Front and the Austrian Freedom Party. In 2016 the ECR included parties such as the Danish People's Party (4 MEPs), the Finns Party (2), the Alternative for Germany (2), the Independent Greeks (1) and the Latvian National Alliance (1).[4] The EFD includes two parties that are usually included in the far right party family. The biggest party in the group is the UK Independence Party which has nearly half the MEPs of the entire group. The Sweden Democrats have two additional MEPs and co-exist with the Italian Movimento 5 Stelle.

A number of more extreme far right parties have not managed to find a home in any European Parliament political groups. The non-attached parties include the three members of Jobbik, the three members of the GD and the one member of the German NPD. Interestingly, among the non-attached members of the European Parliament are Jean Marie Le Pen and Bruno Gollnisch, who were elected with the National Front but have distanced themselves from the more moderate turn of Marine Le Pen. To signal this moderate turn, after the European Parliament elections in 2014,

---

[4] In March 2016, the two MEPs of the Alternative for Germany were expelled from the group.

the new leader of the French National Front ruled out the possibility of collaborating with the GD, Jobbik, Ataka and the NPD.[5] In an attempt to break this isolation, these more extreme parties – except Jobbik – formed a new European party in February 2015, the Alliance for Peace and Freedom (APF). The members of the party include the really marginal Spanish National Democracy and Czech Worker's Party of Social Justice. In 2016, the People's Party – Our Slovakia and the Cypriot National Popular Front were affiliated with the Alliance. The former joined the Alliance in 2017 and the latter subsequently distanced itself from it, along with the GD.

Political Action

One of the most important distinctions between extremist and radical right-wing parties relates to their propensity to undertake contentious forms of political action. Radical right-wing parties are mostly known for their ideas rather than their action and make comparatively small investment in organizing disruptive political activities. Based on the limited evidence made available by the numerous studies on far right parties on the range and frequency of political activity they undertake, there seems to be notable variation among the various parties in what they do. The Dutch Party for Freedom is probably at one end of the spectrum when it comes to organizational investment in contentious political action. Unlike other successful far right parties in Europe, the Party for Freedom has purposefully avoided setting up an elaborate party organization, resembling, instead, the business-firm party model (Mazzoleni and Voerman 2016). In the recent past, parties resembling the latter model, like the Swedish New Democracy (Taggart 1996; Widfeldt 2014) or the Greek Popular Orthodox Rally (Ellinas 2010), quickly faded away, unable to sustain their initial electoral gains. But the Party for Freedom has been successful as a member-less party. The party is known for only having a single member, Geert Wilders, and to lack an extensive organizational network beyond its parliamentary caucus (Vossen 2011). Although party statutes allow party membership, Wilders is reported to have stopped membership after its founding as part of an effort to set up a very slim and highly centralized organization. "Consequentially, a party on the ground does not exist and no local or regional branches of the PVV have been set up" (de Lange and Art 2011: 1240).

[5] Ataka ended up without any representatives in the European Parliament.

Most of the other major far right parties are different from the Party for Freedom in trying to set up organizations with features reminiscent of the mass party model rather of the business-firm party model. Parties such as the Danish People's Party, the Norwegian Progress Party and the Swiss People's Party have actively invested in the development of effective – in some cases, highly centralized – national party organizations and in the proliferation of local organizational networks. This explains why in an era of membership decline (see Chapter 3), some of these parties managed to expand their membership base (Widfeldt 2014; Heinisch and Mazzoleni 2016). At least on paper, membership expansion has given these parties more significant presence on the ground. In practice, though, it is unclear how to interpret the growth of party membership. For one thing, the link between membership and activism is not very strong. One of the few measures of levels of activism across Danish parties, for example, finds that the members of the Danish People's Party are the least active among members of all parties. As for the activities in which they are encouraged to participate, these are typical in most parties: attending meetings, distributing pamphlets and putting up posters (Pedersen et al. 2004). For the Zurich section of the Swiss People's Party, local activism has meant the organization of public activities that "included 'senior afternoons,' with free coffee and cake; matinees; local regulars' table; information events; or the widely known 'farmers' breakfasts,' with free sausages and popular music" (Skenderovic 2009: 144).

Whereas some far right parties have invested resources in organizing conventional types of political activity, like matinees and breakfasts, others started out with more controversial, contentious and sometimes violent action before adopting a more conventional mode of political activism. The French National Front is probably the best such example. Some of the leading figures of the party in the 1970s had their origins in the banned Occident and Ordre Nouveau, both of which became known for their violent activism and paramilitary action (Marcus 1995: 13–22). In the 1970s, though, the party managed to rid itself of this violent element and in the 1980s, especially after its local and national breakthroughs, it transformed itself into a highly organized political machine with well-trained activists and iron discipline that helped moderate its early profile (Mayer 1998; DeClair 1999). The Sweden Democrats followed a similar trajectory to that of the French National Front. The strong ties the party initially had with former Nazis gave rise to violent street confrontations with counterdemonstrators. The public meetings of the Sweden Democrats "were often marred with violence" and by the "plethora of militant racists, skinheads and/or Nazis" (Widfeldt 2014: 182). It took a number of expulsions and the imposition of strict rules – such as bans on wearing uniforms in party meetings – for the party to start changing its activist profile. Part of the modernization strategy of the Sweden Democrats involved shifting to modern campaign techniques via the internet and the media, rather than on traditional labor-intensive leafleting and meetings (Widfeldt 2014: 185). Like the French National Front and the Sweden Democrats, in its early years the Belgian Vlaams Belang (then Vlaams Blok) was similarly involved in more contentious activities before going through a phase of professionalization that turned the party into a modern, highly centralized machine. The militant profile of the party was largely due to its reliance on a network of right-wing extreme nationalist groups, which usually undertook more confrontational and, sometimes, violent activism. These groups include *Voorpost*, *Were Di*, the Language Action Committee and the National Young Students Union. Through the association with the Flemish nationalist subculture the party was also involved in a number of cultural activities at the local level. It took about a decade for the party to go through a period of modernization that partly changed its action profile (Mudde 1995; Art 2008; 2011).

Extremist right-wing parties differ from radical right-wing parties because they are intensely and systematically involved in contentious and violent forms of political action of the type usually associated with social movements rather than political parties. They are known as much for their street action as they are for their extreme discourses. The oldest and most well-known of these parties is the German NPD. The party has gained notoriety for its street-level activism, violent demonstrations and protest marches that bring it into direct confrontation with counter-demonstrators (Chapter 10). The British National Party, also known for the contentious and violent activism of its "political soldiers," experimented with a similar change in street-level activism in the 1990s and 2000s. Rather than solely relying on violent confrontation and loud demonstrations, which attracted negative attention to the party and undermined its electoral prospects, British neo-fascists started embracing social activism as a means to legitimize themselves in various communities. They fine-tuned their programmatic messages to the needs of local communities and organized campaigns on locally important issues, such as the closure of local industries or public facilities. Moreover, BNP activists were involved in local community work, such as garbage collection and graffiti cleanups (Copsey 2004: 55–60; Goodwin 2011: 46–47, 71–75)

The two Italian neo-fascist parties, Casa Pound and Forza Nuova, display notable similarities with the NPD and the BNP in terms of their street-level activism. Founded in 2003 and named after the American poet and Mussolini supporter Ezra Pound, the "house" of Pound is more a movement than a party. Born in Rome with the squatting of a public building and becoming a national organization a few years later, the party is known for its contentious modes of political participation. While intermittently participating in local, regional and national elections, the party also organizes protests, demonstrative and expressive actions and unauthorized marches and riots. Casa Pound has undertaken a number of squatting activities and violent riots that led to clashes with antifascist groups and police units. Beyond these violent street politics, Casa Pound is also involved in cultural activities with a well-known music band, *Zetazeroalfa*, bookshops, pubs and various publications. The party takes social activism very seriously, seeking to challenge the traditional domin- ance of the Left on social action. Besides this political and cultural action repertoire, then, Casa Pound projects itself as a promoter of "para-welfare" activities that involve the distribution of food, the provision of health assistance, aid to disabled and elderly people and a form of civil protection. It is keen on establishing a community of activists that spans across various aspects of political and social life (Gattinara et al. 2013; Froio and Gattinara 2015). Forza Nuova is also known for its contentious and sometimes violent political activism. Founded in 1997 by two figures associated with the terrorist activity of the neo-fascist Italian Social Movement (MSI), the party has been organizing demonstrations at both the local and the national level. In recent years it has been implicated in protest action against minorities, including the storming of a television studio hosting a Muslim leader and an incident that involved the throwing of a banana against the first black minister of Italy during a public event. As the next chapter shows in more detail, the GD is similar to the Italian, British and German extremist right-wing parties in being active on the streets.

The type of political activism undertaken by extremist movement parties in Western Europe seems to have been adopted by a number of East European parties as well. The best example of these parties is the Hungarian Jobbik, which has been known for its association with the banned paramilitary-type organization Hungarian Guard. Founded in 2007 by the leader of Jobbik, Gábor Vona, the Guard gained international spotlights for its military-uniformed marches, fascist-looking emblems and vigilante-type activities against the Roma (Karácsony and Róna 2011). The paramilitary action of the Guard brought about its disbandment in 2009 – a court decision that was subsequently upheld by the European Court of Human Rights. The Court noted that the military- and Nazi-looking marches effectively intimated the Roma population where it took place (EHCR 2013). After its disbandment, the Guard continued to exist as an association organizing mostly cultural activities. Jobbik, however, is reported to continue to rely on paramilitary action for mobilizing anti-Roma activism in the Hungarian countryside. One of those activities, in 2011, led to the fleeing of the Roma from the town and the resignation of the mayor (Varga 2014). The People's Party – Our Slovakia is similarly active on the streets against the Roma population. Its leader, Marian Kotleba, has been detained several times by police during anti-Roma events organized by various extremist groups, such as the banned Slovak Togetherness association. In the past years, his party was involved in the organization of several marches in Roma-inhabited villages, claiming to offer protection to local citizens against Gipsy crime and police inactivity (Kluknavská 2015: 151). The Czech Worker's Party of Social Justice has similarly been reported undertaking "civic patrols" in villages with Roma minorities. As in Slovakia, the party is a successor to another political party, the Worker's Party, which was outlawed in 2010 for its extreme ideology and links to Nazism.

Conclusion

This chapter has borrowed from the existing literature on party families to demarcate the conceptual contours of the far right and to distinguish between extremist and radical right-wing parties. This literature has focused on the ideologies, programs, electorates, histories and international links to analyze the far right. A lot less attention has been paid to an additional criterion, the political *praxis* of really extreme parties. The involvement of extremist right-wing parties in contentious and violent political action serves as a useful criterion that distinguishes them from radical right-wing parties. Using this and the other criteria, the chapter classified dozens of far right parties in Europe, distinguishing between the two subtypes (Table 2.3). The GD, to which the book now turns, as well as the NPD and the LSNS analyzed in Chapter 10, are among the most extreme parties in the universe of far right parties in Europe.

Table 2.3 *Extremist and radical right-wing parties, 2016*

Country	Biggest FR party	Acronym	Nationalism	Anti-immigration or anti-minority	Origins	International association	Contentious/violent political action	Classification
Austria	Freedom Party of Austria	FPÖ	Ethnic	Yes	Parliamentary, extremist	ENF	No	Radical
Belgium	Flemish Interest	VB	Ethnic	Yes	Extra-parliamentary, extremist	ENF	No	Radical
Bulgaria	Attack	Ataka	Racial/biological	Yes	Extra-parliamentary, non-extremist	None	No	Radical/extremist
Cyprus	National Popular Front	ELAM	Racial/biological	Yes	Extra-parliamentary, extremist	None	[Yes]	Radical/extremist
Czech Republic	Worker's Party of Social Justice	DSSS	Racial/biological	Yes	Extra-parliamentary, extremist	APF	Yes	Extremist
Denmark	Danish People's Party	DPP	Ethnic	Yes	Parliamentary, non-extremist	ECR	No	Radical
Finland	Finns Party		Ethnic/civic	Yes	Parliamentary, non-extremist	ECR	No	Radical
France	National Front	NF	Ethnic	Yes	Extra-parliamentary, extremist	ENF	No	Radical
Germany	National Democratic Party	NPD	Racial/biological	Yes	Extra-parliamentary, extremist	APF	Yes	Extremist
Germany	Alternative for Germany	AfD	Civic	Yes	Parliamentary, non-extremist	ECR	No	Radical
Greece	Golden Dawn	GD	Racial/biological	Yes	Extra-parliamentary, extremist	APF	Yes	Extremist

	Independent Greeks	IG	Ethnic/civic	Yes	Parliamentary, non-extremist	ECR	No	Radical
Hungary	Jobbik	Jobbik	Ethnic	Yes	Extra-parliamentary, non-extremist	None	Yes	Extremist/radical
Italy	Forza Nuova	FN	Ethnic	Yes	Extra-parliamentary, extremist	APF	Yes	Extremist
	Casa Pound Italia	CPI	Ethnic	Yes	Extra-parliamentary, extremist	None	Yes	Extremist
	Lega Nord	LN	Ethnic/civic	Yes	Extra-parliamentary, non-extremist	ENF	No	[Radical]
Netherlands	Party for Freedom	PVV	Civic	Yes	Parliamentary, non-extremist	ENF	No	Radical
Norway	Progress Party	FrP	Ethnic	Yes	Parliamentary, non-extremist	None	No	Radical
Slovakia	People's Party - Our Slovakia	L'SNS	Racial/biological	Yes	Extra-parliamentary, extremist	[APF]	Yes	Extremist
Sweden	Sweden Democrats	SD	Ethnic	Yes	Extra-parliamentary, extremist	EFD	No	Radical
Switzerland	Swiss People's Party	SVP	Ethnic	Yes	Parliamentary, non-extremist	None	No	Radical
United Kingdom	UK Independence Party	UKIP	Civic	Yes	Parliamentary, non-extremist	EFD	No	[Radical]
	British National Party	BNP	Racial/biological	Yes	Extra-parliamentary, extremist	None	Yes	Extremist

[borderline case]

CHAPTER 3

The Organizational Development of Extremist Right-Wing Parties

Organizational development is one of the most important lines of research inquiry into political parties (Webb et al. 2002). Any attempt to understand the internal dynamics of extremist right-wing parties needs to begin with a consideration of how this voluminous literature can help develop an analytical framework for understanding the evolution of such parties. Party organizational development refers to changes in the basic features that make up these systems of collective decision-making across time. The understanding of organizational development requires a systematic consideration of how internal party features relate to each other and evolve – a task that the party literature has successfully undertaken over the years. Based on this literature, there is now a considerable volume of works looking "inside" parties for clues regarding their developmental trajectories. The range of party organizational features used to trace party development ranges considerably. The litany includes internal organizational structures and dynamics (e.g., Janda 1983; Szczerbiak 2001; Grzymala-Busse 2002; van Biezen 2003; Sartori 2005); party membership and activism (e.g., Kitschelt 1989; Scarrow 1996; Szczerbiak 1999; Mair and van Biezen 2001; Whiteley 2011); party links with collateral organizations (e.g., Poguntke 2006); societal rootedness (e.g., Mainwaring 1999; LeBas 2011); and resources (e.g., van Biezen 2004). The examination of these organizational features has provided precious insights into the wide array of political organizations that make up the party universe in different times and countries. The organizational polymorphism evident in the party universe has not helped explicate a general theory of organizational development (Krouwel 2006: 249) but it has led to a literature seeking to link these distinct organizational forms with the capacity of political parties to respond to environmental change.

The links drawn between party organizational development and political outcomes have been both direct and indirect. Using party organization as an intervening variable, works on the European and Latin American

Left have shown how parties can respond differently to common environmental challenges, depending on their internal make up. The main idea is that organizational features that permitted strategic flexibility allowed Leftist parties to deal more effectively with environmental obstacles or opportunities, indirectly affecting their capacity to remain or become potent forces in their respective political settings (Koelble 1992; Kitschelt 1994; Grzymala-Busse 2002; Levitsky 2003). Some works are even bolder in their attempts to link organizational development with political outcomes, using party organization as an independent variable to directly account for electoral results. Although the organizational features used to capture organizational strength differ, the idea here is that strong party organizations deliver better electoral results than weaker ones (Crotty 1968; Janda 1983; Tavits 2013). Though somewhat detached from the broader literature on party organizations, scholarship on radical right-wing parties in Europe similarly suggests a strong link between organizational form and electoral performance. Single- and cross-country analyses show that strongly organized parties fare better at the polls than less organized ones (Betz 1998; Lubbers et al. 2002; Carter 2005; Art 2008; de Lange and Art 2011). The level of organizational rootedness and development of these parties can go a long way to account for their persistence after initial electoral breakthroughs (Mudde 2007; Ellinas 2010; Bolleyer 2013).

This book differs from these works in treating organizational development as the main dependent variable rather than as an intervening or independent variable. Taking an analytical step back from existing work on political parties, it problematizes and systematically traces variation in the developmental trajectories of party organizations. In doing so, the book joins scholarly attempts to understand parties from "within" (Berman 1997) but treats organizational phenomena as outcomes that merit attention of their own. Instead of granting organizations autonomy from their environment *a priori*, this book investigates how various sets of environmental and endogenous influences affect organizational processes and outcomes. Although organizational development is one of the oldest strains in the now vast literature on political parties, there are few efforts to systematically understand why some parties evolve into strong organizations that get to enjoy relative autonomy from their environment, while others remain organizationally weak, or in many cases (Bolleyer et al. 2018) simply fail. Agreeing with Tavits (2013: 6–7) that there is very limited theoretical work on the origins organizational strength, this book focuses on understanding the varying capacities of political parties to become organizationally successful.

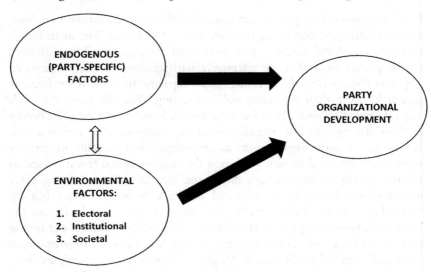

Figure 3.1   Factors affecting party organizational development.

The "Logics" of Organizational Development:
An Analytical Framework

Some of the most important advances in organizational theory have largely come from the understanding of the complex ways in which organizations interact with their environments and from the appreciation of how various environmental features affect organizational change (Aldrich 2008; Scott 2008). Party organizations are similar to other organizations in that their evolution depends on how they shape and are shaped by their environments. Hence, any attempt to systematically trace their evolution must take into account both endogenous and environmental factors affecting organizational development. Drawing from the theoretical and empirical insights of earlier and more recent scholarship on political parties, this section develops an analytical framework for examining different "logics" of organizational development and the next section applies it to extremist right-wing parties. The framework consists of one set of endogenous features and three sets of environmental factors affecting organizational development (Figure 3.1). These four factors are not incompatible but, rather, are key elements in distinct but complex conceptualizations of empirical reality.

Endogenous Factors

A long tradition to the study of party development going back to Ostrogorski (1902) and Michels (1915) looks "inside" parties to understand their organizational evolution. The main idea of this approach is that parties have considerable autonomy from their environments and, hence, get to shape their organizational fate. This organizational approach to party development has been applied in a number of diverse settings. Going beyond the Downsian treatment of "each party as though it were a single person" (1957: 26) and breaking down party units into their component parts, the emphasis on intraorganizational dynamics has helped highlight the wide range of features that come to bear on how parties develop and, ultimately, on how they perform in changing electoral contexts (Koelble 1992; Kitschelt 1994; Grzymala-Busse 2002; Levitsky 2003). No single feature can adequately account for the complex processes of organizational change or the varied evolution of organizational entities. Long lists of attributes associated with strong party organizations (e.g., LeBas 2011; Tavits 2013) are indicative of the richness of intraorganizational life and of the futility of efforts to attribute organizational development to a single party characteristic. It is best, instead, to focus on some recurring themes in this organizational approach to party development.

One such theme is the importance of institutional structures in political parties. Unlike cadre (Duverger 1959) or charismatic (Panebianco 1988) parties, mass parties have been seen as organizational entities with well-systematized processes and procedures and weighty – and, in many cases, slow-moving – bureaucratic structures. Regardless of the electoral effects of this institutional density (Kitschelt 1994; Levitsky 2003), parties that sought to structure the behavior and interaction of their leaders, members and supporters through well-entrenched institutional mechanisms became associated with developmental continuity. Unlike the organizational volatility evident in new entrepreneurial (Harmel and Svasand 1993; Bolleyer 2013) or business-firm (Hopkin and Paolucci 1999) parties, Duvergerian mass parties displayed organizational stability, inertia and persistence that helps account for their developmental trajectory. Although the postwar period witnessed the near extinction or death of this party model (Krouwel 2006; Katz and Mair 2009), most parties continue to rely on a dense set of institutional arrangements, including features (e.g., democratic centralism in orthodox Leninist parties, Ellinas and Katsourides 2013) that one would have anticipated to fade away with time.

A second theme cutting across many works adopting an organizational approach to party development is periodization. Efforts to understand endogenous organizational evolution naturally focus on various phases of party development (e.g., Harmel and Svasand 1993). The formative phase of party development is one of the most important in the periodization of party evolution. In line with Duverger (1959) and Panebianco (1988), efforts to understand party trajectories emphasize the initial period during which the party was founded. As LeBas points out in her analysis of African oppositional parties, "In order to understand differences in party organization and party system development, starting conditions matter" (2011: 35). This does not mean that parties are to forever follow a set developmental path. It does mean, however, that we cannot fully understand party developmental trajectories without a thorough consideration of party formation. Subsequent phases in organizational evolution are also important but difficult to clearly demarcate. Panebianco focused on the organizational consolidation or institutionalization of party entities and Pedersen linked developmental phases with electoral size (1982). As political organizations mature and, more importantly, as they undertake representative or executive tasks, their internal configuration of power changes (Katz and Mair 1993; van Biezen 2000).

A third theme related to the organizational approach focuses on party leaders and members. According to this perspective, organizational development is a function of the strategic choices made by political agents seeking to maximize their goals (Aldrich 1995). In some settings, practical leaders (Mudde 2007) set up extensive organizational networks to facilitate party institutionalization while in others, leaders rationally choose to keep organizations slim, to better control internal competitors and militant activists (Kopecky 1995: 519; Tavits 2013). The ideological purity of the latter – "true believers," as Panebianco calls them (1988) – can have an important effect on organizational development, limiting the room for organizational reform and pragmatic reorientation of goals, strategies and programs to changing environmental conditions (Kitschelt 1989; Art 2011). Party leaders who push for organizational reform and change old party structures can bring about the transformation of even the most bureaucratic parties and help them remain competitive in fast-changing environments (Grzymala-Busse 2002).

Electoral Factors

Parties are not entirely autonomous from their environments and the attempt to understand how they develop necessitates the disaggregation of the complex environments in which they operate. The most obvious element in these environments is electoral change. The broader literature on political parties mentioned above tends to treat party organization as an independent variable and then proceeds to examine its direct and indirect effects on electoral outcomes. Electoral environments, though, can also have an independent effect on party organizations and their development. Elections are key in how we conceptualize parties (Sartori 2005) and, hence, changes in how elections are contested can be expected to bring about modifications in how party organizations develop to effectively compete in these electoral environments. At a broader level, the shift from mass bureaucratic parties to electoral-professional parties is largely – albeit not entirely – a function of changes to the overall electoral environment, especially those associated with the advent of television (Panebianco 1988: 262–267). Parties have responded to these changes by diverting organizational resources to new technologies, divesting from traditional forms of activist recruitment and mobilization, and professionalizing and centralizing their organizational structures (Farrell and Webb 2000). Organizational development, then, has mirrored the evolution of pre- to post-modern campaigns, which tend to last longer, involve outside profes-sionals and consultants and, ultimately, cost more (Norris 2004).

The evolution of electoral campaigns can go a long way to account for party organizational change but the organizational polymorphism of modern parties shows that these broad changes cannot tell the entire story of how parties develop. Beyond the broad effects of modern campaigning on the overall development of party organizations, one can expect more specific effects depending on the particular electoral context. One element of the context is the competitiveness of the electoral environment. In electorally marginal settings, where even minor voter gains might make a big difference in the overall outcome, parties might set up more robust organizational infrastructure. In the United States, for example, parties are known to be more active in battleground than in safe states. This is not because of the strength of local organizations but because central parties are effective in diverting resources and mobilizing grassroots activists where they can make the biggest difference (Beck and Heidemann 2014). Alter-natively, it can be expected that local parties are much stronger in trad-itional party electoral strongholds. In such non-competitive settings, it can be expected that local parties have significant financial and human resources at their disposal and evolve differently than local organizations relying on central party support. As Seyd and Whiteley note in their analysis of the British Labour Party, "when Labour is the dominant local party, the environment is much more favorable, both to the party organization and to mobilizing the vote, than when it is weak" (1992: 191).

Electoral success or failure can also shape the organizational development of political parties. The literature on activism suggests that electoral performance is strongly linked with party organizational capacity by affecting grassroots mobilization. Studies mostly undertaken in the British context show that party activists can be incentivized by electoral success and demoralized by electoral failure. Electoral performance yields spirals of mobilization or de-mobilization in political parties that affects their national and local organizational development and their subsequent electoral performance. In highly competitive electoral contexts, activists could also overwork during the campaigns and subsequently go through a phase of campaign "burnout" or simply become less active (Whiteley and Seyd 1998; Fisher et al. 2006). An additional dimension of the electoral context is incumbency, especially in single-member district electoral systems that tend to be associated with the cultivation of a "personal vote" (Cain et al. 1984). The personal vote of an incumbent member of parliament can help make local campaigning more effective (Whiteley and Seyd 1994: 247). Similarly, the prospect of incumbency might help energize activism and improve party organizational structures. Overall, the electoral environment can be expected to affect the way party organizations evolve and need to be taken into account in analyses of organizational development.

Institutional Factors

A second set of environmental factors revolves around the institutional environment in which parties develop. The main focus in this second environmental approach is on the role of the state in party development. This role is not as well specified in the early works on organizational development compared to the electoral environment analyzed earlier. Duverger, for example, draws an indirect link between state and organizational development when he discusses the organizational evolution of communist and fascist parties. "Both try to adapt themselves equally for conditions of open struggle and clandestine combat in case the State should react against them with prohibitions and proscriptions" (1959: 2). But the analysis of cadre and mass parties does not explicitly or systematically draw on the relative position of each vis-à-vis the state. More recent scholarship has made bold attempts to follow broader trends in comparative politics and "bring the state back in" to the analysis (Shefter 1994: xi). Examining the development of American political parties, and borrowing from work on their European counterparts, Shefter linked the development of strong party organizations to the degree of access outsider parties have to state resources or to the fear insiders have of losing their own access (1977). His analysis helps highlight not only the role of the state in facilitating party development but also the relative porousness of the state apparatus and its susceptibility to political control.

This permeability of the state apparatus lays the basis for the advent of what Katz and Mair termed the "cartel party." Observed as early as the 1950s by Kirchheimer (1957), the cartelization of politics limited competition between parties and allowed them to complicate the entry of new competitors in the political arena. Parties are thought to have used their access to the state to grant themselves financial, communicative and patronage resources and to draft laws regulating the political market in ways that benefit them. "The state, which is invaded by the parties, and the rules of which are determined by the parties, becomes a fount of resources through which these parties not only help to ensure their own survival, but through which they can also enhance their capacity to resist challenges from newly mobilized alternatives" (Katz and Mair 1995: 16). Unlike mass parties, which were well embedded in society, the parties have now come to be seen as public utilities, especially in terms of their financing (van Biezen 2004). Their "capture" of state and dependence on state resources has limited the propensity for party activism, stifling voluntary participation of the party grassroots (Whiteley 2011). This reliance of parties on the state for financing and regulation is increasing across time (van Biezen and Kopecky 2014), confirming the main expectation of the cartel thesis that, over time, the role of the state in party development is growing. Like the societal approach discussed next, the institutional approach sees parties being pushed across a common development path, coming closer to the state and developing away from society.[1]

Societal Factors

Although not always identified as such, the societal approach to organizational development examines how parties link with society. The party organizations formed in the nineteenth and early twentieth centuries had

---

[1] When applied outside the framework of the cartel party, the institutional approach to party development has allowed for more divergent developmental outcomes, focusing on how the type of the communist regime (Ishiyama 1997); the institutional context of democratization (van Biezen 2003); or the practices of authoritarian states (LeBas 2011) have shaped the development of political parties.

different links to society, famously noted by the distinction Duverger highlighted between cadre and mass parties. Caucus-based cadre parties were seen as having weak ties to society, unlike branch-based mass parties which were thought to be "externally created" by civil society groups (Duverger 1959: xxx–xxxiii). Such groups included trade unions (e.g., many European socialist parties), peasant associations (e.g., the Scandinavian agrarian parties), church organizations (e.g., a number of Christian Democratic parties) and intellectual societies (e.g., the Fabian Society's influence on the genesis the Labour Party). Duverger suggested that gradual extension of suffrage to broader segments of European societies brought about the predominance of the mass over the cadre party organization, with possible contagion from the Left to the Right of the political spectrum. This contagion – evident in the adoption of branch-level organization by denominational and fascist parties (Duverger 1959: 26–27) – pointed to the functional appeal of this mode of party organization, which seemed to cut across ideological doctrine. The organizational effectiveness of the mass party is thought to have helped stabilize mass democracy (Mair 1990) and, arguably, facilitated the freezing of party systems Lipset and Rokkan subsequently observed (1967). But in the postwar period, mass parties started transforming themselves to catch-all parties, a process driven by social transformation. "Under present conditions of spreading secular and mass consumer-goods orientation, with shifting and less obtrusive class lines, the former class-mass parties and denominational mass parties are both under pressure to become catch-all people's parties" (Kirchheimer 1966: 190).

The main theme cutting across the societal approach to party development is the growing distance separating parties from their members and voters. Macro-level processes of social transformation are seen pushing party organizational trajectories on a similar path, away from organized social groups and individual party supporters. Modernization has blurred preexisting social boundaries, limiting the political relevance and mobilizing potential of class identification. Social cleavages, which structured political competition in Europe for most of the twentieth century (Lipset and Rokkan 1967), became increasingly less important or supplanted with new cleavages (Inglehart 1990; Bornschier 2010). The fading of traditional cleavages and the formation of new ones has further complicated party efforts to link with increasingly more heterogeneous electorates. Along with the erosion of class identification came the weakening of voter loyalty and increasing voter mobility. A growing number of voters have stopped identifying with a political party signifying a process of voter dealignment

(Dalton 1984; Flanagan and Dalton 1984), which raised concerns about the very viability of party organizations (Lawson and Merkl 1988). The weakening social linkage of political parties has been confirmed by a significant body of evidence showing a near universal decrease in voter turnout (Wattenberg 2000), party identification and dealignment (Dalton 2000) and electoral volatility (Dalton et al. 2000). More alarmingly, parties have been losing their ties not only with voters but with their members as well. Repeated studies have documented that in the last quarter of the twentieth century European political parties have been consistently losing members (Scarrow 2000; Mair and van Biezen 2001). By the beginning of the twenty-first century, a large cross-national study of party membership in Europe concluded that it fell "to such a low level that membership itself no longer offers a meaningful indicator of party organisational capacity" (van Biezen et al. 2012). Another study, which focused on the ties of political parties with collateral organizations, similarly showed that "the organizational anchorage of Western European party systems has clearly declined over the past decades" (Poguntke 2006). Although there is notable variation in the degree of party institutionalization and social rootedness of political parties in Africa (LeBas 2011), Asia (Hicken and Kuhonta 2011) and Eastern Europe (Tavits 2013), party organizations across different newer democracies are thought to be driven away from the old mass party model.

The Organizational Development of Extremist Right-Wing Parties

The focus on the developmental trajectories of extremist right-wing parties provides an opportunity to refine endogenous and environmental accounts of party development. The very nature of these parties offers possibilities to rethink some of the basic parameters used to analyze party development and to reconsider the processes associated with the evolution of party organizations. This section casts new light on the theoretical understanding of party development by examining the issues posed by the evolution of extremist right-wing parties and by incorporating insights from the social movement literature to enhance the conceptualization of party development.

Endogenous Factors

The very nature of extremist right-wing parties invites the reconsideration of the organizational approach to party development. This approach primarily rests on the analysis of mass parties involved in institutionalized politics. Two main characteristics of extremist right-wing parties set them apart from other parties and affect how they develop. First, extremist right-wing parties are "charismatic" parties headed by individuals who have near absolute discretion in the provision of selective incentives to party members and activists, without following formal intra-party rules, procedures or processes (Panebianco 1988: chapter 8). The internal life of extremist right-wing parties revolves around the party leader, who tends to avoid setting up the institutional infrastructure found in most modern parties. The leader demands and commands the absolute loyalty of the party functionaries and militants who, in turn, compete for party resources and for the selective incentives the leader distributes. Lacking the institutional infrastructure to distribute resources and incentives and to resolve internal conflicts, these parties can be expected to display organizational instability.

The second feature of these parties can be expected to exacerbate this instability: extremist right-wing parties are interesting organizational phenomena because they tend to also be "movement parties" (Kitschelt 2006) functioning on the frontier between political parties and social movements. A considerable body of works on individual (Barnes and Kaase 1979; Muller 1979; Norris 2002; Dalton 2006) and on group behavior (Kitschelt 1989; McAdam et al. 2001) shows that this frontier is not clearly demarcated. The organizational evolution of ecological (Berman 1997) or radical Left (della Porta et al. 2017) parties over the years highlights the fuzziness of this frontier but also shows its transitory nature, since most of these parties gradually made the transition from extra-institutional and disruptive street protest to institutionalized and formalized channels of political representation. The developmental trajectory of extremist right-wing parties can be expected to be different from Green or radical Left parties in that they are not known to grow out of social movements and because they are best known for their violent rather than their contentious street activity. But extremist right-wing parties are similar to other movement parties in adopting the action repertoire of social movements while also seeking to win legislative presence through their participation in elections (see also Chapter 2).

Realizing the movement component of extremist right-wing parties allows the utilization of insights from the social movement literature to understand their development. The resource mobilization perspective developed in this literature seems particularly useful for understanding how the nature of the extremist right-wing parties affects their developmental trajectory. Viewing movements as purposeful organizations that seek to mobilize resources to achieve their ends (Zald and McCarthy 1979; Tarrow 1994), resource mobilization theory turns attention to the range of organizational assets these parties have at their disposal. Due to their nature and their position outside the system, these parties naturally resort to the recruitment, socialization and training of militants with biographical availability to undertake risky action (McAdam 1986). The mobilization of this type of resources has developmental implications for the movement parties because militant activism is not usually accompanied by the establishment of highly elaborate mechanisms to control it. In charismatic parties where the control of resources and incentives lies with the party leader and close circle of devotees, militants often vie for attention by taking increasingly more risky and often violent political action. The competition for militancy makes the organizational development of these parties subject not only to their own programmatic, tactical and strategic choices, but also to those of institutional and societal actors who seek to confront them.

Electoral Factors

The electoral environment can be expected to have a different effect on extremist right-wing parties than on other parties. Unlike most conventional parties, extremist right-wing parties usually lack the financial and communicative resources associated with modern or post-modern campaigns and, hence, they are less likely to have developed in accordance with the patterns observed in most modern democratic systems. As outsiders to the political system, extremist right-wing parties are most likely to primarily rely on volunteer activists rather than professional politicians or outside consultants; to employ traditional leafleting and meetings to communicate with existing and potential voters; and to spend considerable time in the streets rather than in the parliament or television. Put simply, extremist right-wing parties are still in the pre-modern era or very early stage of election campaigning (Farrell and Webb 2000; Norris 2004). The changes to party organization caused by the transformation of the broader electoral environment are less likely to be found in extremist right-wing parties.

Although still caught in a pre-modern era of campaigns, extremist right-wing parties are not necessarily immune to the effects electoral factors have on their organizational development. But the size of these effects can be expected to be smaller than for most other parties. As discussed above, the very nature of these parties limits their adherence to the vote maximizing logic one can easily assume for most parties. Although electoral considerations and dynamics are still an important factor for understanding their development, they are less important than in most other parties. Their emphasis on constituency representation (Kitschelt 1989; Art 2011) undermines their capacity to easily adapt to the electoral context. In this sense, the electoral incentives and disincentives in a given context are less likely to affect how these parties evolve either because the organization and its leadership are unwilling or slow to adapt to the context or because the activists do not pay much attention to these incentives. In its purest form, the expectation is that an extremist right-wing party organization can be expected to develop similarly in the most and least competitive electoral contexts. A milder and more realistic expectation is that the competitiveness of the electoral environment does not have a major effect in the organizational evolution of these parties. When it comes to the activists, it can be expected that their mobilization is relatively independent of electoral prospects and outcomes. Put simply, electoral success or failure cannot be expected to match the spirals of mobilization or de-mobilization observed elsewhere (Whiteley and Seyd 1998; Fisher et al. 2006). And incumbency cannot really be expected to change patterns of mobilization (Whiteley and Seyd 1994).

Institutional Factors

The evolution of extremist right-wing parties provides an opportunity to also reconsider the role of the state in party development. The institutional approach to party development views parties as coming closer to or colonizing the state at the expense of their ties to society. Regardless of their organizational form, modern parties are seen as using their proximity to executive power and legislative authority to extract financial and communicative resources or regulatory discretion – sometimes distorting competition against new or smaller parties. Extremist right-wing parties challenge the notion of increasing cartelization because their ideas and practices (Chapter 2) tend to generate varying degrees of institutional hostility against them. Their antithesis to democracy generates hostile institutional environments that affect how they develop (Art 2011). Militant democratic responses to extremism are not a new phenomenon. In the interwar years a number of European democracies used repressive measures to defend themselves from subversive fascist or communist movements or groups (Loewenstein 1937a; 1937b; Capoccia 2005). In postwar years, militant democracy policies have targeted party organizations in such countries as Belgium, the Czech Republic, Germany, Israel, the

Netherlands, Slovakia, Spain and Turkey (de Witte and Klandermans 2000; Pedahzur 2004; Bale 2007; Downs 2012; Capoccia 2013). Hostile institutional environments raise important normative questions about the limits of democratic liberalism (Kirshner 2014) but they also bring attention to the lack of systematic knowledge on how militant democracy actually affects the targeted parties.

A better understanding on the effects of institutional hostility on extremist right-wing parties requires an in-depth analysis of how these parties evolve during these periods of democratic militancy. This analysis can benefit from the consideration of the social movements literature. Because social movements are outsiders to the polity (McAdam et al. 2001: 11), their relationship with state authority has received systematic attention and yielded important findings that can be utilized to better understand the evolution of extremist right-wing parties (della Porta 1995; Jenkins 1995). The analysis of party development in general and extremist right-wing development in particular can begin with, but must also go beyond the careful consideration of differences in the formal institutional structures of states (Birnbaum 1988; Kriesi 1995: 84–85). Besides formal structures, though, one must also take into account the scope for administrative and political agency on state capacity for repression. The boundaries between states and their societies are usually porous enough to allow for both types of agency. The scope for administrative agency is highlighted by work on nationalist mobilization in the former Soviet Union, which shows that "what often allowed challenges on the street to intensify in the first place was the fact that sympathizers of the crowd existed within state institutions" (Beissinger 2002: 97). Administrative agency also comes into play by works on the policing of protest, which demonstrate how types of policing can have a different effect on social movement activism (della Porta and Reiter 1998) or how state repression trickles down through law enforcement mechanisms (Davenport 2009). This work also shows how the interaction between political and administrative agents can affect the capacity of the state to repress its challengers. The degree of control political agents have over administrative agents (e.g., over police commanders or front-line officers, Earl 2006) can account for their varied capacity to deal with extremist right-wing activists as well as with social agents who counter-mobilize against them.

Societal Factors

The evolution of extremist right-wing parties invites a reconsideration of the societal approach to party development as well. Whereas the basic premise of this approach is that political parties increasingly move away from society, extremist right-wing parties are trying to move in the opposite direction, challenging the perceived cartelization of party politics (Katz and Mair 1995: 24). Although none of the postwar extremist right-wing parties is close to being a Duvergerian mass party, all have actively tried to infiltrate society by adopting organizational modes and political frames that resemble those of earlier periods of party development. The emphasis on the establishment of local cells, branches or militias, for example, is reminiscent of parties with extra-parliamentary origin (Duverger 1959). Lacking access to resources that cartel parties take for granted, extremist right-wing parties seek territorial diffusion, through which they hope to recruit more activists and gain more resources. Moreover, extremist right-wing parties undertake street-level political and social action, aiming to supplant capital-intensive communicative methods with labor-intensive activism. Their adoption of movement tactics and frames is in line with the reinvention of political activism evident in modern democracies (Norris 2002), albeit casting a different light on its normative link to democratic politics. Extremist right-wing parties are seeking to capitalize on partisan dealignment and political disaffection evident across many democracies by presenting themselves as bottom-up, street-based movements that seek to replace traditional top-down, party-based political participation. The adoption of extra-institutional modes of political action challenges the dominance of the Left in protest politics – an observation that has not gone unnoticed (van Dyke and Meyer 2016: 2).

Attempts by extremist right-wing parties to grow roots in European societies bring about the mobilization of other social groups against them that eventually affects their organizational development. The societal reactions against extremist right-wing parties are largely related to their organizational nature. Because of their movement and charismatic nature, these parties try to infiltrate local societies through political activism that leads to street-level counter-mobilization by opposing societal groups. In other words, organizational efforts by extremist right-wing parties to penetrate local societies generate mechanisms of social hostility against them. The historical legacy of extremism in Europe constitutes a reference point that brings together distinct or loosely connected networks of social movements or groups to counter these efforts. The range of social actors mobilizing against the extremists varies considerably from antifascist groups to anarchist networks, immigrant associations, advocacy groups and citizen initiatives. These actors bring together a diverse range of organizational, intellectual and spatial resources to combat extremism in their neighborhoods and cities. Their efforts to contain extremist right-wing parties take different forms depending on the institutional, social and cultural context. In some cases, antifascist actors employ institutional means to pressure institutional actors – for example, the police or the courts – to take action against extremism. In other cases, they seek to mobilize broader segments of society to get involved in political protest against right-wing extremism. A small minority employs more contentious and, sometimes, violent means to disrupt the organizational presence of extremist right-wing parties. In some cases, these groups target the parties themselves, for example causing physical damage to party premises. In other cases, social repression targets party activists (Linden and Klandermans 2006; Birchall 2010; Copsey 2011; Art 2011). The dynamics of movement and counter-movement mobilization raise important issues for party and movement development that merit systematic attention. With regards to party development, it is important to examine variation in attempts to socially confront extremist parties and explore the factors affecting why in some settings these parties persist while in others they seem to succumb to social pressure. This highlights the organizational resources and tactics extremist parties and their societal challengers have at their disposal to deal with hostile social environments. The systematic examination of the resources and tactics of the multitude of actors involved in these phenomena turns attention to the micro-processes – rather than the macro-variables (McAdam et al. 2001) – of political contention.

The Local Development of Political Parties

The analysis of endogenous and environmental factors affecting the development of extremist right-wing parties would be incomplete if it were to solely focus on national or central party structures. Much of the literature on political parties does exactly that, disregarding subnational or local party organizations. There are a number of reasons for this neglect. The organizational evolution of modern parties away from the Duvergerian mass party model has diverted attention to national and central party organizations and away from their local branches or cells. Modern catch-all, electoral-professional, cartel, cadre or business-firm parties are not known for their local organizational strength (Krouwel 2006). As parties loosen their traditional ties with society and increasingly rely on the state for resources (Katz and Mair 1995), they have less need for local organizational roots. Moreover, the changing nature of electoral campaigns pushes parties to professionalize, personalize and centralize authority, thereby limiting the relevance of their subnational or local organizations. As mentioned earlier, electoral pressures have pushed parties to hire outside consultants and external advisors, thereby centralizing channels of information around the central party leadership or to those few with access to the campaign headquarters. In addition, the presumed "Americanization" of electoral campaigns has granted leaders an enhanced role in these campaigns at the expense of permanent party officials or the party itself. Furthermore, the growing role of the media in national electoral campaigns has increased the amount of resources required to contest elections, augmenting the importance of state funding or large donations and diminishing the significance of local fund raising. All in all, the campaign process is seen as facilitating the centralization of party organizations at the expense of their local units (e.g., Farrell and Webb 2000; Norris 2004). Although parties still care about their membership (Scarrow 1996), "it is still possible to argue that local party organization is most likely not as important to the national political party as was once the case" (Webb 2002: 28).

The scholarly neglect of subnational or local party organizations merits some discussion, as the available evidence does not always support the claims upon which it is based. Contrary to what one would expect, the evidence of party "nationalization" or centralization is not overwhelming. As discussed earlier there is now a lot of data documenting the decrease in party memberships and the growing tendency of parties to hire campaign professionals and external advisors. But it is not clear whether this is evidence of organizational centralization per se. Indicators of party centralization across countries (e.g., candidate selection) show considerable variation that raises doubts about the emphasis placed on party centralization. The conclusion of a cross-country study of centralization that "there are no really strong associations between explanatory variables and the degree of centralization" (Lundell 2004: 41) points to the need to further examine centralization, especially across time. An analysis of party centralization across time requires access to intra-party information that most analysts lack but this does not mean that the subnational party units can be so quickly discounted in exegeses of party development. Even if one accepts the strong evidence of declining party memberships as a strong indication for the waning of the Duvergerian mass party, this does not justify claims about its death. The point Scarrow makes is still valid today: "it is important to remember that diminished importance is not obsolescence" (1993: 378). The emphasis communist parties place on their local branches and cells suggests that, although less important than they once were, subunits continue to matter for central party leaderships and need to be incorporated in analyses of how parties develop. In fact, the Leninist organizational models used by the remaining orthodox communist parties in Europe, which are still based on the principle of democratic centralism, are instructive into how centralization can co-exist with strong local presence and that, contrary to what the party literature tends to assume, the two are not necessarily antithetical. The grassroots organizations of Green parties in Europe are also indicative of the need to better appreciate party subunits – a point well documented in earlier literature (Kitschelt 1989) but largely ignored due to the "whole nation bias" in the broader party literature.

Although scholars tend to disregard subnational party organizations, national party leaders have good reasons not to. Local organizations can become breeding and training grounds for new recruits and future party politicians. Parties that solely rely on central recruitment mechanisms are limiting the pool of potential activists and reducing the probabilities for attracting new talent to their ranks. Subnational units can also facilitate organizational innovation by providing settings for trying new ideas, techniques or, even, alliances. Local organizations might prove particularly useful when the national party is in retreat, for example after major electoral losses. Organizational subunits can allow parties to customize their national message to local societies, taking into account subnational particularities and adjusting general themes into locally relevant issues. Through their attempts to reach local societies political parties can reach segments of society that are otherwise hard to reach, such as young voters or rural populations who might not follow national campaigns (Geser 1999). Finally, local organizations can be at the forefront of party activism trying to improve the electoral reach of the national party. Party activism can make a difference in electoral results (Huckfeldt and Sprague 1992; Seyd and Whiteley 1992; 1994; Gerber and Green 2000) and national parties have strong incentives to build networks of local subunits and activists to help get out the vote. The volunteer work of party activists is too precious for national parties to ignore (Clark 2004), even in an age of partisan dealignment.

All these good reasons for having strong local subunits have not gone unnoticed by political parties. In Eastern Europe, for example, where parties are thought to be less institutionalized than in Western Europe, national parties try to build broad local networks. Extensive local presence is a source of organizational, and, ultimately, electoral strength. Parties that, among other things, have strong subunits perform better in national elections than those that are organizationally weaker. Local party organizations can be consequential for how parties develop. They can help parties improve their electoral standing but can also change the internal configuration of power, challenging the national or central party and leadership (Tavits 2013). Local activist militancy can also make parties less flexible, thereby limiting their capacity to effectively adjust to changing environments (Kitschelt 1989). These last two reasons might account for why some central party organizations are more willing to invest in establishing strong subnational units than others (Kopecky 1995). But the notable variation in the territorial expansiveness of political parties in Eastern Europe (Tavits 2013) is suggestive of the need to subject local party development into theoretical and empirical inquiry, rather than neglect it.

The Local Development of Extremist Right-Wing Parties

For extremist right-wing parties local organizations are more important than they are for other parties. Extremist parties usually lack the financial or communicative resources their competitors have to compete for social support. They are hence much more reliant on their organizational subunits for reaching and infiltrating local communities. Organizational subunits are also important for extremist right-wing parties because, as mentioned earlier, they often face hostile political environments. Environmental hostility in the form of militant democracy policies often targets the national party organization. This creates the need for local party units that will keep the "party torch" alight when the national party is facing state hostility that threatens its survival. In adverse political environments, party subunits can continue their local activism and, hence, allow national parties to claim political relevance at a time of retreat. Vibrant local units make it harder for the state to repress extremist right-wing parties and complicate militant democracy strategies to combat extremism. Simply put, local party organizations can be a form of "organizational hedging" for parties facing uncertain institutional or social environments, especially where they can successfully combine a broad repertoire of conventional and contentious activities. The establishment of local organizations is also in accordance with the organizational identity of extremist right-wing parties. Parties cannot claim to be movements unless they have strong presence on the streets. A network of local organizations allows parties to recruit, socialize and train activists to undertake street-level action. Because movements are associated with grassroots mobilization, subnational organizational presence allows extremist right-parties to project the image of politically ascending and territorially diffused grassroots movements.

Party subunits are more important but also present greater challenges for extremist right-wing parties than for other parties. Local party units can become organizational liabilities because of organizational features particular to these parties. The emphasis extremist right-wing parties ascribe to the leadership or *Führer* principle requires the near complete subordination of the subunits to the central party, especially to the leader. Yet, "charismatic" parties are not known to establish the institutional mechanisms necessary to effectively and smoothly achieve this subordination. Instead they rely on informal relations unmediated by formal hierarchical structures. "As opposed to other forms of power, charismatic power gives rise to an organization of social relations characterized by an absence of 'rules,' internal 'career patterns,' and a clear division of labor" (Panebianco 1988: 144). The informal relations charismatic parties rely upon are not conducive to the establishment of an organizationally stable network of similarly structured local units. The "charismatic" nature of the national party is a source of local organizational polymorphism and instability. Lacking institutionalized mechanisms for controlling their peripheral units, extremist right-wing parties cannot bring about the level of organizational isomorphism one would expect from such highly centralized organizations. Extremist right-wing parties need local organizations more than other parties but, unlike in the case of communist parties, local organizational presence can turn from asset to liability. A related challenge for extremist right-wing parties is the nature of activities these local units undertake and the hostile environment in which they take place. Street-level activism in hostile environments generates a set of socializing experiences for local militants, creates activist comradery and builds intragroup solidarity – all of which have organizational consequences. Street clashes with antifascist activists and police units can facilitate the formation of local group identities. Moreover, the emphasis the party places on this type of aggressive or violent activism, along with existing environmental hostility, make the outcome of these encounters less predictable than that of other types of local activism. The unpredictability of this type of activism makes local party units even harder to control. The encounters between local activists, antifascists and police set in motion different processes and yield varied outcomes, which further complicate the relation between national parties and their local organizations. Overall, then, extremist right-wing parties need to develop strong subnational units to facilitate their persistence in hostile environments but these local organizational efforts pose important challenges for the central party, and more interestingly, yield distinct developmental outcomes.

The Subnational Comparative Method

To examine the development of extremist right-wing parties this book borrows elements from the subnational comparative method (Snyder 2001). Rather than focusing on the development of extremist parties at the national level, the book examines the trajectories of hundreds of local organizations of extremist right-wing parties. To gain insights on the endogenous, electoral, institutional and societal "logics" affecting party development, the book examines the local organizations set up by three of the most successful extremist right-wing parties in postwar Europe.

The subnational method rests on comparative insights from different phenomena ranging from subnational authoritarianism to economic reform, in dissimilar settings such as the "Solid South" (Gibson 2005), Mexico (Snyder 1999) and the European Union (Kelemen 2015). Whereas much work in comparative politics treats countries as single units and seeks to identify variation between them, the subnational comparative method rests on the empirical observation that sometimes there is so much variation within countries that cannot be captured if countries are treated as wholes. This method solves many of the problems associated with comparative political research but it is not as frequently used. This "is partly the result of pragmatic considerations" associated with the difficulty of obtaining data at the subnational level (Lijphart 1975: 167). Once the data availability problems are surpassed, though, this method can help overcome the "whole nation bias" (Rokkan 1970: 49) still characterizing comparative political studies.

The subnational comparative method is well suited for the analysis of extremist right-wing parties. Although radical right-wing parties have some presence in almost all European countries, extremist right-wing parties are not as common. Examining local party organizations of extremist parties multiplies the number of cases, thereby solving the small-N problem associated with the analysis of such parties. This approach is also useful because it limits the number of explanatory variables. As discussed earlier, one set of variables that can potentially explain party development relates to the formal institutional set up of the state. The subnational method allows tracing variation when these formal institutions are kept constant. It also allows keeping cultural and historical variables constant, or at least, it helps identify subcultural factors. Moreover, the subnational method casts new light on two important party-specific variables that the literature on far right parties considers important. The examination of local organizations invites a reconsideration of the effect of leader characteristics or charisma on the development of extremist right-wing parties (Eatwell 2006; Mudde 2007; van der Brug and Mughan 2007; Arter 2016). If under the same leader a party displays notable subnational developmental variation, then one must look beyond his or her personality, talents or flaws to understand these developmental trajectories. Overall, then, by increasing the number of cases and limiting the potential explanatory variables, subnational comparisons allow scholars to identify complex processes that are harder to spot with fewer cases and more variables. This enhances the ability not only to more accurately describe but also to more adequately theorize about these processes.

More importantly, the subnational method permits the consideration of variation within countries. Mostly dealing with the national or central party organizations, the literature on radical or extremist right-wing parties tends to aggregate intraparty features to assess the overall organizational capacity of these parties. This assumes a certain level of uniformity in national party organizations that misses the nuances of subnational organizational life. The case of Germany illustrates this point. Most analyses of the German case rightly note the failure of extremist right-wing parties to gain representation in the national legislature since 1949. Nevertheless, some of these parties have had occasional breakthroughs in some regional parliaments. Coding the German case as "negative" captures the overall failure of these parties but misses the small but notable subnational variation, especially between Western and Eastern regions. Works focusing on the regional organizational strongholds of these parties underscore the importance of going below the national level to better understand their development. The examples of the French National Front in Dreux (Gaspard 1995), the Belgian Vlaams Belang in Antwerp (de Witte and Klandermans 2000) and the Golden Dawn in Agios Panteleimonas (Dinas et al. 2013) provide useful suggestions on how local party organization affects national party evolution (see also Kitschelt with McGann 1995). But their emphasis on organizational strongholds tends to overlook the overall failure of subnational organizations in some regional or local settings. Examining the subnational level allows a better understanding of not only developmental success but also of developmental failure.

The subnational comparative method can offer insights into the development of extremist right-wing parties but also raises two problems that need to be addressed. The first relates to the relationship between the national and the subnational units. Local units might display varying degrees of independence from the central party and, hence, the analysis of their development needs to take into account the relation between the national party and its subnational units. This book, then, examines local party organizations by themselves but also takes into account the input the central party has in its organizational evolution. The second problem relates to the generalizability of the findings. Despite their advantages, subnational comparisons cannot yield generalizable insights unless they are undertaken across different national contexts. This is not an easy task because the level of resource investment required to systematically collect evidence at the subnational level limits the capacity to undertake cross national comparisons. In accordance with Snyder (2001), this book addresses this problem by devoting the penultimate chapter to probe the generalizability of the findings in different national settings. The book compares the development of local organizations of the Greek Golden Dawn with the subnational organizations of the German National Democratic Party and Kotleba's People's Party Our Slovakia. Although a systematic study of the latter two parties is not possible within the confines of this project, the book relies on field work in subnational strongholds of the two parties and compares cases of subnational success and failure. This allows the study to explore whether the outcomes and processes identified in the postauthoritarian setting of Greece can also be identified in different settings, postwar Germany and postcommunist Slovakia.

CHAPTER 4

The Organizational Development
of the Golden Dawn

This chapter uses a unique collection of hundreds of issues of Golden Dawn (GD) publications and dozens of interviews with the GD leadership and activists to systematically trace its evolution from a street-level gang to the third biggest political party in Greece. The first part of the chapter briefly traces the development of the GD in the 1980s from a small National Socialist ideological movement to a marginal political party. The second part focuses on the ideological, programmatic and, more importantly, the organizational development of the party since the early 1990s. The third section focuses on its local party organizations and their activities providing a rare overview of internal organizational life.

The Early Years of the Golden Dawn

The GD was founded in December 1980, initially as a magazine and since 1983, as a political party, under the leadership of Nikos Michaloliakos. He describes this period as one during which they "flirted" with various ideologies of the interwar period. "We started with a magazine in which each of us wrote whatever they wanted. We flirted with various ideas of the interwar period, like Fascism, National Socialism, even Peronism. We even had Che Guevara on one of our front covers – as you know, he started out as a nationalist."[1] As most covers of the magazine during the 1980s clearly signaled, the association of its founders with National Socialism was much more than a flirt. In its early years, the magazine was subtitled "National Socialist Periodical Publication" before becoming a "Popular Nationalist Publication."[2] Despite the seeming turn to this ill-defined notion of "popular nationalism," throughout the 1980s the magazine became the voice of Greek National Socialists. In 1988, the magazine boasted to have

---

[1] Nikos Michaloliakos, interview with author, Athens, October 2012.
[2] For example, covers of issue 2, January 1981, and issue 11, November 1983.

published more than 400 articles and analyses on the ideological principles of National Socialism; the most important National Socialist personalities, such as Adolf Hitler, Rudolf Hess, Joseph and Magda Goebbels and Leon Degrelle; the principle of racialism in National Socialist ideology; and "the Jewish question." According to the editorial team of the magazine, which included the long-time associate of Michaloliakos and current parliamentary spokesperson of the GD, Christos Pappas, its articles can help readers form a comprehensive view on National Socialism. "Hence, by coding the principles and positions of our ideology, [the reader] can take active role in the struggle we give against the Established System of democracy and Bolshevism, and their Jewish patrons."[3]

Although the Golden Dawn magazine proclaimed early on that its main goal was to "stay out of every form of political struggle"[4] it soon became the ideological mouthpiece of the "Popular Association – Golden Dawn," founded as a political party in 1983. By December 1983, the publication and the "Popular Association" became indistinguishable, establishing offices in Athens and Thessaloniki and holding office hours for the public four times a week. The publication and the office operations were suspended for more than two years in 1984, when Michaloliakos became the leader of the youth organization of the National Political Union (EPEN). The Union was founded by the imprisoned colonel of the Greek junta, Georgios Papadopoulos, whom Michaloliakos met in prison in 1976, when he was arrested and imprisoned for violence.[5] Michaloliakos left EPEN in 1985, due to concerns of other leading members of the party regarding his National Socialist beliefs as well as due to the support of EPEN for Israel. "EPEN did not put forth any ideological tendencies that opposed the paradigm of the French Revolution. It was more of an attempt to return to tradition. Their patriotism cannot be characterized as nationalism."[6] After 1986, the magazine reappeared with similar content and by the late 1980s the party started preparing its entry into the electoral arena. As Pappas recalls, "we opened new offices in Kefallinias Street in the spring of 1986, continuing in the same spirit our ideological work."[7] The first party congress in 1990 decided to adopt "popular

---

[3] "Golden Dawn: A Review of the Publication of our Magazine," *Golden Dawn* [Magazine], issue 36, June 1988, pp. 16–17.
[4] "Our Publication," *Golden Dawn* [Magazine], issue 1, December 1980, p. 3.
[5] Nikos Michaloliakos, "George Papadopoulos, as I met him," *Golden Dawn* [Newspaper], issue 286, July 2, 1999, p. 5.
[6] Michaloliakos, interview with author, October 2012.
[7] Christos Pappas, interview with author, Athens, December 2015.

nationalism" as the basis for its ideological platform, seeking to moderate its explicit association with National Socialism. By the early 1990s, the party attempted to link its now vague, popular nationalist ideological platform with issues of the day, such as the popular mobilization over the use of the name Macedonia by the former Yugoslav state and the influx of migrants from the Balkans. The second party congress in 1992 decided to launch a weekly newspaper, also named Golden Dawn, and to prepare for contesting national elections. Michaloliakos identifies the founding of the newspaper as a critical moment in the party trajectory: "Our political struggle started in 1993. We started in a Leninist way: we decided to issue a newspaper and to build a party around it. By the 1990s, we had settled the ideological issues and positioned ourselves in favor of popular nationalism."[8]

Becoming a Party

The early 1990s signal the beginning of a new phase in the trajectory of the GD. This phase is marked by the attempt to rid itself of the stigma of National Socialism and to participate in elections. The GD participated for the first time in the European election of 1994 and, subsequently, in the national election of 1996. The party continued to contest European elections in collaboration with others (with the First Line in 1999 and the Patriotic Alliance in 2004). But it did not contest national elections for another thirteen years, until 2009, when it received merely 0.29 percent of the vote. In 2002 the party participated in the local elections with five candidates for the Athens ticket of the Popular Orthodox Rally and in 2010 it managed to elect its leader in the Athenian municipal council. The double elections of 2012 put the GD on the electoral map as a sizable electoral force and by the double elections of 2015 it managed to become the third biggest political party in the increasingly more fragmented Greek party system (Table 4.1).

Ideology and Program

In terms of ideology, in the early 1990s the party abandoned its explicit embrace of National Socialism and adopted a biological form of nationalism, usually associated with extremist right-wing parties (Chapter 2).

---

[8] Michaloliakos, interview with author, October 2012.

Table 4.1 *The electoral performance of the GD, 1994–2015*

Election	Date	Votes	Percentage	Seats
European	June 12, 1994	7242	0.11	0
National	September 22, 1996	4487	0.07	0
European[a]	June 13, 1999	48532	0.75	0
European[b]	June 13, 2004	10618	0.17	0
European	June 7, 2009	23609	0.46	0
National	October 4, 2009	19624	0.29	0
Local[c]	November 14, 2010	10222	5.29	1
National	May 6, 2012	440996	6.97	21
National	June 17, 2012	426025	6.92	18
Local[c]	May 18, 2014	35919	16.12	4
European	May 25, 2014	536913	9.39	3
National	January 25, 2015	388387	6.28	17
National	September 20, 2015	379722	6.99	18

[a] with First Line (Πρώτη Γραμμή).
[b] as Patriotic Alliance (Πατριωτική Συμμαχία).
[c] Athens municipal election.
Source: Greek Ministry of Interior, http://www.ypes.gr/el/Elections/

Throughout the 1990s and 2000s, party publications avoided direct appeals for National Socialism, sidestepped their previous praise for Hitler and other Nazis and evaded uninhibited calls in favor of the racial purity of the Aryan race. Instead, the party sought to position itself as a nationalist political force that rejected nearly all aspects of the established political system and as a third force between communism and Western democracy.[9] Despite the notable shift away from the explicit embrace of National Socialism, the party literature displays notable continuity with the ideological platform developed in the 1980s. Addressing a relatively small readership of party devotees and militants, the party publications sustain the ideological rootedness of the party in the political ideas first explicated by the party leadership in the 1980s. The most notable element of continuity is the explicit adoption of the principle of "racialism"

---

[9] This idea of nationalism being the third force of history – between communism and liberalism – remains one of the main tenets of the party identity (e.g., Golden Dawn 2012b). In an earlier formulation of this idea, the party rejects both communism, defeated by capitalism, and Western democracy. It recognizes nationalism as a continuation of interwar regimes, such as fascism in Italy and National Socialism in Germany. See "What nationalism is not," *Golden Dawn* [newspaper], issue 100, May 1995, p. 2.

(φυλετισμός), a key constituent of National Socialist ideology.[10] As presented in a number of newspaper articles published across the years by the GD newspaper, racialism is "the attempt to maintain the purity of the Race, as is natural, that is, as nature commands."[11] According to Michaloliakos, "the first constituent element of a group of people, denoted as Nation, is common descent, common blood, race and biological kinship."[12] The GD selectively uses quotes from Pericles, Isocrates, Plutarch and many other ancient Greek philosophers to claim that they were also racialists.[13] It also traces its Swastika-looking party symbol to the ancient Greek meander found on many ancient Greek sculptures. The emphasis the GD places on race remains a defining characteristic of its ideological platform even after its major electoral breakthrough in 2012 and despite the vehement reaction this generates among its opponents. The ideological pamphlet prepared for the eighth party congress in 2016 has a number of references to race and upholds that the "the idea of the Nation, of the Race, is dominant for the people of the Golden Dawn" (Golden Dawn 2016). Although the party presented itself in this congress as a "modern and dynamic ideological movement," it remains grounded by its ideological rootedness to National Socialism. This explains why key party documents, like the description of its identity, state that "the party does not ignore the law of diversity and difference in Nature. Respecting the intellectual, national, and *racial inequality* of humans we can build a just society based on equality before the law" (Golden Dawn 2012b, emphasis added).

The first program of the GD first appears prior to the 1996 national election and remained unchanged until 2011. In this one-page program, the party took a hardline position on all major "national" issues, such as the Macedonia issue, the plight of the Greek minority in Albania, the ongoing disputes with Turkey over the Aegean, the Muslim minority in Western Thrace and the occupation of the northern part of Cyprus by Turkey. Among other things the party proposed a long-term strategy for the incorporation of northern Epirus, in southern Albania, to Greece.

[10] A number of articles in the Golden Dawn magazine, in the 1980s, acknowledge the importance of race in National Socialist ideology. See, for example, "Ideological," *Golden Dawn* [magazine], issue 4, April 1981, p. 3.
[11] A. P. Mattheou, "Racialism: The big truth," *Golden Dawn* [newspaper], issue 57, p. 7.
[12] Nikos Michaloliakos, "Nationalism and Race," *Golden Dawn* [newspaper], issue 427, June 20, 2002, p.16.
[13] Periandros Androutsopoulos, "The racialism of the ancients," *Golden Dawn* [newspaper], issue 237, April 24, 1998, p. 9.

The party also sought to capitalize on growing Greek anxiety over the influx of immigrants, mostly from Eastern Europe.[14] The programmatic platform of the GD started changing in 2011, when Greece began implementing the economic adjustment program agreed with its Eurozone partners and the International Monetary Fund in exchange for a series of new loans that would allow it to refinance its ballooning debt. In its revised two-page program, the GD wanted the Greek government to denounce the agreement with the creditors (what became known as the "memorandum"), which included draconian budgetary cuts and tax hikes. The party also put forth social policies for those most affected by the economic crisis, such as debt relief, minimum income and protection of primary residence. In the 2011 program the party sought to capitalize on growing public resentment against established political parties and politicians by demanding cuts in their public subsidies and salaries. The party also proposed a redirection of economic policy to boost national production, especially in the primary sector. Despite these changes, large parts of the 2011 program were similar or identical to the 1996 program, especially those regarding "national" issues and illegal immigration.[15]

The party presented its first full-fledged program in 2016, more than two decades after it started participating in the electoral process. Prepared for the eighth party congress, the thirty-two-page program reflected a move to moderate some of its signature positions and to extend its programmatic reach in new political terrain. Whereas in 1996 the party wanted to deport "all foreigners," the new program focused on illegal immigration and called for the provision of residency permits only to those non-EU nationals that meet the necessary requirements. In the new program, the GD avoided irredentist claims but sustained a hardline stance toward Turkey. The 2016 program reflected the growing emphasis the party placed on infiltrating rural constituencies and devoted more than four pages to outlining a number of proposals for boosting national agricultural production and autarky. Apart from subsidies and debt relief for farmers, the party proposed setting up a registry for "primeval Greek animal races" to facilitate their reproduction. The GD considered the expansion of national

---

[14] Popular Association – Golden Dawn, "Political program," *Golden Dawn* [newspaper], issue 164, September 13, 1996, p. 5. The same program reappears in the party literature in 1998 and 2005; Popular Association – Golden Dawn, "Political program," *Golden Dawn* [newspaper], issue 240, May 15, 1998, p. 6; Popular Association – Golden Dawn, "Political program," *Golden Dawn* [newspaper], issue 596, November 24, 2005, p. 10.

[15] Golden Dawn, "Proposals for a new national policy," *Golden Dawn* [magazine], issue 747, November 9, 2011, p. 8–9.

productive capacity a prerequisite for having a national, rather than a European, currency. The new program also captured the reorientation of its foreign policy toward Russia, and to a lesser extent China. The GD proposed a strategic alliance with Russia, which can help better secure Greek interests, including those related to the extraction of its energy resources and protection from Turkey. The party also proposed introducing simple instead of reinforced proportional representation and direct election of the president from the people. To address political corruption it suggested repealing the immunity of members of parliament. A self-declared paganist ideological movement in the 1980s, the GD now declared that there should be no separation between the Church and the state.

Organizational Development

The GD has developed from a street gang to the third biggest Greek political party under the permanent leadership of Nikos Michaloliakos, the general secretary of the party since its founding in 1983. Born in 1957, Michaloliakos boasts tenure in the Greek nationalist movement since the age of sixteen. He was imprisoned for a violent incident in 1976 and served time for illegal possession of explosives in 1978 (Psarras 2012). He has authored a number of historical, ideological and political books in which he outlines his ideology and worldview and has been in charge of the party magazine and newspaper for most of this time. The formal party structure, documented in the party statutes the party submitted to the Supreme Court in August 2012 (Golden Dawn 2012d), revolves around the party leader. The party statutes note that "the general secretary is the highest party organ in the period in between the regular congresses, and his decisions are compulsory and bind all party organs" (Golden Dawn 2012d, p. 10). Moreover, the statutes vest Michaloliakos with the "absolute discretionary authority" to choose the political council among those elected in the sixty-member central committee. The general secretary also appoints the general manager of the party and appoints candidates for elections. The authority of Michaloliakos within the party seems to go well beyond what the official party statutes already grant him. Whereas the statutes specify that new cells can be established with a decision by the central committee, "everything comes down to the decisions of the leader. *We* have a leader."[16] Similarly, while the statutes outline an elaborate

---

[16] Nikos Michos, MP of the GD from 2012 to 2017, interview with the author, Athens, July 2013.

process for the recruitment of new members, Michaloliakos seems to have a major role here as well: "For someone to become a member there is a process. One of us undertakes the responsibility to recommend a new member to the leader."[17] Although the official statutes make no reference to the "leadership principle" or *Führerprinzip* that such parties are known to adhere to (Mudde 2007: 160), party functionaries consider this principle as one of the main strengths of the party. "We abide by the 'leadership principle.' This is one of the party's strengths, not weaknesses."[18] Many local party organizations have a picture of the leader on their walls and party events often end with acclamations to the GD "chief" (αρχηγός) – as party devotees call their leader.

Although the congress is the top party organ, higher in the party hierarchy than the general secretary, the meager information the party makes available about the proceedings of the eight congresses it has held since 1990 show the limited role it plays in major party decisions. On paper, the congress must be held every three years among three hundred members of the party sent by the local party organizations, depending on the registered members each local branch has. In practice, the congress has been held at less regular intervals, further pointing to the failure of the party to set up well-institutionalized processes and structures. In April 1997, the party announced that its fourth congress would be held later that year but it was not held for another three years. The last congress, held in March 2016, was also delayed for three years by the criminal prosecution and imprisonment of most GD parliamentarians and dozens of local militants.[19] Moreover, although the congress is supposed to determine "the broader political planning and strategy of the party," it was kept aside for some of the most critical decisions in the party trajectory. For example, in 2000, the fourth party congress, approved the formation of alliances with other nationalist forces – something the GD had *already* done for the 1999 European election by joining with the First Line (Πρώτη Γραμμή) of Kostas Plevris.[20] In 2004, members of the GD leadership formed another party, the Patriotic Alliance, to run in the 2004 European election and, subsequently in the 2007 national election.[21] The form the electoral

---

[17] Michos, ibid.   [18] Ioannis Lagos, interview with the author, Athens, July 2013.
[19] Party activist, interview with the author, September 2015.
[20] Plevris is well-known Holocaust-denier and former leader of 4th August party, the only party that existed during the military junta.
[21] The Patriotic Alliance (Πατριωτική Συμμαχία) was led by Demetrios Zafiropoulos, a member of the Political Council of the GD and publisher of the newspaper, Free World (Ελεύθερος Κόσμος). It

participation of the GD took was determined by the appointees of Michaloliakos in the Political Council, not the congress.[22] In December 2005, after a number of attacks against party branches, Michaloliakos decided *by himself* that the party should freeze its political activities. In a brief announcement published in the party newspaper, he declared: "I hereby decide the suspension of all political activity of the party Golden Dawn – Popular Association."[23]

Apart from some scattered references to the proceedings of party congresses, the party literature provides very limited information about the composition or operation of the rest of the various party bodies. The central committee is made up of sixty members elected by the party congress. The analysis of its membership shows that the 2016 congress re-elected thirty-seven, or 62 percent, of those sixty members elected in the 2010 congress.[24] Important party functionaries, such as Christos Rigas and Frantzeskos Porichis, have since left the party. Both the 2010 and the 2016 congresses of the GD elected only two women to the central committee – Eleni Zaroulia, the wife of Michaloliakos, and Alexandra Mparou, then-wife of MP Nikos Michos.[25] The central committee has provided most albeit not all members of parliament. Twelve out of the eighteen MPs elected in September 2015 are also members of the central committee elected by the 2016 congress.

Appointed by the secretary general among members of the central committee, the Political Council is the most obscure among the top bodies of the party. The size of the Political Council remains unspecified in the official statutes. It has grown from six members reported in the third party congress of 1995; to seven members in the sixth party congress of 2007; to nine members in the seventh congress of 2011. With few exceptions, the

sought to bring together various nationalist forces, including former junta loyalists. Its founding congress was held on April 21, 2004 – the date the military junta took control of Greece in 1967. The Patriotic Alliance had parallel structures and in some cases shared offices with the GD. A number of GD members took part in the 2004 European election and 2007 national election on the Patriotic Alliance ticket (various issues of the *Golden Dawn* newspaper, e.g., 519, 529, 539, 544, 547, 551). As the GD subsequently revealed, the Patriotic Alliance was founded "after a decision of the congress of the Golden Dawn" (issue 610, p. 3). Zafiropoulos subsequently left the GD along with other members of the central committee that disagreed with the party leadership (issue 610, p. 3; Psarras 2012).

[22] Golden Dawn announcement, "About the elections," *Golden Dawn* [newspaper], issue 504, January 15, 2004, p. 9.

[23] Nikos Michaloliakos, "Statement of General Secretary," *Golden Dawn* [newspaper], issue 597, December 1, 2005, p. 3.

[24] Analysis performed by author based on lists published in by the Volos local organization (http://xavolos.blogspot.co.uk/2011/02/blog-post_3802.html) and issue 974 of the party newspaper.

[25] Both Michos and Mparou left the party in 2017.

GD conceals information about the members of the Political Council. In the past, its members have included Antonios Androutsopoulos ("Periandros") who participated in the Council *in absentia* while wanted for seven years by the police for almost killing leftist activists in 1998 and subsequently sentenced twenty-one years in prison (Psarras 2012). The subsequent founder of the GD's sister party in Cyprus, the National Popular Front (Εθνικό Λαϊκό Μέτωπο, ΕΛΑΜ), Christos Christou, has also been a member of the Political Council.[26] Based on the scattered information made available by the party, the 2010 Political Council included Ioannis Vouldis, George Germenis, Elias Kasidiaris, Ioannis Lagos, Artemis Mattheopoulos, Elias Panagiotaros, Frantzeskos Porichis, Michael Tsakiris and Nikolaos Chrysomallis. Nearly all joined the party in the 1990s and are close associates of Michaloliakos. With few exceptions, such as Porichis and Vouldis, all others continue to have a key role in the daily operation of the party, most in the Attica region and some (Chrysomallis, Mattheopoulos, and Tsakiris) in Northern Greece.

Since the early 1990s the GD has also formed a number of auxiliary organizations, as part of an ongoing experimentation with different organizational means to infiltrate Greek society. One of the oldest and still active of these organization is the Youth Front (Μέτωπο Νεολαίας), which has been at the forefront of many street-level political activities since the late 1990s. Since 1998 the Front has been publishing another GD magazine, *Counter-Attack* (Αντεπίθεση), and since 2000 it has been organizing an annual Festival of the Greek Youth. Another systematic attempt to infiltrate the Greek youth was through the formation of the football fan clubs Bulldogs and Blue Army (Γαλάζια Στρατιά) – following the model of nationalist or fascist football clubs elsewhere in Europe (e.g., Italy's Lazio).[27] The Blue Army gained considerable political visibility in the 2000s when it rejected all efforts by the Hellenic Football Association to cooperate with its Turkish counterpart. "Among the fans, it was easier to find political soldiers. On the spectator stands [κερκίδες] you find the *Lumpenproletariat*."[28] As early as 2010 and especially after its 2012 electoral breakthrough, the GD also organized the Women's Front (Μέτωπο Γυναικών). The Front was particularly active in Nikaia, organizing weekly speeches and self-defense lessons for women and led by Nicole Mpeneki, the partner of Ioannis Lagos. After her arrest and imprisonment in 2013 as

---

[26] Interview with GD activists, January 2015.
[27] "In the stadiums of Europe," *Golden Dawn* [newspaper], issue 329, June 2, 2000, p. 4.
[28] Activist, interview with the author, August 2015.

part of the criminal prosecution of party leaders and members, the Front stopped systematically reporting its activities.

In addition to its youth and women movements, in recent years the GD has also started establishing local or regional professional organizations, seeking to gain institutional representations in various occupational sectors. One of the first of such efforts was with taxi owners, who formed the Popular Association of Attica Taxi Owners (Λαϊκός Σύνδεσμος Ιδιοκτητών Ταξί Αττικής, ΛΑΣΙΤΑ). In June 2013, this GD association received 13.75 percent of the vote and elected three representatives to the board of the professional association.[29] In 2014, GD participated in the election to the Thessaloniki Bar Association with the Movement of Nationalist Lawyers that caused a stir in the profession.[30] The Nationalist Lawyers received 106 votes or 2.59 percent of the total and failed to elect any members in the Bar Association.[31] In late 2015 and early 2016, the GD also set up a number of local farmer associations in such places as Imathia and Lakonia. And in February 2016 it set up the Association of Greek Workers Saint Nicholas close to the dockyards of Perama, a traditional communist bastion.[32]

The Local Organizations of the GD across Time and Space

One of the most consistent features in the organizational development of the GD is the emphasis it has placed in setting up local party organizations. As early as 1981, when the Golden Dawn was just a "National Socialist review," it set up offices in both Athens and Thessaloniki hosting ideological lectures. By 1988, the party set up an additional branch in Volos and held regular office hours a few times a week. In December 1992, the party reported having two additional local organizations in Patra and Kalamata. The third party congress of 1995 decided that in the next two years the party should try to "infiltrate this society for good" by "housing our combative cells in the countryside and developing them into strong local branches."[33] Indeed, by 1997 the party newspaper lists thirteen local

---

[29] See www.xryshaygh.com/enimerosi/view/lasita [last accessed in May 2016].
[30] "The nationalist faction divides the Thessaloniki lawyers," *To Βήμα*, February 3, 2014; downloaded from www.tovima.gr/society/article/?aid=563704 [last accessed in May 2016].
[31] Final results of the first-round election for the president and members of the Thessaloniki Bar Association, February 25, 2014; downloaded from https://goo.gl/AzcHRX [last accessed in May 2016].
[32] See https://goo.gl/6L27e3 [last accessed in May 2016].
[33] Periandros Androutsopoulos, excerpts from speech in the third party congress, "Congress: turning-point in the road of popular nationalism to victory," *Golden Dawn* [newspaper], issue 103, April 7, 1995, p. 7.

branches as the GD continued to grow its network of local organizations despite the electoral setback in the 1996 election. In the next decade, the network of local branches gradually shrank and the pattern of local organizational development changed. Instead of investing its organizational resources in increasing its brick-and-mortar presence in various localities, the GD set up local cells that did not have a physical presence. By the early 2000s, the party reported the formation of local "cells of militant action." Rather than the name of the party, some of these cells had different names, like White Power in the Southern Athenian suburbs, Elioforos in the Western suburbs, Keratsini Guard, "Christos Kapsalis" in Mesologgi, Blue Eagles in Chania, Patriotic Union of Ilia and National Guard of Evia.[34] During this period, the now fewer brick-and-mortar organizations tried to infiltrate local societies through new means, such as the publication of their own newspapers. The branches in northern Greece published the *Northern Lights* and the Kalamata branch the *Greek Worker*. In 2001 the GD boasted having nine local branches and twenty local cells, including one in Cyprus. The fifth party congress of 2003 stressed the importance of expanding the local presence of the GD, organizing many open events and sustaining the street-level activism of party militants. Moreover, the party decided to establish two "executive offices" to handle its growing local presence, one for central and northern Greece and the other for southern Greece.[35] By 2005, the party had seven local branches and more than thirty local cells. In December 2005, Michaloliakos decided to suspend "all political activity" and overnight all local party branches and cells were no longer listed in the party newspaper. Nevertheless, the GD continued to organize some local events through affiliated organizations, such as the Nationalist Cultural Movement of Thessaloniki and the Committee of National Memory.[36]

The GD started to rebuild its local organizational network in 2007, a little more than a year after the decision to officially suspend its political activities. Ahead of the sixth party congress, the party newspaper signaled a

---

[34] For example, see *Golden Dawn* [newspaper], issue 342, September 29, 2000, p. 14; and issue 490, October 9, 2003, p. 2.

[35] "Golden Dawn, 5th party congress: Nationalism yesterday, today, always," *Golden Dawn* [newspaper], issue 480, July 17, 2003, p. 9.

[36] The Committee of National Memory appears in the party literature as early as 1997, as the organizing body of a number of open GD events, such as the commemoration of the Imia event, when three Greek navy officers were killed in an incident with Turkey. According to the party newspaper, the Committee "is the frontal organization of the Golden Dawn for the national issues." Golden Dawn, "Announcement, 2.2.2011," *Golden Dawn* [newspaper], issue 712, February 9, 2011, p. 3.

change of course away from earlier attempts to unite nationalist forces, which it admits were a mistake.[37] In the past decade the party had collaborated with the First Line for the 1999 European election, cooperated with LAOS for the 2002 municipal election in Athens and helped establish the Patriotic Alliance to align forces with former junta loyalists. It now, however, decided to run a separate and autonomous electoral course. By the 2007 congress, the party had four local branches in Athens, Thessaloniki, Piraeus and Kalamata. During the congress, Michaloliakos noted the importance of diverting organizational resources to new technology, especially the internet, but also reminded party members of the need to continue door-to-door and person-to-person political action.[38] But it took another four years before the party could start, again, to expand its local network of local branches.

> The Chief was very restrictive when it came to setting up new branches. He had a bad experience with local branches in the past, because he had given power to people who subsequently tricked him. This started changing only after 2010, when the memorandum came along. After the summer of 2010, for the next eighteen months, the Chief started touring all around Greece. He worked on the local branch network a lot. The electoral result in 2012 did not come just like this. The Chief worked on it a lot.[39]

After its relatively successful participation in the 2010 municipal elections and the onset of the economic crisis, the party began opening local branches beyond the three main cities and Kalamata. Ahead of the seventh congress of 2011, the party announced a new organizational structure, with fourteen regional administrations approximating the thirteen geographical regions of Greece. Each regional administration became responsible for the local branches and cells of that region and was charged with the registration of new members and new cells.[40] In preparation for the next election, the seventh congress decided to intensify political activities, ideologically train new members and functionaries, set up a press office in each region and commence tours of Michaloliakos across the country.[41] Through these tours of its core leadership the party managed to set up new local cells, many of which subsequently evolved into branches. Before its

[37] "The Golden Dawn is not a ghost!," *Golden Dawn* [newspaper], issue 610, February 7, 2007, p. 3.
[38] Golden Dawn, "Popular Association – Sixth Congress," issue 616, May 3, 2007, pp. 9, 11.
[39] Interview #44, member of central committee, September 2016.
[40] Golden Dawn, "The Popular Association organizes its party mechanism," *Golden Dawn* [newspaper], issue 709, December 29, 2010, p. 2.
[41] "Toward a new Golden Dawn for Hellenism," *Golden Dawn* [newspaper], issue 710, February 9, 2011, p. 7.

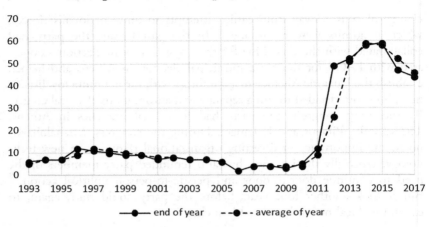

Figure 4.1   GD branches across time (1993–2017).

electoral breakthrough in the double 2012 elections, in May and June, the party had brick-and-mortar presence in fifteen different locations across Greece.

The electoral breakthrough in the 2012 national elections gave a strong push to the organizational expansion of the GD. Within less than a year after the elections, the party expanded its local presence to fifty-two branches. The General Secretary and members of the Political Council continued touring Greece inaugurating the opening of new local branches, some in the presence of hundreds or even thousands of supporters. The criminal prosecution and temporary imprisonment of the party leadership and functionaries in the fall of 2013 placed the local organizational expansion of the GD on hold. But in the following year, and as the core party leadership remained in prison, the party managed to open new branches in a number of locations, mostly in northern Greece. In 2014, the local organizational network of the GD peaked at sixty branches, the party acquiring brick-and-mortar presence in forty-five out of fifty-six electoral districts. In 2015, and despite the release from prison of its leader and top functionaries, the GD stopped its organizational expansion, establishing a new office at its national headquarters in Ampelokipoi. By 2017 the branch network shrank to forty-four. Figure 4.1 shows the evolution of the organizational network of the GD, as reported in nearly all newspaper issues published since 1993.

The local organizational presence of the GD displays no particular geographical patterns. Apart from major urban and suburban areas, the party set up branches in significantly less populous areas, in some of the islands and in districts where it already had one branch. It remained absent from most of Epirus and from many of the smaller islands. The contraction of the local branch network took a toll on branches in rural and suburban areas but it also affected the presence of the party in some populous cities, such as Larissa and Serres. All in all, in the ten years since the party officially resumed its local operations, it set up 74 branches in 45 out of 56 electoral districts and in 73 out of 325 municipalities. In the biggest district, Attica, the party set up as many as seven branches, and in most others it had a single branch. By September 2016, when the GD celebrated the printing of the thousandth issue of its newspaper, its local presence shrank to 48 branches in 36 out of 56 electoral districts and 47 out of 325 municipalities.

Conclusion

In the past decades the GD evolved from a network of National Socialist ideologues to the third biggest political party in Greece. This chapter has examined the trajectory of this party from the 1980s onwards, emphasizing critical aspects of its organizational development. After a necessary detour into the ideological and programmatic development of the GD, the chapter focused on its organization. The establishment of local organizational structures has been a key element in its development and became a central tenet of its organizational evolution after its electoral successes in the 2010s. The chapter traced the local organizational development of the party across time and space. The evolution of local party units displays a lot more variance than their common existence in a highly centralized "*Führerpartei*" would suggest. The purpose of the next chapter is to systematically trace the varied organizational trajectories of local party subunits.

CHAPTER 5

Variation in Local Organizational Development

The local organizational life of political parties displays notable variation that merits systematic examination. The factors affecting this variation constitute the main focus of the next four chapters of the book. The purpose of this chapter is to provide the basis for the subsequent analysis by documenting the divergent trajectories of subnational organizational units. The first section analyzes the basic characteristics of all local party organizations the Golden Dawn (GD) set up, laying the groundwork for the subsequent analysis of variation in their organizational evolution. The second section provides insights into local organizational life by analyzing the range of activities they have undertaken over a period of twenty-three years. The third section uses these data to show the distinct trajectories of the various local units of the GD and analyze variation in organizational outcomes. It first presents evidence regarding the degree of continuity these local structures display bringing to the surface cases of organizational persistence and fatality. It then delves deeper into the organizational life of local party branches and presents data regarding their activism.

The Local Party Branch

As discussed in Chapter 4, even before the GD started organizing as a political party, it paid particular attention to developing a network of local branches that would help it grow roots in local societies. These branches display remarkable variation across time, not only in numbers but also in activism, size and resources. Nevertheless, they also share a number of basic characteristics that are worth noting. The local branches are set up after permission from the party by people who are thought to be loyal to its ideology and cause. The local leadership of the party is not elected but appointed by the party through a process that involves the central as well as the regional party leadership. Party interviewees are not shy of the fact that the GD does not have a democratic electoral process for the selection of local leaders. Local branches usually have five-member councils, what the party calls a "pentameles" (πενταμελές), though this number varies depending on local conditions.

The local branches are supposed to be active in the local community through the organization of various activities. Even before 1993, when the GD started organizing as a political party, its local branches were expected to regularly host political, ideological and historical speeches (see next section). "The local branches operate based on statutes and central [party] directive. They are obligated to open the offices two or three times a week and to undertake an informational activity in their areas at least once a fortnight."[1] Party functionaries place a high value in the brick-and-mortar presence of the GD in local communities. The activities organized in the local branch facilitate the ideological and political training of local activists, which subsequently helps their mobilization in outdoor activities. Moreover, the local office becomes a place for the social interaction of loyal activists and for the establishment of strong social bonds between them. "It is both a home and a castle at the same time."[2] The importance of a local branch is also symbolic: "The local office adds prestige. Like a flag on a castle, it signals that this area belongs to someone. The branch becomes a point of reference. It is also important for political propaganda purposes. It is important for the opponent to know that something is happening, that you are constantly organizing and being active. It is a matter of strategy."[3]

Most local branches are relatively modest in size both in terms of people and other resources. With the exception of the branches in main urban centers, the ones in Athens, Piraeus or Thessaloniki, the number of people regularly attending indoor branch events rarely exceeds more than a few dozen people and those undertaking outdoor activities are even fewer, especially in challenging local environments. "The stable force of each office is fifteen to twenty people. These are the activists."[4] These figures are in line with the attendance records kept by one of the most active branches of the GD as well by the numbers observed in various local branches and reported by local branch heads.[5] Although in most branches the number of

---

[1] Interview #42, member of local branch council, September 2016.
[2] Interview #32, member of local branch council, August 2016.
[3] Interview #31, member of local branch council, August 2016.
[4] Interview #42, member of local branch council, September 2016.
[5] The author saw the attendance records in one of the most active local branches. The attendance sheets showed that the number of attendees in the events organized once or twice a week by the party were between fifteen and twenty-five. Also, interview #32, member of local branch council, August 2016.

attendees is relatively small, in the big urban branches the figures are naturally higher. The attendance of local events in some of the main urban branches suggests that the number of regular participants ranges from fifty to eighty people.[6] This number can grow to more than one hundred people depending on the speaker.

Many local branches are located in central city locations in upper floors of apartment complexes and are usually limited to a single office apartment with two or three rooms. Each branch has a common space for the regular speeches of the party and a small office for the branch head or other functionaries. The biggest branch is the one in Athens taking several floors in an apartment complex, one of which serves as a bookstore. Depending on the location and size of the branch, the operational cost of most branches ranges from €300 to €600, which includes money for rent, utilities, printing and gas.[7] Both the central and local party leadership stress that the branches should be financially independent. The operational cost tends to be covered by the contributions of the local functionaries and the attendees of local events. The few people who end up footing most of the bill for the operation of the local branch often mention how much more they could do had they had more resources at their disposal. "The most difficult point in the development of the local branch is now because there is no money and we are begging for contributions using coupons and asking colleagues [lawyers] who belong to the GD to chip in. We barely cover the costs and have no money for more actions."[8] Although local branches are supposed to be self-funded, they occasionally receive external support for individual activities, either from the party or through the salaries of elected party officials. "Our branch has followed the basic guidelines of the party and is self-funded but there is also help from our MPs."[9]

Life in Local Party Branches

The analysis of activities organized by local GD branches provides a rare glimpse into local organizational life. In the past three decades, the GD

---

[6] The author observed four local events organized by the Athens branch in July and September 2016 and December 2017; one organized by the Piraeus branch in September 2016; and one in Ampelokipi in December 2017.

[7] Interview #31, member of local branch council, August 2016; interview #34, member of local branch council, August 2016; interview #40, member of local branch council, September 2016.

[8] Interview #27, member of local branch council, July 2016; interview #34, member of local branch council, August 2016.

[9] Interview #32, member of local branch council, August 2016; interview #33, member of local branch council, August 2016.

has reported in its newspaper the organization of hundreds of activities, furnishing researchers with a large amount of unique and unexploited data regarding its action repertoire. The analysis of this repertoire can facilitate a better understanding of the nature of the party and, more importantly, help explore the factors affecting its organizational development. The vast majority of political activities have been undertaken by local party organizations, usually under the guidance, coordination and sometimes involvement of the central party leadership.[10] The party has long recognized "the Local Branch as the basic unit of the political battle of the Movement."[11] And it considered the expansion of the network of local organizations as important "for consolidating our presence on the street and the acceptance of our political discourse."[12] In the past decades, local organizations were formally charged with the responsibility of recruiting new members and organizing local party activities.[13]

The range of 2,786 political activities reported in 939 out of 1,000 issues of the *Golden Dawn* between 1993 and 2016 can be broken down into three broad categories: speeches, lectures and meetings; political activism; and social activism. The most frequent type of activity organized by local organizations is lectures given by national or local party functionaries on current affairs. In these lectures, the GD would seek to reinterpret current affairs and to reiterate its key programmatic claims while countering the claims of its opponents. Out of the total of 2,786 local activities, there were 585 lectures on current affairs, comprising 21 percent of all activities (Table 5.1). Emphasizing the importance of ideologically training its militants and supporters, the local branches have also organized speeches across Greece on such themes as "racial purity," "Shakespeare and the Jews," "the idea of nationalism today," "the great fraud of the myth of democracy," "the continuity of the Greek race," "the northern tradition of the Aryans," "the ancient Greek spirit," "Church and

---

[10] The degree of involvement of the central leadership has varied across time, in part due to the rapid expansion of the local organizational network of the party after 2011. Michaloliakos, interview with the author, Athens, October 2012.

[11] Golden Dawn, "General Principles," *Golden Dawn* [newspaper], issue 272, March 19, 1999, p. 4.

[12] Periandros Androutsopoulos, excerpts from speech in pre-congress conference in Athens, "The third congress of the Golden Dawn, congress of struggle!" *Golden Dawn* [newspaper], issue 90, January 6, 1994, p. 3.

[13] Golden Dawn, 2012d, "Statutes of the political party with the name 'Popular Association – Golden Dawn,'" retrieved from https://goo.gl/eBrUoy [last accessed in May 2016].

Table 5.1 *GD activities, 1993–2016 (n = 2786)*

Type of activity	Number	% of total
Speech/lecture/meeting	**1356**	**48.7**
Speech on current affairs	585	21.0
Ideological lecture	184	6.6
Historical lecture	273	9.8
Electoral campaigning	118	4.2
Video presentation	89	3.2
Organizational meeting	41	1.5
Meeting with institutions/interest groups	66	2.4
Political activism	**1316**	**47.2**
Canvassing	640	23.0
Commemorations/celebrations	413	14.8
Demonstration/protest/march	171	6.1
Camps/training	29	1.0
Inauguration of new office	63	2.3
Social Activism	**114**	**4.1**
Food	67	2.4
Clothing	8	0.3
Blood donation	23	0.8
Other	16	0.6
Total	**2786**	**100.0**

Zionism," and the "meaning of ideology and its terms."[14] The dataset of local party activities includes 184 speeches that focused on ideological issues, 6.6 percent of the total number of activities. The local branches are also at the forefront of efforts by the GD to appropriate the most important moments in Greek history and to reinterpret some of the most controversial ones. The party supplements the reproduction of official Greek history with the reinterpretation of other periods of Greek history, such as the interwar Metaxas dictatorship, the civil war and the military junta of 1967.[15] Overall, over the years the party put together 273 historical lectures or 9.8 percent of the total number of activities reported in the party newspaper.

In addition to various speeches, local party militants are also expected to organize and participate in political activism. Over the years, the GD has gained notoriety for organizing hundreds of such events, in part because

---

[14] The speeches were announced in the party newspaper. See issues 112 (1994), 202, 208 (1997), 409, 417 (2002), 603 (2006). Recent themes retrieved from the party website: https://goo.gl/11T5BD, https://goo.gl/s50SnB.

[15] See, for example, issues 85, 603.

some have been associated with violence. One of the most typical activities undertaken by party militants is the dissemination of party material. Like activists in many parties, groups of GD militants – often less than a dozen people of all ages – are shown in party publications dressed in black or in camouflage disseminating party pamphlets, distributing campaign posters and handing out the party newspaper in local coffee shops and busy streets. In recent years party canvassing has become "localized," the party message adjusted to local conditions.[16] "When we go to the commercial center of Thessaloniki, for example, we print pamphlets for issues related to shops and of concern to the shop-owners. In Thrace, the issues are different – it is the presence of the Turks and the Turkish consulate in Komotini."[17] In the Athenian district of Agios Panteleimonas, where citizens faced a serious problem with the influx of immigrants in various neighborhoods, the party sought to mobilize support through the dissemination of a pamphlet called "The voice of the residents of Agios Panteleimonas" (Dinas et al. 2013: 7). Overall, the dissemination of party material is by far the most frequent activity undertaken by local branches, with as many as 640 activities reported in the party newspaper, 23 percent of the total.

One of the most notable, consistent and controversial features of the GD's repertoire of political activities are commemorations and celebrations. Usually held at various historical sites, the participation in these events ranges from a few dozens to hundreds or even thousands of people, depending on who organizes them.[18] The party started taking part in broader nationalist mobilizations and in various commemorations in the early 1990s. Its local branches took part in mobilizations for the Macedonia issue, in the commemoration of those who fought in December 1944 against the communists in Athens and in the funeral of three Greek naval officers lost in a 1996 skirmish with Turkey over the island of Imia.[19] In subsequent years, the party started organizing commemorative events of its own, turning Imia into an annual commemorative event that drew dozens, hundreds and, more recently, thousands of people. Some of these events have become known as "events of hatred," commemorating the civil

---

[16] Golden Dawn activities, *Golden Dawn* [magazine], issue 12, December 1983, p. 5.
[17] Artemis Matheopoulos, member of political council and central committee, former MP, interview with the author, June 2015.
[18] Some of these events are organized by the national or regional party organizations.
[19] "Rally for the Macedonian issue in Lamia" and "Patra – Kalamata," *Golden Dawn* [newspaper], issue 59, March 25, 1994, p. 2; "Glory and honor to the heroic X," *Golden Dawn* [newspaper], issue 134, December 15, 1995, p. 2; "Fallen for the homeland," *Golden Dawn* [newspaper], issue 141, February 9, 1996, pp. 1–2.

war battles in Grammos and Vitsi and atrocities against civilians in Meligalas. To the repertoire of these very controversial events, the GD has occasionally added political activities to honor personalities from Greek history such as Alexander the Great, the last Byzantine Emperor Constantine Palaiologos and the fighter in the Macedonian Struggle Pavlos Melas. The GD has also sought to reinforce its ownership of events glorified in official Greek history, such as the battle of Thermopylae. The party has been commemorating the heroic battle of the ancient Spartans against the Persians since 1997 and over the years it has become a showcase of its capacity to mobilize hundreds of militants bearing Greek flags and torches to put together a display of military order and discipline.[20] To bolster the morale of its militants, many of these commemorative events are subsequently shown as videos and thoroughly analyzed in various local branches. As Table 5.1 shows, the party newspaper reported 413 celebrations or commemorations, 14.8 percent of the total.

In addition to commemorations and celebrations, the party has also been organizing demonstrations and marches with more specific programmatic focus, such as those against immigration. In 2001, for example, the party organized a march in the center of Athens against a new immigration law. In a number of similar events held throughout the 2000s GD militants started appearing with shields bearing the emblem of the party, army camouflage and boots, thick crash helmets and heavy flag poles that were occasionally turned against antifascist mobilizers. At around this time, the many reports the GD published in its newspaper regarding these events started mentioning the "security patrols" the party put in place to protect GD demonstrators from their opponents.[21] In some of these events, the GD demonstrators were also accompanied by motorcades, which became an even more prominent feature of the action repertoire of the GD in subsequent years, especially in Piraeus. Towards the end of the 2000s, local party militants started taking part in demonstrations in various Athenian neighborhoods held by supporters and opponents of the abrupt influx of immigrants in their localities. To the surprise of the national party leadership and the militants themselves, the groups of GD militants received favorable reception by some local residents. As one of the leaders of the group of GD

---

[20] In the late 1990s, only two dozen militants would participate in the event. By 2015, the event became an attraction for hundreds of party loyalists and a display of the discipline, hierarchy and order the party wants to instill on its militants. See "We are the new Spartan Phalanx," *Golden Dawn* [newspaper], issue 290, August 13, 1999, p. 3; and https://goo.gl/tgE3Mm [last accessed in May 2016].

[21] See many pictures in issues 379, 408 and 421.

militants who infiltrated the Agios Panteleimonas neighborhood recalls: "I was in charge of the team that entered Agios Panteleimonas for the first time. There were about 500 residents demonstrating against the situation with immigration and about 2,000 counterdemonstrators. The GD decided with an order from the chief to send its own team in the area. It was the first contact the party made with the residents."[22] Another participant similarly remembers that "the action in Agios Panteleimonas started in 2008, with the first event that took place in November that year. It was the first time that the Golden Dawn went somewhere where it was applauded by the people. We started having events with the residents there who were not our members but later joined us."[23] Throughout the next years, local militants and, sometimes, the GD leadership participated in dozens of such events. On a number of occasions, these events became associated with vigilante-type activities and with criminal activity against immigrants and antifascists. The onset of the Greek economic crisis provided the impetus for more demonstrations and protests, this time against the austerity measures agreed between the government and its creditors as part of its rescue program. GD militants joined the large masses of people demonstrating against the memorandum associated with the Greek bailout, especially in 2011. After the imprisonment of the party leader and top party functionaries in 2013, most of the demonstrations and protests demand the release of its "political prisoners" – seeking to bolster the anti-systemic profile of the party. Overall, there are 171 protest activities reported in the party newspaper between 1993 and 2016, 6.1 percent of the total.

Apart from political activism, local branches of the GD are also involved in social activism. Mostly marginal in the political program and ideology of the GD in the 1980s the 1990s, social issues started gaining more attention toward the mid-2000s. Attentive of the social turn the NPD had made in Germany at around this time (Art 2011), the GD started signaling to its militants the need to pay more attention to social problems. In its first congress, the Patriotic Alliance, which was founded by the GD to contest the 2004 European election, asks its supporters to keep in mind the tactics of the NPD as part of an effort to make the GD more socially acceptable. "We have to immediately examine with special attention how we can organize those social groups that can give mobilizational yields."[24] As part

[22] Former Golden Dawn functionary, interview with the author, December 2015.
[23] Golden Dawn activists, interview with the author, January 2015.
[24] "The first congress of a great course," *Golden Dawn* [newspaper], issue 549, December 16, 2004, p. 7. In the same issue, see also Iason Anagnostou, "Nationalism and the social issue."

of its social turn, the party started organizing May First demonstrations, purposefully seeking to trespass the ideological and programmatic territory of the Left.[25] More importantly, the local branches of Thessaloniki started experimenting with various forms of social activism, such as the small-scale collection and distribution of clothes to the homeless.[26] By the end of the decade, a number of branches – mostly in major urban centers such as Athens and Piraeus – started replicating the social activism of the Thessaloniki branch. In addition to clothes, some branches, like the newly established branch of Nikaia, would also start collecting small amounts of food. They would distribute it door-to-door to a few families, take pictures and post them online, to publicize the social face of the GD. After the electoral breakthroughs of the party in the 2012 elections and helped by the flow of public money in the party coffers, the GD shifted to large-scale food rationing to "Greeks only." In the next year, dozens of such events were held in a number of local branches across Greece, attracting hundreds, and in some cases thousands, of people lining up to get grocery bags of food. As one MP in charge of the Evia branch notes, "Our activists go door to door collecting food from suppliers and households and we distribute it whenever we have enough. In Chalkida [Evia] so far we have distributed food to 3,500 families. We do this once a month or every two months. This Saturday we will also have chicken."[27] In December 2012 the party started setting up medical centers under a program called "Greek doctors" and by September 2013, the party made plans to further expand its social activism – again, to Greeks only. "We distribute food, we give blood, we started establishing centers for providing medical advice and we want to set up childcare centers. At the local center food distributions take place regularly. If you go to local organizations you will see that there is food for 30 or 40 families, whatever we can."[28] As part of its social activism the GD also established a "Jobs for Greeks" program, through which they "convince" employers to replace their foreign employees with Greeks. Overall the party newspaper reported 114 social activities

[25] "Nationalist May First: So that Greece belongs to the Greeks," *Golden Dawn* [newspaper], issue 570, May 10, 2005, p. 1; "Nationalist May First," *Golden Dawn* [newspaper], issue 616, May 3, 2007, p. 9.
[26] "The Golden Dawners of Macedonia are showing the way," *Golden Dawn* [newspaper], issue 613, March 21, 2007, p. 7.
[27] Nikos Michos, member of central committee and of parliament, interview with the author, Athens, July 2013.
[28] Ioannis Lagos, member of political council, central committee and of parliament, interview with the author, Athens, July 2013.

organized by its local branches, or 4.1 percent of the total number of local activities reported.

Variation in Local Organizational Development

This overview of the range of activities organized by the GD across the past decades provides useful insights into what local party branches do but it does not adequately capture variation in how these branches evolve over time. To get a fuller picture of local organizational development, this chapter now focuses on the "lives" of the seventy-four branches the GD set up since 2007. The goal of this section is to trace the trajectories of these local units and to gauge various aspects of their organizational life that are deemed constitutive of their development. In most national settings, a number of indicators measuring various aspects of internal party life, such as party membership, resources and staffing (see Tavits 2013: 17–18, for an overview) are generally available – at least, for national party organizations. In Greece, such gauges of party development are not readily available, and at the local level, they are non-existent. To trace the evolution of each of the seventy-four local branches set up by the GD in the past decade this section relies on an original dataset that includes information on the organizational evolution of all branches set up from March 2007, when the party officially resumed the operation of its local branches, to September 2016, when the four-year data collection effort ended. The dataset includes two different, albeit related, gauges of organizational development: branch longevity and activity. The first gauge best captures the trajectory of party structures and the second measures party activism.

Branch Longevity

The first source of insights into the organizational development of local party branches is the degree of longevity displayed by the local branches of the GD. "Organizational longevity refers to the durability or continuance of organizations" (Montuori 2000: 61). Longevity, then, is a measure of both the *age* of each local organization and also its capacity to endure – to display *continuity* even in relatively adverse internal or external environments. With regards to age, the gauge of longevity is relatively simple: the longer the life cycle of a branch, the higher the organizational longevity. As far as continuity is concerned, a local branch might be relatively old but might have been shut down at some point during the period under examination, while another branch might be around for the same time without discontinuity. The latter displays higher levels of longevity than the former.

The GD officially announces the opening of new branches in its newspaper but shies away from officially reporting branch closures. To assess the life cycle of each branch, this section relies on the listings of all party branches in each issue of the party newspaper between March 2007 and September 2016.[29] Based on these listings, the age of each branch is calculated by measuring the number of days between the first and the last mention of each branch in the party newspaper. When a branch stops being listed in the party newspaper, this is considered evidence of branch discontinuity. In nearly all cases, branch discontinuity was verified with at least one interview and in most cases with more than one. Figure 5.1 shows the age of the seventy-four local branches of the GD. The average age of each GD branch throughout the period under study is about 42 months or 3.5 years (1,262 days; median: 1,365 days). Although most of the branches were set up in the short period between the electoral breakthroughs of the party in 2012 and the early months of 2013, they display considerable differences in age.

The analysis of newspaper listings also reveals considerable evidence of discontinuity in the lifecycle of the local branches. Out of the total of 74 branches, 30 of them stopped appearing in the newspaper listings at some point after their initial listing. To the 30 branches that displayed discontinuity in their operations, one must also add those of Lagadas in Thessaloniki and Volos in Magnesia, which opened and shut down relatively quickly, without making it to the newspaper listings. The map in Figure 5.2 distinguishes between branches that displayed discontinuity and those that have had a continued local presence. Although the party avoids explicit references to branch closures, the analysis here shows that they are common: 43 percent of the branches opened since 2007 displayed discontinuity and 35 percent proved to be organizational failures – they did not reopen after their closure. Overall, then, there is notable variation

---

[29] Each issue of the *Golden Dawn* lists all office branches along with their addresses. The analysis relies on all listings starting from issue 613 (the first after the GD resumed its operations) to issue 1,000 (the arbitrary cut-off for the conclusion of the four-year data collection effort). Out of a total of 388 issues, 34 or 8.7 pecent of all issues are missing, mostly intermittently. The analysis here includes two branches that were not listed in the newspapers but for which there is strong evidence of their existence (office pictures, inaugural events, etc.), Volos in Magnesia and Lagadas in Thessaloniki.

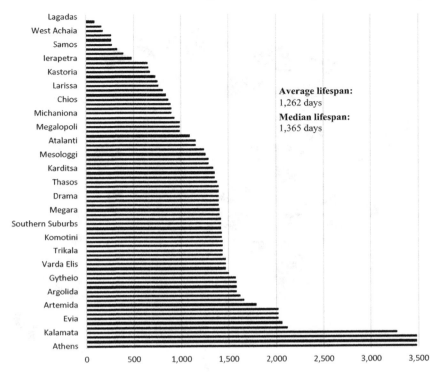

Figure 5.1 The lifespan of seventy-four local GD branches, 2007–2016 (number of days).

in the relative longevity of GD branches, both in terms of their age and also in terms of continuity.

Branch Activity

Party structures can tell part of the story of local party organizations but cannot fully capture internal organizational life. In addition to branch lifespans, then, it is also important to take into account what local organizations do throughout their period of existence. This requires opening the black box of local party organizations and examining the internal branch dynamics. To get a better sense of organizational lives, it is important to go beyond evidence of physical existence. The analysis of the brick-and-mortar presence needs to be supplemented with a systematic examination of the organizational outputs of a local branch. As we know from Duverger (1959: 23–36), the very essence of branch or cell

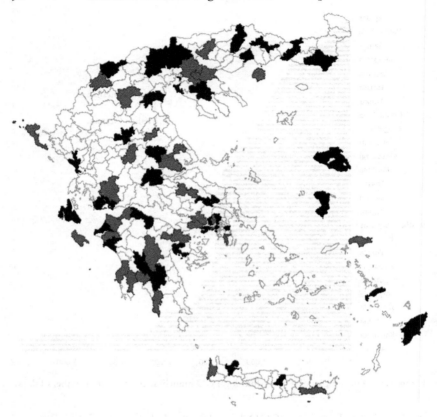

Figure 5.2   All local branches set up by the GD in 73 out of 325 Kallikratian
municipalities since 2007. Those in black were in operation in
September 2016 and those in gray had shut down at least once during this period.

life is the organization of meetings or activities that bring together
existing or prospective party members or supporters, for education,
training or, simply, for human interaction. It is important, then, to also
keep track of these activities to acquire a fuller understanding of local
organizational life.

    To analyze the internal life of the seventy-four local branches of the
GD, this book utilizes the unique dataset presented earlier of all the
activities organized by local branches and reported in the party newspaper. The analysis here relies on 1,131 activities reported between
March 2007 and September 2016 – the period after the GD officially

resumed its operations until the 1,000th issue of the newspaper, when the data collection ended.[30] The analysis of these activities yields interesting insights about the life of each of the seventy-four local branches the GD set up in the past decade. Based on these data, the most active branch of the GD was naturally the one in Athens, which also hosted the central party headquarters until 2013. The Athens branch organized a total 218 activities throughout this period, or 19.3 percent of the total activities used for this analysis. The Thessaloniki and Piraeus branches have also been relatively active, with a total number of 121 and 97 activities, respectively. Twenty-six branches were also relatively active throughout this period, with ten to forty-five reported activities during this period. The remaining forty-five branches organized fewer than ten activities throughout this period. Interestingly, six of these branches did not report any activity throughout their lifespan and another eight branches only organized a single – usually their inaugural – event. Put simply, in a notable number of localities, the brick-and-mortar presence of the GD was just that, bricks and mortar. These branches proved to be "empty shells" barely organizing anything – sometimes not even a report-worthy inaugural event.

The count of activities reported in the party newspaper is a good first cut to the level of activity organized by each of the seventy-four local branches but it cannot adequately capture the variation among the various branches, unless their respective lifespans are taken into account. The longer a branch has been around, the more the activities it can be expected to have organized. It is hence necessary to consider the level of activity undertaken by each branch given its age. Taking age into account, each branch is assigned a score for *intensity* – how many activities it was reported to have organized every three months of its existence. The seventy-four branches display notable variation in the intensity of their organized activities across this period. Naturally, Athens is the most active branch of the GD, organizing an average of 5.6 activities per quarter. The branches in Thessaloniki, Nikaia in Piraeus, the northern Athenian suburbs and the main Piraeus branch organized

---

[30] The dataset of local party activities includes a total of 2,799 activities. For 496 activities there is no particular references to the local organizer, hence they cannot be used in the analysis of the activities undertaken by the 74 local branches. Another 268 activities were organized by sectoral organizations (e.g., the youth organization), not local branches of the GD. This leaves 2,035 activities. Out of these 2,035 activities, 1,131 or 56 percent were reported after issue 613, when the party officially resumed its operations.

between 2.5 and 3.5 activities every three months. The Artemida branch in Attica, the one in Pyrgos of Elis and that in Kavala also rank among those with the highest levels of activity. Another six branches organized between one and two activities per quarter, fifty-two branches organized less than one activity and eight branches did not organize any activities. The average intensity score of each branch is 0.69 activities per quarter and the median intensity score is 0.40.

Apart from the intensity of local branch activity, the analysis of organizational development must also take into account the consistency of this activity. The consistency of branch activity captures the degree of routinization or regularity of branch operations and in this sense it goes beyond periodic spurts in local party action. This regularity is critical for understanding local party trajectories: a local branch routinely organizing a biweekly speech or protest displays different developmental characteristics than a branch with a large concentration of activities in a short period of time, for example, right before elections. The degree of consistency is calculated by measuring the number of gaps in the quarterly activities of each of the seventy-four branches. Based on this analysis, the most consistent branch was that in the Northern Suburbs, which organized at least one activity in all nineteen quarters of its existence and received the maximum consistency score of one. The Athens branch, which organized at least one activity in all but one of the thirty-nine quarters of its existence, received a consistency score as follows: $(39-1)/39 = 0.97$. The average consistency of the seventy-four branches is 0.34 and the median consistency is 0.31. Only twenty out of seventy-four branches had a score between 0.50 and 1, which means that they organized an activity only in half of the quarters throughout their lifespan. The vast majority of GD branches organized a noteworthy activity even less systematically than that and eight branches did not report any activity.

Figure 5.3 shows the association between the intensity and consistency measures for each of the seventy-four local branches of the GD. As the graph indicates, there is a strong correlation between the two measures of activity (0.84). Branches that organized a relatively large number of local activities were likely to have done so consistently. Naturally, those branches that rarely organized any activities received low scores of both intensity and consistency. Although the two measures are strongly correlated, there are also notable exceptions to these patterns. For example, the Nikaia branch averaged more than two activities per quarter but not very consistently. This is because most of its activities were organized in the last few months before its sudden closure.

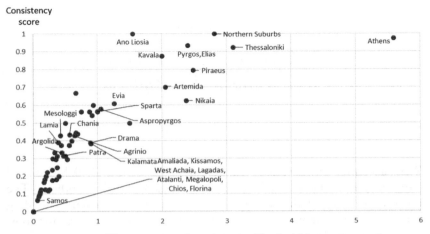

Figure 5.3   The intensity and consistency of local activism, 2007–2016
(n = 74 local branches).

Conclusion

The life of local party organizations is one of the most intriguing yet neglected areas of inquiry into the organizational development of political parties. Since Duverger pointed to the necessity of undertaking "a series of monographs on the life of a Socialist branch" (1959: 27), there have been very few efforts to understand how parties evolve at the local level. This chapter constitutes the beginning of the examination into the local organizational life of one of the most extreme parties in Europe. The local organizations of the GD display similar features in terms of their composition, purpose and size. They are expected to organize a range of conventional and contentious activities, ranging from ideological and historical lectures to controversial commemorations and protests. But they display notable variation in their organizational life. Some local structures display high levels of longevity and manage to endure across time, while others shut down in the face of internal or external challenges. The analysis of all local activities reported in the GD newspaper for nearly a decade also reveals differences in the vibrancy of internal organizational life. Some parties are quite active in the local community, organizing dozens of activities across their lifespan. Others exist only on paper, barely organizing anything beyond their inaugural event. The next four chapters explore distinct sets of factors affecting the evolution of local party organizations.

CHAPTER 6

Endogenous Drivers of Local Organizational Development

What accounts for the varied local development of the GD? Why do local party organizations succeed in some settings but fail in others? The purpose of this and the subsequent three chapters is to start providing explanations for the varied trajectories of subnational party organizations. This chapter looks at how endogenous factors affect local organizational development and the subsequent chapters examine environmental (electoral, institutional and societal) factors. The first part of this chapter seeks to utilize insights from the broader literature on political parties and the extant literature on far right parties to analyze how endogenous (party-specific) factors might account for variation in local organizational outcomes. The remainder of the chapter presents the evidence. The second section looks at factors that are specific to the national party and the third section examines whether organizational outcomes are endogenous to the local units themselves.

Party-Specific Factors Affecting Local Organizational Outcomes

The idea that organizational development is endogenous to the party is one of the oldest in the study of political parties (Michels 1915; Panebianco 1988). This idea turns attention to the internal life of political parties rather than to the environmental factors shaping their development (Berman 1997). Looking inside parties for clues related to their development is not an easy task: parties lead rich lives affected by a wide variety of characteristics, processes and dynamics. The focus of this book on local rather than national organizational development further complicates this already delicate task. More so, because the analysis focuses on an extremist right-wing party in a setting with no reliable data on such factors as party membership or financing, which are usually useful for this type of analysis.

To investigate local organizational development, this section utilizes insights from the literature to generate expectations regarding the effects of national and subnational party factors on local organizational outcomes. Much of the work examining endogenous drivers of party development relies on analyses of Duvergerian mass parties (1959). Although not always optimal for electoral efficiency (Kitschelt 1994; Levitsky 2003), these somewhat rigid and sometimes overly bureaucratic organizations grant parties organizational continuity that helps reduce the anxiety for survival that smaller or newer organizations face. Although Duvergerian mass parties are facing a major decline (Katz and Mair 1995; 2009), some of their main features, such as institutional density and differentiation, persist across the party political spectrum. Some of the best known and most successful radical right-wing parties display organizational features that resemble postwar mass parties (Heinisch and Mazzoleni 2016).

Although extremist right-wing parties share the emphasis mass parties place on grassroots support, they lack the institutional density and differentiation that characterizes most postwar mass parties. As Chapters 2 and 3 suggest, it is important to appreciate two characteristics of extremist right-wing parties, which set them apart from other political parties. First, extremist right-wing parties are "movement parties" (Kitschelt 2006; della Porta and Diani 2006), operating on the frontier between social movements and political parties. Unlike other parties, movement parties are active in the conventional politics of party competition as well as in the contentious politics generally associated with social movements (Tarrow 2011). Extremist right-wing parties participate in the electoral process just like other parties, drafting electoral programs and taking vote maximizing positions in the competitive space. But they are simultaneously out in the streets, not only propagating these positions but also signaling them through controversial and sometimes violent political action. Street-level protest is both a necessity and a tactic. Street-level politics partly substitutes for the lack of communicative (Panebianco 1988; Farrell and Webb 2000) and institutional (Katz and Mair 1995) resources that more established parties usually have at their disposal. Contentious political action is also a way to send ideological and programmatic cues and turn attention to the antithesis of the party to established politics and practices – to its "anti-systemic" nature. Although the centrality of such action in the presence of a party varies across time, the undertaking of contentious activity is critical for the categorization of a party as a movement party and it is important for the distinction made in Chapter 2 between radical and extremist right-wing parties. Radical right-wing parties such as New Democracy or the Pim Fortuyn List displayed organizational deficiencies similar to those Kitschelt associates with movement parties (2006). But these had more to do with their "entrepreneurial" origins (Bolleyer 2013) than with the organizational consequences of their street-level practices. Put simply, these were not movement parties. In the case of extremist right-wing parties, the link between contentious action and organizational development is more direct. The emphasis these parties place on street-level politics has consequences for their subsequent development.

Second, extremist right-wing parties are also "charismatic" parties lacking the institutional infrastructure that generally characterizes Duvergerian mass parties. The reference to charisma is used here to describe the institutional infrastructure of the party and the role of the leader within the party organization rather than to describe the personal charisma of the leader. Whereas environmental or radical left movement parties are characterized by relatively open structures of bottom-up participation and active linkage mechanisms (della Porta et al. 2017), the movement parties analyzed here are relatively closed organizations ran from the top. The internal life of extremist right-wing party movements revolves around a party leader who commands respect, legitimacy and authority among the party members. The overtowering presence of the leader eliminates the need for institutional mechanisms for distributing resources and resolving conflicts. Resource allocation and conflict resolution takes place through personal ties with the leader in a fashion similar to that described by Panebianco in his analysis of "charismatic parties." The net effect of leadership dominance in these parties is the total lack of the certainty and predictability in intra-party outcomes that tend to characterize mass parties. "The charismatic organization therefore substitutes total uncertainty and instability for the stability of the expectations that guide bureaucratic and traditional organizations" (Panebianco 1988: 144). Extremist right-wing parties are not the only ones to award their leader near absolute discretion. Business-firm or entrepreneurial parties might also display some of the organizational characteristics noted here. The important difference between extremist and other parties is the combination of "charismatic" organizational elements with contentious political practices.

The practice of street-level politics by "charismatic" organizations affects the recruitment patterns in extremist right-wing parties. The involvement in both conventional and contentious politics generates a need for attracting a heterogeneous mix of people to the party, which is consequential for its subsequent development. On the one hand, these parties need to recruit politically skillful people who can effectively participate in conventional politics. These tend to be relatively good speakers and writers and people with a pragmatic approach to politics that allows some room for compromise in exchange for political gains. Their involvement in conventional politics might be short-term and opportunistic or they might have longer-term horizons for the advancement of their policies or themselves (Kitschelt 1989; Art 2011). These individuals are the "ambassadors" of the party (Scarrow 1994) to national publics and local communities. On the other hand, extremist right-wing movement parties need to recruit people who will participate in contentious political action. These tend to be individuals with biographical availability (McAdam 1986) for riskier, more confrontational and sometimes violent types of street activity. They are the political soldiers of extremist right-wing parties. This latter group is made up of the "ideologues" that both Kitschelt and Art examine but also by non-ideologues who join the street activity because they are part of activist or other (e.g., football) networks that have a proclivity for, or are drawn by their networks into riskier types of political action.

In "charismatic" parties with fluid organizational structures, like the ones discussed here, the two types of recruits cannot easily co-exist and can often lead to internal feuds that get to affect how parties develop, both nationally and locally. Without proper institutional infrastructure to handle conflict resolution and resource allocation, the militant activists are likely to make their way to the higher echelons of the party leadership. There are a number of reasons favoring a higher-than-usual concentration of militant activists in the top echelons of an extremist right-wing party. The first is that the leader of the party is likely to prize militancy over more conventional types of political activity. Given the importance of loyalty in charismatic parties, the leader is likely to reward contentious over conventional forms of political involvement because they signal higher levels of loyalty. Riskier than other types of political activity, contentious activity demonstrates a degree of loyalty to the party that militant activists can subsequently capitalize on when selective incentives are distributed. The second reason relates to the shared experiences of people involved in contentious types of activity. Experience of fighting in the streets with leftists or the police cement the loyalty of the militant activists to each other and grant them important experiental "capital" that helps them build informal networks within the party.

The combination of these factors does not only explain why militant activists end up having key positions in the party but it also accounts for why extremist right-wing parties have a high tolerance for overzealous or extremist fanatics whose actions jeopardize the legitimacy of the party. Political leaders prizing contentious activism are reluctant to sanction political followers when their contentious activity goes far beyond what even they consider reasonable. And the shared experiences of political soldiers in the streets across the years shield them from expulsions or other penalties they would otherwise face for violent and sometimes outright criminal activity. Overall, then, political soldiers have a much weightier role in extremist right-wing than in other parties and this affects how they subsequently develop. Their presence can be expected to exacerbate the organizational instability intrinsic to charismatic movement parties because the way they practice politics can embroil the party in damaging forms of violent activism and criminal acts or because militant activists form networks within the party that tend to complicate efforts for institution-building and process-routinization, both necessary for further party development.

The subnational units of the party are likely to mirror the relative focus of the central party on contentious politics. As the core party leadership, the local branches of extremist right-wing parties can be expected to be headed by people whose political experience largely revolves around their involvement in contentious political action. As mentioned earlier, this is partly because participation in these events cements personal ties with the core party leadership that subsequently affect the distribution of selective incentives (e.g., heading a branch) by the leader. Moreover, the involvement in contentious, controversial and violent action demonstrates loyalty to the party. Given the outsider status of the party and the hostile environment in which it has to operate, this loyalty is a critical element in decisions to grant people the authority to run a local branch. Beyond this initial choice of local party heads, the subsequent development of a local branch depends on what it actually manages to achieve on the ground. The development of local party units is contingent, in part, on the choices the central party makes regarding resource allocation. It can be hypothesized that those branches most active in the streets are likely to attract more central party resources than those that are less active. The central party is unlikely to invest resources for local branches that prove to be empty shells or, even, for subunits that mostly focus on conventional rather than contentious politics.

The organizational trajectory of local branches depends not only on features or actions of the central party but is also related to the characteristics of the local units. If these characteristics could be foretold by the very profile of extremist right-wing parties, one would not observe the organizational polymorphism and developmental divergence of local party units described in Chapter 5. To the extent that this polymorphism and divergence is endogenous to the local branches, it is worth considering how branch-level characteristics might shape the organizational trajectory of subnational units. One of these characteristics relates to the *experience* of local branches. Experience might help local units maximize their organizational potential and better address the challenges of local organization. Experiential assets can turn into liabilities, though, if these experiences restrain the capacity of local parties to find the right balance between conventional and contentious politics and to adjust to changing environments. A second characteristic is the existence or not of *organizational legacies* in the area where the party seeks to establish a local presence. The existence of past networks of local activists can help or hinder future party development, depending on the local legacy these networks have helped establish. A third characteristic is the association of local party units with *violence* – a characteristic that is particularly relevant in the analysis of an extremist right-wing party. The association with violence can facilitate or undermine the evolution of a local party unit. The next section examines how the main characteristics of the Golden Dawn (GD) have affected its local development and the following section develops and tests these three hypotheses on how specific features of the local party units affect their development.

The GD and Its Local Organizational Development

To examine endogenous factors affecting local organizational development this section analyzes how two main features of the GD – its charismatic nature and contentious activity – have helped shape its local organizational development. Since 1993 the party has been involved in both conventional and contentious forms of political participation. The former is documented by the thousands of meetings in party branches dealing with current, historical and ideological issues. Many of its current members recall being attracted to its ideas through the publication of the magazine or newspaper and subsequently attending some of these relatively closed meetings in the various party units in Athens and elsewhere. The political involvement of the party went well beyond the world of deliberation and the propagation of ideas. Since its early days the party has been organizing a number of outdoor events. As analyzed in Chapter 5, some of these events are similar to those organized by most other parties, like distributing party leaflets and newspapers. Other events have been much more contentious, and, sometimes, violent. Marches during the 1 May labor day celebration or the commemoration of the Imia incident with Turkey; demonstrations against immigration or foreign embassies; and participation in controversial anniversaries of civil war events in Meligalas, Vitsi and Grammos are known for the controversy they generated and for the violent clashes they often caused with anti-fascist or other groups. In addition, throughout the 1990s the party gained notoriety for assaults against leftists and, in the late 2000s and early 2010s, immigrants. Although the participation of the party in competitive politics went through different phases, discussed in Chapter 4, its involvement in street-level contentious and violent activity has been a constant source of trouble for the party. Its decision in 2007 to pursue an autonomous electoral course did not yield a substantial change in the emphasis the party placed on both conventional and contentious politics. Even after its electoral breakthroughs in the 2012 elections, the party continued to be involved in various forms of contentious politics.

The establishment of the GD as a movement party is closely associated with the profile of its leadership, particularly of its leader Nikos Michaloliakos, who has been involved in politics through both political ideas and action. Although part of the literature on far right parties focuses on the charismatic qualities of party leaders (e.g., Eatwell 2006; Mudde 2007), the case of the GD is indicative of how much can be learned from the analysis of how leaders' life experiences shape the organizational development of their parties. Prior to 1974, Michaloliakos was a member of the political arm of EOKA B, the organization that sought to topple the elected government of Cyprus in July 1974. During the Greek dictatorship, when he was still a teenager, he was a member of the Party of the 4th of August, along with Kostas Plevris and Andreas Dendrinos, National Socialist ideologues and authors. As Michaloliakos recalls:

> My first entry to a political office was of that of the Committee for the Coordination of the Political Struggle (Επιτροπή Συντονισμού Πολιτικού Αγώνα) – the political arm of the EOKA B. It was headed by Nicos Kartsomenakis. In 1973 I started being involved in the Party of the 4th of August. It was basically the office of a newspaper, since parties were prohibited due to the regime. The office undertook nationalist propaganda ... I stayed in the 4th of August until it shut down around 1978–1979.[1]

His involvement in the propagation of national socialist ideas continued in the 1980s with the founding of the *Golden Dawn* magazine.

Apart from ideological propaganda, though, Michaloliakos was also interested in political action. Even in his late fifties, Michaloliakos still considers himself both an ideologue and activist. Asked whether he always combined the two, he responds "Absolutely. Yes. I have taken part in

---

[1] Interview with author, October 2016.

many political activities. During the invasion in Cyprus in 1974, when major demonstrations took place outside the British Embassy and the Embassy was blocked. I was arrested then."[2] During the late 1970s, the political activity of Michaloliakos went beyond participation in demonstrations. He was implicated in a number of violent incidents, indicted for the possession of explosives and eventually imprisoned for a few months in the most well-known Greek prison, Korydallos, where he met the former dictator George Papadopoulos (Psarras 2012). Throughout the 1980s, Michaloliakos remained both an ideologue and an activist but, compared to the turbulent late 1970s, his activism was subdued. Rather than taking to the streets to propagate the National Socialist ideas of the *Golden Dawn* magazine, he assumed a mostly organizational role, setting up the basic organizational structure – along the lines of military hierarchy – of the party that was still in the making (Psarras 2012). In the 1980s, members of the Golden Dawn – then just an association – occasionally took to the streets to propagate their ideas but this activity was very limited. Things changed in the 1990s, when the GD took a decision to become involved in politics. The timing of the decision was critical: the massive mobilization for the Macedonia issue granted nationalists an opening for entry into the political mainstream (Ellinas 2010). The GD sought to capitalize on the changing political opportunity by commencing the publication of its newspaper but also through participation in the Macedonia protests. Groups of GD activists started taking part in the demonstrations held in various Greek cities for the Macedonia issue under the party banner.[3] The participation of the GD in these protests earned it notoriety for the violent – and in a number of cases, criminal – activity of its members toward antifascist or other leftist groups. It was this type of activity that quickly stigmatized the party as a neo-Nazi gang (Psarras 2012).

The emphasis the GD placed on militant activism necessitated the recruitment of militant street fighters who gained considerable influence within the party throughout its existence. The stigma of a violent gang turned the party into a source of attraction for young males eager to dominate in the streets. One of the rising stars in the party during this period was Antonis Androutsopoulos, nicknamed Periandros, who quickly became a member of the Political Council of the party, lead the Piraeus local branch and subsequently headed the GD magazine. For a number of years, Androutsopoulos was the right-hand man of Michaloliakos and a regular contributor to the party newspaper, where he would sometimes

[2] Ibid.   [3] See, for example, issues 59 and 60, in March and April 1994, respectively.

urge the party activists and followers to project their "utter fanaticism" against party opponents. "We are both nationalists and conspirators. We are full of fanaticism, which we will inscribe with the sword and the pen, and we will spread through ink and blood!"[4] In 1998 this fanaticism almost proved fatal for opponents of the GD when Androutsopoulos and other GD activists nearly killed a leftist student in one of their many encounters during this period. Fleeing trial for more than seven years, Androutsopoulos was convicted to twelve years in prison in 2006. For several years, while Androutsopoulos was wanted by Greek police for his criminal activity, he was still a member of the Political Council of the party and would also contribute a number of articles to the newspaper and speeches read in his absence during various party events. His conviction put an end in his party career but did not alter the emphasis the party placed on both ideological and physical struggle. Some of the best-known activists of the party during this early period, such as Ioannis Vouldis and Nikolaos Chrysomallis, remained prominent members of the party for years.

Along with these older activists, towards the late 1990s and in the early 2000s, a new group of militants started gaining prominence within the party, reinvigorating its focus on street-level dominance. The fan clubs of various football teams became a pool for the recruitment of new activists in the GD. Although in earlier years the party avoided mixing football and politics, toward the late 1990s it actively pursued the formation of nationalist cells within these fan clubs. The opening to football fans was because, after the fleeing of Androutsopoulos, the party lost part of its street-fighting capacity. But it was also because the GD sought to capitalize on trends in various European football clubs where racist attacks of their fans against foreign or black players started troubling the European sports authorities. "The formation of nationalist fans' cells in all clubs is something we should pursue and promote at every cost. All comrades involved in football must definitely network in the stadiums and move in this direction."[5] Some of the best-known members of the core party leadership, such as Elias Panagiotaros, Ioannis Lagos and Antonis Gregos, are thought to have had close links with the football fan clubs of Panathinaikos, AEK and PAOK, respectively (Hasapopoulos 2013). Panagiotaros acquired a prominent role in the Blue Army (Γαλάζια Στρατιά), a nationalist

---

[4] Periandros Androutsopoulos, "Our Fanaticism," *Golden Dawn* [newspaper], issue 183, January 31, 1997, p. 5.

[5] "News from all Greece: Kalamata," *Golden Dawn* [newspaper], issue 306, December 24, 1999, p. 2.

association of football fans founded in 2000 to support the Greek national team. Under the banner of this football association, the GD would seek to turn football fanaticism into political hatred against Albania and Turkey, claiming in 2002 that the Blue Army succeeded in blocking the common organization of the European football tournament by Greece and Turkey.[6]

The recruitment of football hooligans by the GD was a double-edged sword. The hooligans provided necessary manpower for the street-level activism of the GD but could also be a source of trouble. Unlike other activists, the hooligans were not necessarily ideologically trained or politically astute. As one of the recruiters of such hooligans in Thessaloniki recalls:

> Those coming close to the GD were not politically conscious. They understood the need for street-level mobilization but not necessarily the political aims of this mobilization ... Not many of them showed up in the party offices and did not really care for speeches and discussions. In a political activity involving the posting of pamphlets, the football fans (γηπεδικοί) would not come. They only would only occasionally come for spraying [graffiti]. Those recruited in the 2000s were often troublemakers. At the time, we did not have the luxury to get rid of the hooligans. These were individuals used to being in the street because of their activity in the stadiums. In the 1990s it was fans of Aris and in the 2000s this started changing and it was from PAOK, from the western neighborhoods [of Thessaloniki].[7]

The 2000s witnessed the formation of another cohort of activists who also ended up in prominent positions in the party. Some of these activists were Greek Cypriot students studying in Athens and Thessaloniki. Christos Christou joined the GD while a student in Athens and became a member of the Political Council before returning to Cyprus to found the National Popular Front, a sister party of the GD (Katsourides 2013).[8] He was a close associate of Michaloliakos as late as 2012, when he permanently returned to Cyprus and started getting more systematically involved with ELAM. Another example is Evelpis, who became affiliated with the local branch of the GD in Athens and quickly became a member of the central committee of the party. He subsequently returned to Cyprus and also acquired a prominent role in ELAM as a member of the Political Council and a key organizer of many national and local events. Aggelos Ioannou

---

[6] "Co-organization 2008 no more: Victory for the Blue Army," *Golden Dawn* [newspaper], issue 450, December 29, 2002, pp. 1 and 9.
[7] Interview #30, member of central committee, August 2016.
[8] Christos Christou, interview with author, September 2011.

joined the GD in 2006 while studying law in Thessaloniki. He was previously a member of the Pancyprian United Organization of Students, one of the autonomous organizations affiliated with the student movement Grivas founded in 1968. After the 2012 elections Ioannou was hastily recruited to the central party in Athens to help the GD in the Greek parliament. He subsequently became a member of the central committee and then returned to Cyprus in 2016 as a parliamentary officer for ELAM. Andreas Herakleous also joined the GD in the 2000s and became a member of the central committee in 2011. He returned to Cyprus in 2016 to become a member of the central committee of ELAM. Ioannis Oskis joined the GD later that decade and became one of the leaders of the activist groups that marched into Agios Panteleimonas in the "cleansing" operations that gained the GD notoriety and fertilized the path for its electoral breakthrough (Dinas et al. 2013). Oskis returned to Cyprus to become a member of the Political Council of ELAM. Along with Christou and Herakleous, Oskis was a member of the personal guards of Michaloliakos – a term used for loyal members of the party who escorted and consulted the GD leader on a regular basis. Andreas Yiallourides joined the GD in 2008 while studying in Athens. He subsequently became a parliamentary assistant for one of the party's MEPs and a member of the central committee of ELAM. Alexander Kritikos joined the GD in 2009 and quickly got involved in its various activities in Athens, including the patrols in Agios Panteleimonas. He subsequently returned to Cyprus and became a prominent ELAM functionary. The Cypriot recruits of the GD in the 2000s gave a significant boost to the party in the many street battles it gave in Athens and Thessaloniki before nearly all left and took key positions in ELAM in Cyprus.[9]

Along with this cohort of Cypriot activists came Elias Kasidiaris, who quickly established himself as one of the most prominent members of the core party leadership. Kasidiaris started being involved in the party in the early 2000s and in the next few years he became the party spokesman and a member of the Political Council. His involvement in the party offers a glimpse of the dual nature of politics the GD practiced throughout this period. Toward the end of the decade, Kasidiaris became one of the key communicators of the party program and ideology, through regular contributions in the party newspaper. In his regular column in the newspaper he would write about current political issues, explain GD positions and

---

[9] The information comes from interviews #4, #13, #14, #17 and #48 with existing or former members of the central committee of the party and other functionaries.

actions and offer an alternative view of history – for example, by writing a favorable portrait of Hitler and National Socialism.[10] In addition, Kasidiaris was in charge of training new party activists in what the GD called "cells" – small groups of trainee activists who had to go through a party-defined process before being admitted. Despite the emphasis the GD placed on the capacity of these militants for street-level activism, Kasidiaris also understood the need for people in the party with skills other than their physical capabilities. To assess such skills, Kasidiaris trained people in politics, history and ideology and occasionally gave them an IQ test before recommending them for the central committee of the party.[11] Kasidiaris was also in charge of leading activists in outdoor activities in areas such as Agios Panteleimonas, where the GD undertook vigilante-type activity against immigrants and leftists.[12] In its newspaper, the GD made sure to remind these activists that "war takes place at all levels and hence, our warriors need to be trained in all fields that the circumstances command."[13]

The dominance of the party leadership by street activists continued into the 2010s. Most of the people Michaloliakos picked for the Political Council in the seventh party congress of 2011 were better known for their street action than their political skills. When the party achieved its national electoral breakthrough in May 2012, it was primarily run by activists very close to the party leader who had joined the GD in the 1990s and 2000s. As a disgruntled former party member critically notes, "this is a rare case of a party that turned the leader's bodyguards into parliamentarians."[14] The peculiar mix of street tactics with parliamentary politics quickly material-ized when, less than a month after his election to the parliament, Kasidiaris physically assaulted two female politicians during a live television program. The party called this an "unfortunate incident" but its top leadership refused to change tactics. In part, this was because opinion polls showed a small spike in GD support after the incident, allowing the party to sustain its percentage in the June election. More importantly, though, incidents like this constituted the natural development of a party run by street fighters that suddenly gained parliamentary representation. One of the most prominent members of the party, Christos Pappas, paralleled the way the party behaved at the time with the behavior of a "wild foal."[15]

[10] Elias Kasidiaris, "Hitler beyond history," *Golden Dawn* [newspaper], issue 719, April 20, 2011, p. 2.
[11] Interviews #4 and #47.   [12] Interview #14.
[13] E.K., "How can I become a member of the Golden Dawn?" *Golden Dawn* [newspaper], issue 553, January 13, 2005, p. 11.
[14] Interview #11, former party functionary.
[15] Christos Pappas, interview with the author, December 2015.

As Ioannis Lagos said, "yes, the incident of Kasidiaris helped but he did not do it for the votes. This is how we are, a bit more aggressive. We will continue doing this. We are who we are. We are not like those [politicians] in parliament."[16] Indeed, in the period that followed the entry of the party into parliament, there were a number of violent incidents involving prominent party members, like the political council members and MPs George Germenis and Elias Panagiotaros (Ellinas 2013).

In most political parties violent incidents involving party members would lead the adoption of strict sanctions against them. In movement parties with charismatic features such sanctions are harder to put in place and to impose. Not surprisingly, then, those who undertake these actions are not penalized by the party leadership and tend to linger around, thereby reinforcing party misbehavior. In the case of the GD, things were even more complicated because some of those who exposed the party with their actions were not just ordinary activists but part of its core leadership. Penalizing some of the topmost members of the party would undermine its street tactics at a time when they seemed to attract many younger activists necessary for sustaining party mobilization. Sanctioning top party members was also difficult because of the very close links they had among themselves. Having matured politically in the Athenian – and to a lesser extent, the Thessaloniki – streets, the top members of the party could not easily sanction their own. The tenure of party members in the streets helped them form shared experiences that cemented very close personal links between them. These links made it difficult to cut loose not only top party functionaries but also lesser members when they misbehaved.

> There are a few people who would come at the meetings of the local branch and then, under the banner of the GD, they would leave the offices and do "other things." At some point I asked the central party leadership to get rid of them. Indeed, the disciplinary committee decided to expel them. But then, I would see them in various events. Basically, they had backing from an MP or other member of the top leadership.[17]

Article 8 of the party statutes details the reasons for losing party membership, which include "behavior and activity which are antithetical to the ideological and political positions and principles of the party."[18] According to Michaloliakos, "there are penalties for those who misbehave, even expulsion from the party."[19] But apart from many voluntary departures

---

[16] Ioannis Lagos, interview with the author, July 2013.   [17] Interview #28.
[18] Party statutes, 2012.   [19] Michaloliakos, interview with the author, October 2012.

from the party throughout its history, until 2018, when an MP was cut loose for calling on the army to arrest the Prime Minister, there was no evidence suggesting expulsions caused by the misbehavior of party members.[20] The difficulty in sanctioning party militants is evident not only in the party subunits closer to the leadership, like some of the branches in Attica, but in other parts of Greece as well. Even in a party that admits to adhering to the "leadership principle," disciplinary procedures are not always easy to enforce. As one branch leader critically notes, "for some of the phenomena observed here, there should be disciplinary procedures to end them. If there was a proper disciplinary body in the party, these issues would end pretty quickly. It is tiring."[21] Not surprisingly, despite all that has transpired since the electoral breakthrough of the GD in 2012, in the next years its top leadership remained almost unchanged. With the exception of Frantzeskos Porichis who left the party, in the subsequent years all other members of the 2011 Political Council continued to have a key role in the daily operation of the party.[22]

The dominance of militant street activists in the top leadership positions had significant consequences for the initial local organizational expansion of the GD. When the party started growing its local presence after 2010, it initially relied on its network of activists to staff the councils of local branches. The ideal profile of a local head was that of an activist whose loyalty was successfully tested in the streets. As Michaloliakos put in 2012, "it is important *who* wants to set up a branch. That is, if this comes from a person who has been a member of the Golden Dawn for some time and who is a fervent or active member. We do not want opportunists in the party."[23] Although the party does not provide elaborate information on the people heading the local branches, an analysis of the members of its 2011 Central Committee and the names published in thousands of local activity reports highlights the links between the pre-existing network of GD activists and its local organizational expansion. Based on this analysis, at least seventeen local branches were headed at some point by a member of the 2011 Central Committee – the Committee announced prior to the

---

[20] In June 2018, Constantine Barbarousis called on the army to arrest the Prime Minister. He was immediately expelled from the GD parliamentary caucus and was subsequently arrested and criminally charged for treason.

[21] Interview #31.

[22] Vouldis stepped down from the Political Council and continued to head the Athens local branch. He was elected as MP in May 2012 but later lost his seat in the first district of Athens.

[23] Interview #1, Nikos Michaloliakos, party general secretary, October 2012.

2012 electoral breakthroughs, when the party had no parliamentary presence.[24]

The recruitment of local party leaders from its network of activists aimed to sustain the coherence of the GD, at a time when its increasing electoral traction brought thousands of people closer to the organization. "We want to sustain the coherence of the party and not open our doors to just anyone. For the new offices we set up we rely on people we know, who are tested members of the movement, people we can trust. This does not mean we exclude good people but that we rely on a core of party members."[25] The reliance on tight networks of party activists was particularly strong prior to the electoral breakthrough of the party. The branch in Athens was headed by Ioannis Vouldis, one of the most experienced GD activists and member of the Political Council and the Central Committee. The Thessaloniki branch was led by Artemis Matheopoulos, who had considerable experience both as a street activist and as an organizer. Matheopoulos joined the GD in the early 2000s and was subsequently a member of the Political Council, the Central Committee and the Greek Parliament. He had an instrumental role in overseeing the local organizational expansion of the party in northern Greece. The branch in Evia has been led since 2011 by Alexandra Mparou, a seasoned GD activist who served in the central committee of the party since 2007 and "was always there when the smoke of the tear gas spread."[26]

After the 2012 elections, the party continued to rely on its network of activists for its local organizational development. The main activist network in Athens provided the personnel who headed the local branches in the Attica region. The people the party chose to head most of the branches set up in Attica had frequented the Athens branch and were also members of the Central Committee. Some had multiple roles in the party contributing to the party publications and propaganda and helping with various organizational tasks. Costas Alexandrakis, one of the seasoned activists of the Athens branch, was appointed as head of the local branch in the Northern Suburbs.[27] Nikos Lemontzis got to head the local branch in Ano Liosia.[28] George Papageorgiou was appointed secretary of one of the

---

[24] Analysis of thousands of activity reports published on the party website between 2012 and 2017 under the heading "Events" and of the members of the 2011 Central Committee. The Committee members were published for the first time in GD's history. See https://goo.gl/Mrp7P3.

[25] Ioannis Iagos, interview with author, July 2013.   [26] Interview #3.

[27] See https://goo.gl/mNyhGv.

[28] See, for example, https://goo.gl/49Mhx8; https://goo.gl/QvevPB; https://goo.gl/wuNkWf.

most active local branches, in East Attica.[29] Michalis Giannogkonas
received a major role in the West Attica branches of Aspropyrgos and
Megara, and in 2015, his duties were extended to neighboring Corinth, in
Peloponnese.[30] The network of activists in Athens was also involved in the
organization of the Piraeus branch. In the 2000s the two branches were
closely associated, with some people attending the events of both. One
example is Sotiris Develekos, who joined the GD in the 2000s and
subsequently acquired a prominent role in the organization of the Piraeus
branch. Develekos was a member of the Central Committee and a close
associate of Ioannis Lagos, who was entrusted the organization of the
various branches of the GD in Piraeus.[31] Another example is Makis
Mparekas who got to head the Piraeus branch in 2012.[32] In a pattern
similar to that observed in the case of Athens, the Piraeus branch provided
considerable organizational support to neighboring branches, such as those
in Perama and Salamina. Some of the members of the Piraeus local branch,
like Pericles Moulianakis, were at times also members of the councils in
some of these branches.[33] Activist networks provided the people who
staffed local branches elsewhere, as well. In northern Greece, for example,
the local branches set up during the period of organizational expansion
relied on the network of seasoned activists of the Thessaloniki branch. One
of these activists, Christos Hadjisavvas, helped establish and run the two
branches in Kilkis. Hadjisavvas joined the GD in 1990s and subsequently
frequented the local branch in Thessaloniki.[34] In Patra, Vasilis Mertis was
part of the small cell of activists who decided in 2012 to reopen the Patra
branch. A few months after the opening of the Patra branch, Mertis was
appointed secretary of the neighboring branch in Aigio.[35]

The rapid local organizational expansion of the GD tested the limits of
its reliance on its relatively closed activist networks. The 2012 electoral
breakthroughs of the party brought it closer to tens of thousands of people,
many of whom were eager to become functionaries of the central party and
to staff its swiftly expanding subnational units. The sudden influx of
supporters caused an organizational shock to the party not only because
it was unprecedented but also because the party lacked the institutional
mechanisms to manage this newly generated support. One of the first tasks
of the central party leadership was to identify people within its activist
networks who had the necessary skills and expertise to help the party in its

[29] https://goo.gl/bhq1fh.　　[30] https://goo.gl/mj4MUa.　　[31] Interview #42.
[32] https://goo.gl/ojv1ZR; https://goo.gl/TBpYvs.　　[33] Interview #42.　　[34] Interview #34.
[35] Interview #39.

new role. But the search beyond the physical capabilities or the ideological indoctrination of the activists proved difficult. "If one were to add up all the university degrees the members of the Central Committee had received, there would barely be more than a dozen."[36] In terms of the local organizational development, the sudden influx of supporters meant that the party had to reach outside its relatively closed networks of activists to staff the party branches. Put simply, the party needed to open up and accept in its relatively closed networks new people, with organizational skills and political appeal.

Opening up a relatively closed political organization has significant advantages for a party strictly dedicated to electoral politics. The reliance on people outside the closed network of seasoned GD activists provided an opportunity for the party to broaden its electoral appeal in local societies. Some of the people who were appointed in the councils of local branches were thought to have a relatively good standing in their communities. The links these people had with local societies varied substantially. In some cases, the links deemed critical for running a local branch were the professional ties of the branch heads to the local gym. In settings such as Katerini and Pyrgos, links to a gym provided a pool for the recruitment of street activists that would help make the presence of the GD known in the local community. In other settings, such as Kalamata, Mesolongi and Messini, the professional background of those granted key roles in local branches came from the security forces – they were either former or current army and police officers, thereby bringing institutional legitimacy and, in some cases, organizational skills to the party. In settings such as Kavala people with a capacity to organize and promote the local branch quickly gained the trust of the central party leadership and rose to the top.[37] In rare cases the links with the local society were due to past involvement of people with other political parties. In Corinth, the GD recruited a former PASOK supporter who had visited the Athens branch a few times before becoming a candidate for the 2012 national elections. Although an outsider to the closed network of Athens activists, Efstathios Boukouras won a parliamentary seat in the 2012 election and naturally acquired a major role in the local Corinth branch.[38]

[36] Interview #46.   [37] Interviews #24, #25 and #31.

[38] The prior political involvement of Boukouras with PASOK is highlighted many times in his written defense to the state prosecutors. He was imprisoned along with the rest of the GD leaders and functionaries awaiting trial. During his imprisonment he quit the GD and stopped being a member of the GD parliamentary caucus. For his written defense, see www.tovima.gr/files/1/2014/01/11/ΥΠΟΜΝΗΜΑ.pdf (last accessed March 2017).

Despite the advantages of opening up a party to newcomers, there are also challenges that complicate this process. The task of quickly recruiting and appointing functionaries among hundreds of newcomers without subjecting them to the process that generated the tightly knit networks of militant activists created problems for the GD that began to affect its organizational development. The first set of problems related to the choice of people. Outside its tight networks of seasoned and trained activists, party loyalty – a key criterion for inclusion in the networks – was much harder to establish and the criteria for becoming a bearer of the party flag inevitably loosened. As one of the close associates of Michaloliakos recalls:

> After the elections, the mentality of those close to the leader changed. Some members of the Political Council started advocating the need to open new branches because many people are coming to the party, which needs to create mechanisms to keep them. The purported need for new branches loosened the criteria the party had for opening them. One of the basic criteria – the ability of a branch to be financially viable – no longer held because the sheer number of people who came to local events was large enough that finding €200 to pay the rent was easy. The other criterion – people who were loyal to the party and could be trusted – was stretched to a point that it no longer made much sense. If someone was seen at the annual event for Imia fifteen years ago, then let us give him a branch! Where there were no activists, things were even more complicated. In Corinth, where we had no people of our own, we had to rely on someone who pretended to be one of us for opportunistic reasons.[39]

In the midst of its local organizational expansion, the party frequently warned against opportunism and cautioned against those who see the GD as a "flag of opportunity."[40] In practice, the delicate balance between opening up the party and guarding it from opportunism proved difficult to sustain.

> There are people who seek to take advantage of opportunities. This is what happened in Lagkadas [a town in the North East area of Thessaloniki, where the GD received more than 10 percent in the June 2012 election]. We opened an office there and then we shut it down because the people there had other things in their mind. We could have changed the five-member council but we chose a more drastic measure, to shut the office down altogether.[41]

[39] Interview #44.
[40] See, for example, Nikos Michaloliakos, "The Golden Dawn is not a flag of opportunity," October 30, 2012, https://goo.gl/RYfVKS; "The ideology of the Golden Dawn," December 21, 2012, https://goo.gl/UVQKGK.
[41] Interview #6, June 2015.

The person appointed as branch head was a GD member for a very short time before being entrusted the task of running the local unit. Another example was the branch in Saronikos (in East Attica) which shut down in April 2013, less than a year after it was set up. "An old friend of the party, who was trusted by one of the members of the political council, was appointed secretary of the local branch. He quickly went to appoint his family members in the local council, generating all sorts of problems. The branch had to be shut down. This is an area where the party received good results."[42] Overall, then, the identification of people who would ably lead a branch and infiltrate local communities was a major complication in efforts to open up the party to newcomers.

A more serious set of complications when parties like the GD seek to open up results from the distribution of selective incentives. Although electoral logic necessitates giving incentives to people with a broader appeal in a local community, party insiders are unlikely to easily accept this logic. People who see the growing success of the party as the result of their long-time street militancy are likely to view with suspicion outsiders who quickly earn selective rewards. Those lacking in votes will still want to cash in their years of street activism with a position on the ballot or in the local council. And those who were not around during the years spent in the political wilderness will emphasize their capacity to bring in voters that militant activists scare away. The bigger the stakes are, the sharper the feuds between party insiders and outsiders.

Some of the biggest feuds in the GD were about the prospect of winning a parliamentary seat, which usually grants material and social rewards to the winners. In settings such as Aetolia-Acarnania, Larissa and Pieria such issues caused a series of problems to the local branches and led to the departure of party members. In Aetolia-Acarnania, the election of Constantine Barbarousis to the 2012 and 2015 parliaments generated a feud with Christos Rigas. Although Rigas had been a GD activist since the late 2000s, with presence in the Agios Panteleimon area of Athens, his popularity among voters dwarfed that of Barbarousis, a farmer who looks like a hero of the Greek Revolution and rides horses in his rural commu-nity. After the party leadership decided not to have Rigas head the GD ticket in the local election in Mesologgi, the notorious activist left the party and founded a new one, with the acronym LEPEN.[43] In Larissa, there was

---

[42] Interview #44, September 2016.
[43] Interviews #44 and #46. The electoral information provided in the interviews was corroborated using the official electoral results of the Ministry of Interior.

friction between one of the most known – and infamous – activists of the party, Dimitris Koltsidas, and a newcomer, Chrysovalantis Alexopoulos, who managed to win a seat in the 2012 elections. The latter distanced himself from the party after the 2013 arrests but the friction also led to the departure of Koltsidas in 2014 and the closure of the party branch in one of the biggest Greek cities.[44] Similarly, in Pieria, the Katerini branch was headed by a newcomer to the party, George Papadimitriou, who received by far the largest number of preference votes in the district of Pieria in the 2012 and in the January 2015 elections. Lured by the benefits and prospects of becoming an MP, one of the oldest activists of the party, Nikolaos Chrysomallis, chose to contest with Papadimitriou in the Pieria district but lost by a margin of three to one. Chrysomallis subsequently managed to convince his comrades in the Thessaloniki branch to get rid of Papadimitriou and unsuccessfully headed the party list in Pieria in the September 2015 election. "They colluded in getting rid of nearly half of the local branch members, including Papadimitriou, without anyone noticing."[45] The bitter internal feuds about relatively "safe" parliamentary seats can also account for the departure of two long-time GD functionaries and MPs, Dimitris Koukoutsis and Nikos Michos, in 2017. After more than two decades in the party, Koukoutsis left the parliamentary caucus of the GD due to ongoing rivalry with the new Kalamata council the party leadership appointed in 2016. Similarly, an internal feud in the Evia branch between long-time militant activists Mparou and Michos and the new people Michaloliakos recruited to broaden the local appeal of the party led to the temporary dismantling of the branch and the departure of Michos – the holder of the Evia seat – from the parliamentary caucus of the GD. In January 2018, Michos became the sole representative of the nearly extinct LAOS in the Greek parliament and a very vocal critic of the party leader.[46]

The Characteristics of Local Branches

Local organizational development is endogenous to the developmental trajectory of the central party but it is also related to characteristics of the local organizational subunits themselves. As the analysis above

[44] Interviews #8 and #44. There are also many newspaper articles regarding the Larissa feuds and a video capturing the departure of Koltsidas: https://goo.gl/yjF5vC.
[45] Interviews #44 and #46. The electoral information provided in the interviews was corroborated using the official electoral results of the Ministry of Interior.
[46] Nikos Michos, interviewed by the author, January 2018.

suggests, although the development of the central party has significant consequences for the organizational evolution of its subnational units, their developmental trajectory is not necessarily foretold by central organizational patterns. The organizational histories and characteristics of the branches are also likely to account for their evolution. The analytically difficult task is to distill those elements from these rich local histories that can help yield generalizable patterns about how the characteristics of the local branches shape their development. The remainder of this section undertakes this task, utilizing the qualitative evidence from the interviews with the GD leadership to generate three plausible hypotheses that are then quantitatively tested.

The first hypothesis, directly drawn from the above analysis, is that those branches established prior to the electoral breakthrough of the party will display different evolutionary patterns from those established afterwards. There are a number of reasons to expect a different evolutionary pattern between older and newer branches. First, in older branches one might expect to find a larger frequency of party loyalists than in newer branches. Set up at a time when the collective incentives of being a party member trumped the selective incentives awarded once the party became electorally successful, the older branches are more likely to be headed by long-time militant activists than recently recruited political opportunists. The experience of the militants in party activism along with loyalty to the party ideology is likely to yield stronger organizational outcomes compared to those of newer branches. Second, older branches have stronger ties with the central party, cemented over the years through participation in contentious and violent politics. The link of key local functionaries to the relatively closed GD networks makes it easier for them to tap central party resources. Such resources might come straight from the central party coffers or from members of the network with public salaries due to their elected office.[47] Third, the branches established before the electoral breakthrough had more time to regularize organizational processes and internalize the party ideology and platform than newer subunits, hastily inaugurated at a time when local offices were flooded with many more supporters than the party could handle. Having established some skeletal structures beforehand, older branches were much more likely to have a capacity to frequently organize local events and to handle problems associated with organizational growth.

---

[47] Interview #33.

To analyze whether local party branches set up prior to and after the national electoral breakthrough of the party display different organizational patterns, the branches were divided into two groups, one made up of the fifteen branches set up prior to May 2012 and a second one made up of the remaining fifty-nine local subunits set up afterwards. The first group includes the old branches of Athens, Thessaloniki, Piraeus and Kalamata, and those set up after late 2010, in such settings as Pella, Lamia and in various Attica suburbs. In most of these branches old party members such as Ioannis Vouldis, Artemis Matheopoulos and Apostolos Gletsos had a key organizational role. The second group includes branches headed by newer party recruits, as the cases of Lagkadas and Katerini discussed in the previous section, and older party functionaries such as the cases of the Northern Suburbs and Ano Liosia. A two-sample t-test between the branches founded before and after the 2012 elections yields statistically significant differences in the average age of the branches ($t(15) = -3.668$, $p = 0.002$). The fifteen branches founded prior to the May 2012 election had an average life 2,061 days (about 69 months) and those founded afterwards had an average life of 1,077 days (about 36 months).[48] The branches founded prior to the elections ended up living longer than those founded afterwards but their continuity rates were not significantly different. As expected, branch discontinuity was much more likely in newer (39.3 percent) than in older (13.3 percent) branches but the chi square test yielded marginally non-significant results ($X^2(1) = 2.816$, $p = 0.069$). Moreover, older branches proved to be much more active than the newer ones. The average activities of the older branches was 1.37 per quarter compared to 0.51 of the newer branches. A two-sample t-test shows that the different levels of intensity were statistically significant ($t(15) = -2.210$, $p = 0.043$).[49] The two groups also differed in their activism patterns – their activity consistency scores. Older branches had an average consistency score of 0.53 which means that they organized at least one activity in more than half the quarters of their lifespan. Newer branches received a consistency score of 0.30, which means that they organized an activity in less than a third of their reported lifespan. A two-sample t-test of the two means shows that they are statistically significant ($t(21) = -3.016$,

[48] Since four of the older branches are really old, a similar test was also conducted using the median rather than the mean, also yielding statistically significant results ($W = 139$, $p = 0.000$).
[49] The Athens branch displays much higher levels of activism (5.59 activities per quarter) than the rest of the branches (average of 0.62 activities per quarter). A Wilcoxon test was hence also conducted using the median intensity score instead of the mean intensity score of the two groups. The results remain statistically significant ($W = 217$, $p = 0.002$).

p = 0.007).[50] Overall, then, most measures show statistically significant differences in the organizational development of the branches founded before and after the first national electoral breakthrough of the party in May 2012.

A second hypothesis relates to "organizational legacies," to the organizational presence of a party in a particular local setting in the past. Some comparative evidence from other country cases is suggestive of the link between past organizational presence and present organizational outcomes. At a broader level, there is considerable evidence pointing to the dependence of far right parties on activists with a long history of this type of activism (Klandermans and Mayer 2006; Art 2011). More specifically, in Britain, the local presence of the extreme right National Front in the 1970s can partly account for the subsequent membership levels of the British National Party in various localities (Goodwin et al. 2013). The main expectation is that once a party sets (even thin) organizational roots in a local society, these roots can set the basis for the organizational reactivation of the party in the future. Having such roots can be expected to offer organizational resources to the local branch – for example, a sizable network of loyal and experienced activists – that branches without this organizational legacy lack.

In the case of the GD, the hypothesis is that local branches set up in areas where the party had organizational presence in the 1990s are likely to display different organizational patterns in the 2010s than branches in settings without such presence. As analyzed in Chapter 4, in the 1990s the GD opened as many as thirteen branches across Greece before its network started shrinking back to just a few branches. When the party officially resumed its operations in 2007 and subsequently set on a new wave of organizational expansion, it reestablished organizational presence in all the municipalities where it had presence in the 1990s. Some local branches, such as those in Patra or Chania, were re-established prior to the 2012 election and others were re-established afterward, thereby providing different subsets of branches than those examined in the previous analysis. The two groups display significantly different lifespans. Branches where the GD had presence in the 1990s had an average life of 2,169 days (about 72 months) compared to those without such prior presence (1,104 days or 37 months). A two-sample t-test of the two means shows that they are statistically significant ($t(12)$ = -3.602, p = 0.004). Moreover, discontinuity rates are

---

[50] A Wilcoxon test of the median rather than the mean consistency scores also yielded statistically significant results (W = 215, p = 0.002).

lower in branches with organizational legacies than in those without such legacies. Only two out of thirteen (15.4 percent) branches with organizational legacies shut down compared to twenty-four out of the sixty-one branches (39.3 percent) without a similar organizational past. But although the differences are in the expected direction, a chi-square test of independence shows that the relation between organizational legacy and discontinuity is not significant ($X^2(1)$ = 1.75, p = 0.122). Organizational legacies have a clearer effect on local party activism than on local party structures. Branches in settings where the GD had brick-and-mortar presence in the 1990s are significantly more active than the rest. These branches organized on average 1.55 activities per quarter compared to 0.50 activities organized by branches in municipalities where the GD had no branch in the 1990s. A two-sample t-test between the two groups shows that the differences are statistically significant ($t(13)$ = −1.946, p = 0.027). Similarly, the branches with organizational legacies were twice more consistent than the rest. They organized at least one activity in 58 percent of their lifespan compared to 29 percent of the rest. The difference in the average consistency scores of the two groups is statistically significant ($t(19)$ = −4.145, p = 0.001).[51] Overall, nearly all measures show that in settings with organizational legacies GD branches evolved differently compared to those where the party had no prior brick-and-mortar presence.

A third hypothesis relates to the violent nature of the activism pursued by some but not all of these local units. It is hypothesized that violent branches are likely to display different organizational patterns than nonviolent ones. As discussed earlier and as explicated in Chapter 8, violence is a constitutive feature of the central party. It is hence reasonable to expect violent activism to trickle down to the subnational party units, affecting their organizational evolution. Violent incidents can help bring militants closer together, cementing bonds of loyalty and devotion to the branch and reinforcing its organizational endurance. Alternatively, violence might scare away moderates who, unlike hard-core militants, are more interested in the electoral prospects than the street dominance of the party (Art 2011). Moderates might leave the party, depriving it of the political skills necessary to institutionalize its organizational presence. Violent branches might also trigger institutional and social hostility against them, which might negatively affect their organizational evolution.

---

[51] As before, apart from the differences in means, there was also an analysis of the differences in the median scores of the two groups, yielding statistically significant results for branch age (W = 150, p = 0.001), intensity (W = 125, p = 0.000) and consistency (W = 138, p = 0.000).

Dividing the seventy-four branches into two groups – the twenty-one branches where at least one incident of violence was reported in the party newspaper and the fifty-three branches located in municipalities where no such incidents were reported – allows a comparison of how the two groups have developed.[52] First, violent branches remained open for much longer than non-violent ones. Branches in municipalities where violent incidents were reported had an average lifespan of 1,746 days (58 months) compared to 1,091 days (36 months) of the rest. A two-sample t-test of the two means shows that they are statistically significant ($t(25) = -3.069$, $p = 0.005$). Second, violent branches were less likely to shut down than the rest, though the differences are not statistically significant ($X^2(1) = 0.091$, $p = 0.613$). Third, violent local branches are also more active than the rest. Branches in municipalities where violent incidents were reported organized an average of 1.23 activities per quarter compared to 0.47 activities organized by the rest. A two-sample t-test between the two groups shows that the differences are statistically significant ($t(23) = -2.504$, $p = 0.020$). Similarly, violent branches were much more consistent in their organized activities than the rest. Their mean consistency score was 0.48, which means that they organized at least one activity in nearly half the quarters of their lifespan. The rest of the branches had a consistency score of 0.29. A two-sample t-test between the two groups shows that the differences in the mean consistency scores are statistically significant ($t(36) = -2.772$, $p = 0.009$). Overall, then, the evidence suggests that violent branches are organizationally more active and have longer lifespans than the non-violent branches. But the continuity of local structures does not seem to be directly affected by this violence.

Conclusion

A notable strain in the general party literature suggests that one must look inside parties to understand how they develop (Berman 1997; Webb et al. 2002). Taking cues from this literature, this chapter has focused on how two basic features of extremist right-wing parties help shape their local organizational development. Extremist right-wing parties tend to be movement parties, involved in a dual track of conventional and contentious politics (Kitschelt 2006). Moreover, unlike the ideal Duvergerian mass

---

[52] The party newspaper systematically reproduces and then denies reports published by mainstream newspapers accusing the GD of involvement in various violent incidents. The newspaper reported ninety-one such incidents in the period under study, most of which occurred in Athens.

party and in contrast to radical Left movement parties (della Porta et al. 2016), extremist right-wing parties are charismatic parties. They lack the institutional density and differentiation necessary for effective resource allocation and conflict resolution.

Through the in-depth analysis the GD, this chapter has shown how the combination of these two features affects the local organizational development of an extremist right-wing party. The dual track of politics practiced throughout the years by the GD privileged the advancement of militant activists over political entrepreneurs in the top ranks of the organization. The dominance of militants in the top ranks of the party complicated the integration of the many moderates who started flooding the local party organizations after its initial electoral breakthrough, regardless of the skills they brought to the party. In a party lacking solid institutional infrastructure to handle the process of opening up to new recruits, the sudden influx of moderates or, even, opportunists (Kitschelt 1989; Art 2011) generated internal problems that trickled down to the local organizations. Due to the nature of the party, in most albeit not all of these feuds, it was the militants who won the day. Not strictly built for electoral politics, the GD remained controlled by the street fighters of the 1990s and, mostly, the 2000s.

The main attributes of the central party trickle down to the local organizational level and affect not only aggregate but also individual organizational outcomes. This chapter has utilized organizational data collected for all seventy-four local branches of the GD to assess how specific branch characteristics help account for local organizational trajectories. First, branches founded prior to the breakthrough elections of 2012 were more active than those established during the subsequent frenzy of local expansion. Second, branches set up in settings where the GD had some presence prior to 2007 – branches in settings with an organizational legacy – were also better at mobilizing their activists than the rest. Third, violent branches were significantly more active than the rest, displaying higher levels and more systematic patterns of mobilization. The analysis of all three characteristics suggests that those branches associated with the militant organizational DNA of the party were more likely to grow organizational roots in local societies than the rest. This militant DNA complicated the interaction between the party and its environment and, ultimately, its local organizational development. The next three chapters examine the way environmental factors shaped the local organizational development of the GD.

CHAPTER 7

Electoral Drivers of Local Organizational Development

This chapter begins the examination of how environmental factors shape the local organizational development of extremist right-wing parties by looking into the way electoral dynamics shape organizational choices and outcomes. It first engages with the broader and extant literature examining the link between electoral and organizational factors. The first empirical section of the chapter focuses on how electoral considerations shaped the organizational *choices* the GD made. The second empirical section investigates how various electoral factors, such as electoral performance, district size or local incumbency, helped shape organizational *outcomes*. The next two chapters examine in turn how institutional and societal factors affect organizational development.

Electoral Dynamics and Local Organizational Development

Attempts to trace the link between electoral and organizational dynamics usually treat organization as an independent variable and seek to examine its effects on electoral outcomes. The basic idea is that the organizational attributes of parties directly or indirectly determine their electoral fate. This idea has been shown to hold across different settings and parties in Europe (Kitschelt 1994; Kitschelt and McGann 1995; Grzymala-Busse 2002; Tavits 2013), Latin America (Levitsky 2003; Samuels 2004) and Southeast Asia (Kuhonta 2011). Taking cues from the broader literature on political parties, works on far right parties have partly attributed their varied electoral performance to their respective organizational features. The litany of organizational parameters linked with electoral performance ranges from leadership charisma (Eatwell 2006) and "practical" leadership (Mudde 2007); to the quality and type (Art 2011) or the training (de Lange and Art 2011) of far right activists; to the existence or not of a regional stronghold (Mudde 2007); to the degree of centralization and coherence (Carter 2005); and, more broadly, to the breadth of its grassroots base. The main idea is that the better organized parties are, the better they perform in elections. Direct evidence in support of this argument is thin, in part because of the difficulty in collecting systematic, reliable and meaningful data on the various organizational characteristics that are usually associated with organizational strength (Norris 2005). Given these intrinsic difficulties, some of the best-known analyses of organizational correlates of electoral performance have relied on expert surveys of party characteristics (Lubbers et al. 2002) or the coding of existing literature (Carter 2005). Case studies of durable and "flash parties" have similarly yielded interesting findings (Art 2008). The examination of party trajectories across time suggests that organization is not as important for the electoral breakthroughs of far right parties as it is for their subsequent persistence (Ellinas 2007; Mudde 2007; Bolleyer 2013). Unlike some of the best organized far right parties in Europe, such as the French National Front or the Belgian Vlaams Belang, parties lacking solid organizational structures are most likely to quickly fall into oblivion after their initial electoral breakthroughs. The Dutch List Pim Fortuyn (de Lange and Art 2011) and the Swedish New Democracy (Taggart 1996) are examples of how organizational deficiencies can lead to electoral collapse.

Despite notable progress in understanding the link between far right organizations and electoral performance, there are still some notable gaps in the analysis of organizational and electoral dynamics. The most important of these gaps is the direction of causality. Lacking concrete, reliable and systematically collected evidence regarding the various organizational features of far right parties, it is difficult to avoid making *ex post facto* assessments of organizational effects. Take the French National Front as an example. Founded in 1972, the party is considered by most experts as one of the best examples of organizational strength (Lubbers et al 2002; Carter 2005; Mudde 2007; Ellinas 2010). There is considerable evidence though that, prior to its electoral breakthrough in the 1984 European election and the 1986 parliamentary election, the party lacked the organizational infrastructure subsequently attributed to its success (DeClair 1999; Perrineau 1996). Dreux, the city where the Front received a local electoral breakthrough in 1983, was far from a local stronghold. In the early 1980s, "the extreme right had no headquarters in the city, only two or three known activists. The *Front National*'s office was no more than a mail drop, actually a post-office box rented by a plant manager" (Gaspard 1995: 118). It was only after this and other secondary electoral successes that the grassroots organization of the party started expanding (Birenbaum 1992). What the example of the National Front suggests, then, is that electoral success precedes organizational capacity. This does not mean that electoral success always leads to particular patterns of organizational development. Electoral success can yield divergent organizational patterns depending on prior party histories and subsequent party choices (Bolleyer 2013). It is important, though, to consider not only the effect of organizational capacity on electoral results but also to take into account how electoral results shape organizational outcomes.

The analysis of how electoral dynamics affect organizational outcomes can benefit from the consideration of how elections affect not only national but also subnational party organizations. As discussed in Chapter 3, much of the literature on far right parties relies on the analysis of national party organizations across countries. The focus on national party organizations is quite reasonable, given that many of these parties are unflatteringly thought to adhere to the *Führerprinzip*. The concentration of decision-making authority in the hands of the party leader suggests a very high degree of centralization (Carter 2005) that might render meaningless an analysis of subnational variation in organizational development. Mostly assumed rather than thoroughly tested or comparatively measured, though, the high levels of centralization in far right parties cannot help account for the notable subnational variation in organizational outcomes. Subnational analysis, then, can help throw more light on various patterns of organizational development and facilitate a better understanding of how electoral dynamics affect local organizations.

Reversing the direction of causality and focusing on subnational organizational development allows a reconsideration of some of the main insights on the relationship between electoral and organizational dynamics. A strain in the extant literature suggests that these dynamics are relatively weak in parties such as the ones studied here. Such parties are thought to eschew the logic of electoral competition that even parties founded on ideological principle have been known to eventually adopt (Michels 1915; Kirchheimer 1966; Przeworski and Sprague 1988). Dominated by staunch ideologues, extremist right-wing parties can be expected to value ideological purity over the programmatic flexibility necessary for electoral success (Kitschelt 1989; Art 2011). The examination of subnational organizational development permits an analysis of the extent to which a party is driven by the logic of electoral efficiency. Since all extremist right-wing parties accept the necessity of participating in elections, it can be safely assumed that, to some degree, they consider electoral efficiency as one of their main aims. The question, then, is how their organizational choices conform to vote-maximizing objectives.

At the macro-level, the degree of adherence to vote-maximizing object-ives is likely to change across time as the party goes through different phases of development (Harmel and Svasand 1993). In its formative years, an extremist right-wing party is much less likely to develop its local organizational network on the basis of electoral logic. During its earlier stages of development, a party is likely to make choices about its local organizational presence that do not strictly conform to the dictates of electoral efficiency. It is plausible that local branches will be set up and sustained even in electorally non-competitive settings where the party has limited or no chances of winning seats. Or, more broadly, the local network will expand in a random manner, which cannot be reduced to particular electoral considerations. Once the party grows and especially after an electoral breakthrough (Ellinas 2007), it is reasonable to expect electoral considerations to trump the logic of constituency representation. It is plausible that, after success, a party will invest its newly acquired resources in an electorally efficient way that seeks to sustain or maximize future votes. Should the party choose to invest these resources to expand its local presence – as we know from the study of far right parties in particular (Mudde 2007; Bolleyer 2013) and political parties in general (Kopecky 1995; Katz and Mair 1995), this is not a given – it can be expected that the choice of location is influenced by this electoral success. If a party chooses to better adjust its organization to electoral context, it is likely to set up local branches in settings that hold the best possible electoral promise. The party is likely to assess the electoral prospects of the localities where it sets up a brick-and-mortar presence by taking into account either the previous electoral results or the next ones.

At the micro-level, once these local branches are set up, their evolution is likely to be affected by the electoral context. The literature on local party activism offers useful insights on the relationship between electoral and organizational dynamics. Although this literature mostly looks at how local party activism affects electoral outcomes (Huckfeldt and Sprague 1992; Pattie et al. 1995; Whiteley and Seyd 1994; Gerber and Green 2000; Denver et al. 2004; Fisher et al. 2006; 2016), it also helps elucidate the possible links between electoral variables and organizational results. The first of such links is between *previous* electoral results and the organiza-tional evolution of local branches. Past results can shape the development of local branches by granting new resources to local organizations. As an analysis of BNP activism suggests, it is plausible "that election success attracts publicity, heightens perceptions of party credibility and encourages passive supporters to enrol as members" (Goodwin et al. 2013: 899).

But the opposite is also plausible. Working hard to achieve the electoral success of a local branch might dampen subsequent organizational efforts. After success, activists might be "burned out" from the enormous effort and this might lead to de-mobilization (Whiteley and Seyd 1998).

A second set of expectations comes from the consideration of the effects of incumbency (Cain et al. 1984; Whiteley and Seyd 1994). For parties without prior parliamentary presence, like most extremist right-wing parties, winning a district seat might yield more resources to the local branch. Having access to a member of parliament might lure more supporters to come closer and work for the party. Or, some of the resources that come with incumbency might be channeled to strengthen the local branch. Incumbency might also undermine the organizational capacity of a local branch. Elected office might limit the time the newly elected members might have to devote to the development of their local branch. Or, it might give rise to internal feuds for the distribution of the newly acquired resources that could ultimately undermine organizational coherence, or worse, turn the local unit into a host of internal rivalries.

A third link is between *future* electoral results and organizational development. The development of a local branch might be shaped not only by past electoral results but also by its electoral prospects. Once branches are set up, their organizational evolution might be associated with their varying probabilities in achieving electoral success. Electoral institutions (Karp et al. 2008) can help local branches assess their electoral prospects. As studies of local activism suggest (Seyd and Whiteley 1992; Beck and Heidemann 2014), organizational efforts are likely to be more rewarding (and hence, larger) in competitive or battleground localities, where the chances of winning representation are larger. In line with this basic expectation, it can be hypothesized that organizational evolution is associated with district size. One can expect local organizations to develop differently in very small districts, where there are limited chances of winning a seat, than in larger ones, where there is a real probability of winning representation.

The Evidence

To empirically examine how the electoral results of the GD affected its local organizational development, this section examines first macro- and then micro-level effects. At the macro-level the first part investigates the expansion of the GD's local network before and after its 2012 electoral breakthroughs. The overarching question in this part of the analysis is how electoral considerations shaped temporal and geographical patterns of local organizational development. The second part focuses on the seventy-four local branches the GD set up between March 2007 and September 2016. Using the indicators of organizational development explicated in Chapter 5, this part investigates how electoral variables relate to the organizational evolution of these branches. First, it examines the effects of past electoral results, and then it focuses on how incumbency and electoral prospects shape organizational outcomes.

Electoral Factors and Organizational Choices

To examine how electoral considerations affected the organizational development of the GD, this part examines temporal and geographical patterns in the evolution of its local organizational network. The analysis of temporal patterns relies on the investigation of how the local network of the party developed before and after major elections. To some extent the GD seems to have expanded its network from four branches in 2010 to fifteen branches in May 2012 in anticipation of future electoral breakthroughs. By 2011 the possibility of such a breakthrough was not remote. As discussed in Chapter 4, the party leadership already started sensing a change in the receptivity of its controversial message and activism in the Agios Panteleimonas neighborhood in central Athens, where it invested a lot of its organizational resources. For the first time ever, GD activists who mobilized in the area were applauded by some local residents instead of being booed. The results of the local elections in November 2010, where the party participated in two municipal and two regional elections, provided further evidence for the reversal of the electoral fortunes of the party. In Athens the party list received 5.29 percent and Michaloliakos got elected in the municipal council, receiving 8.38 percent in the sixth district and 6.94 percent in the fourth district – the areas where the GD concentrated its controversial and, in a number of cases, violent activism (Dinas et al. 2013). In Thessaloniki the party list received 1 percent of the vote and in the Western Greece and Peloponnese regions the party candidates received 1.88 percent and 1.45 percent, respectively.[1] Compared to the 0.29 percent the party received in the national election held only a year before, the local elections marked a major improvement and pointed to the

---

[1] In Aitolokarnania support for the National Rally for Western Greece reached 2.57 percent and in Messinia the National Rally for Peloponnese it reached 2.53 percent. National Ministry of Interior website, www.ypes.gr.

electoral possibilities generated by the first bail-out agreement between Greece and its creditors for smaller political parties. The change in the political opportunity structure did not go unnoticed by the party leader:

> We received 5.3 percent in Athens. And afterwards, as early as April 2011, there was intense talk of a snap election because of the political instability. At this point, we ran to every corner of Athens and Greece. We constantly were on the road. Back then, the burden fell on me, as the Golden Dawn did not have three to four well-known party members. I went from Alexandroupolis to Crete, from Cyclades, to Peloponnese, to Thessalia. At the beginning of 2011, I had a tip from a journalist working for a magazine that, based on unpublished opinion polls, the Golden Dawn would enter parliament. Yes, from the beginning of 2011.[2]

Overall, then, there is strong evidence suggesting that the local organizational development of the GD throughout this period went hand in hand with its electoral expectations. In fact, the major expansion of the local branch network in early 2011 took place *after* the electoral inroads in the local elections and the changing electoral environment generated by the onset of the economic crisis.

The 2012 breakthroughs set the impetus for the rapid organizational expansion of the GD. In the first few months after the elections, the newly elected party MPs toured the country to set up new branches, on some occasions inaugurating the operation of three branches over a weekend. By the end of 2012, the party had more than fifty offices across the country. The pace of local organizational expansion slowed down considerably by early 2013, even before the arrests of its top leadership in October 2013. In the first few months of 2013 the party set up six additional offices and by the end of the year the *Golden Dawn* newspaper listed only two additional local branches. The local party network started expanding again in 2014 and reached a peak of sixty branches by the May 2014 European, regional and local elections, in which the party consolidated its position as the third biggest political party in Greece. The pace of expansion after 2013 though was considerably slower: only nine new branches were listed in the party newspaper in the first months of 2014 and two additional ones toward the end of the year. Whereas past elections encouraged local organizational expansion, by 2015, and as the party leadership started being released from prison, the party stopped expanding its local network. Prior to the September 2015 election, the party inaugurated only one new office in Ampelokipi, which is located in the party headquarters, close to

---

[2] Interview #45, Nikos Michaloliakos, party general secretary, interview with author, October 2016.

the center of Athens. Overall, then, by the snap elections of January and September 2015, the close link observed earlier between electoral and organizational dynamics broke down. Despite the anticipation of minor electoral gains in the September election, the party did not open any new branches.

The analysis of specific characteristics of the electoral context can provide further insights into how electoral efficiency guided party decisions regarding where to expand. Three aspects of the electoral setting are particularly relevant for this analysis: the size of the district where the party chooses to set up a branch; the past performance of the party in this setting; and the performance of other parties. First, a party can be expected to set up a branch where it is most likely to win a seat. Although the allocation of seats in the Greek electoral system is not easy to predict *a priori*, one can expect an electorally efficient party to prioritize setting foot in the largest districts and to avoid really small districts. The evidence suggests that the local organizational development of the GD is at least moderately related to electoral logic: the correlation between the size of the district (number of seats) and the number of branches the party established in each district is 0.44 ($p < 0.001$). The party opened multiple branches in some of the largest districts, such as Attica, but it also had multiple branches in relatively small districts, such as Messinia and Elis. Interestingly, the party also chose to invest scarce organizational resources in electoral settings where it had almost no real chance of winning a seat. Eight local branches were set up in districts that award one or two seats, meaning that the GD would have to be the first or second biggest party to win a seat.

Second, a party can be expected to invest organizational resources in settings where it can obtain the best electoral yield. The past performance of a party in a particular setting is usually a good indicator of its future performance. A party priming electoral efficiency can be expected to establish brick-and-mortar presence where it already had relatively high electoral support, in an effort to sustain it. The GD partly conformed to this logic. For example, the party set up branches in suburban regions of Attica, such as Megara, where in the June 2012 election the party had received 8.67 points above the national average – an impressive 15.59 percent. As Figure 7.1 suggests, though, electoral efficiency cannot sufficiently account for the local organizational development of the GD. In nearly half the localities where the GD set up a presence during this decade, the overall performance of the party was lower than its national average at the breakthrough election of June 2012. For example, the party

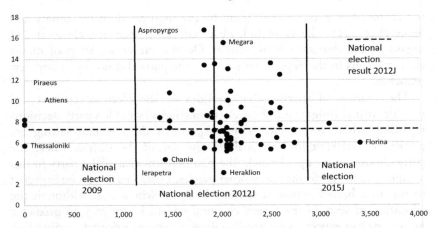

Figure 7.1   The establishment of GD branches across time (days since 2007) and GD results (%) in the June 2012 election.

set up three branches in Crete – Chania, Heraklion and Ierapetra – where the party had received some of its worst results.

Third, a party might make organizational choices by getting signals about its electoral prospects from the performance of its competitors. It is plausible that the GD received signals regarding the electoral prospects of particular localities from the results of other parties from where it expected to draw support. One such party is the Popular Orthodox Rally (LAOS), a radical right-wing party that achieved significant electoral breakthroughs in the 2007 and 2009 national elections, receiving 3.8 percent and 5.63 percent, respectively. Arguably, the GD could choose to set up local presence in settings where LAOS had performed well in 2009 to lure its voters away. However, this is not the case. The seventy-three localities with GD branches were far from LAOS electoral bastions – the average LAOS result in these localities was only 0.02 points higher than the national average of LAOS in the 2009 election. Similarly, the GD does not seem to have spotted right-wing bastions for expansion. The average result of the center-right New Democracy (ND) in the seventy-three localities was 34.60 percent compared to its national average of 33.47 percent in the 2009 election. In nearly half of these municipalities the ND underperformed its national result. Similarly, the vote for the socialist PASOK in these municipalities was only 0.29 points higher than its winning national average of 43.92 percent. More interestingly, the GD seems to have expanded in locations where the communist KKE under-performed its national average in 2009 by 0.71 points (6.83 percent compared to 7.54 percent). The same findings hold for the June 2012 election as well. The average result of the center-right ND in the seventy-three municipalities with GD presence was 29.91 percent compared to the national average of 29.66 percent. These seventy-three municipalities were not left-wing bastions either: in these settings, the three left-wing parties, Syriza, PASOK and KKE, performed slightly worse than their national average. Overall, then, the electoral performance of other parties does not seem to have affected the local organizational expansion of the GD.

The moderate association between electoral context and local expansion does not mean that the organizational choices a party makes are electorally irrelevant. Although the GD did not fully adhere to a vote-maximizing logic, its choices had notable electoral effects. This effect can be tested by examining the association between the local presence of the party and its electoral results. The first opportunity for this test is in the 2015 election, which followed the organizational expansion of the party in seventy-three different municipalities. In the seventy-three municipalities where the GD established brick-and-mortar presence at some point throughout the past years, then, the party received 7.97 percent in the September 2015 election. In the remaining 951 municipalities without such presence, the party averaged 6.92 percent. A two-sample t-test of the two means shows that they are statistically significant ($t(87) = 3.72$, $p < 0.001$). Put simply, in settings where the party set up a local branch it had a better result than in the rest of Greek municipalities. This is also consistent with evidence showing that active party branches achieved better electoral results than less active ones (Ellinas and Lamprianou 2018). In other words, local party supply makes a difference in electoral outcomes and local party organization matters.

Electoral Factors and Organizational Outcomes

Once a party makes a decision where to expand its local network, it is important to investigate how electoral factors shape the trajectory of these local party organizations. This section examines how various electoral variables associated with the four indicators of organizational development explicated in Chapter 5. Moving from the macro- to the micro-level, the aim here is to explore how a number of electoral variables affected the organizational development of the seventy-four local branches.

The first set of variables relates to the electoral performance of local organizational units. Subnational organizations in settings where the party does well in elections can be expected to develop differently than in settings where the party underperforms. In local communities where the party gains electoral traction, local party branches can more easily convince the central party to grant them more resources and, more generally, to help them enhance their local presence. Moreover, in local settings scoring good electoral results, party functionaries can more easily recruit new members and activists (Goodwin et al. 2013). As more people come closer to the party, the pool of people that can be recruited from the local community to help with party tasks widens. By contrast, where the party underperforms, its subnational units will have a harder time to attract resources from the central party and the local community.

To examine the association between electoral performance and organizational development, the analysis takes into consideration the electoral results of the GD in the 2012 national elections, which *preceded* the rapid expansion of its local network.[3] The analysis of the 2012 results shows that where the GD established local offices does not affect the evolution of these offices. These municipalities averaged 7.86 percent in the June 2012 election, with remarkable differences between settings such as Aspropyrgos, where the GD received 16.75 percent, and Ierapetra in Crete, where it merely got 2.25 percent (SD = 2.59). Such notable differences do not seem to have much or any effect on the fate of these local organizations. First, the 2012 result does not have any bearing on whether the branches set up by the party experienced discontinuity after their establishment. Although thirty-two out of the seventy-four branches experienced some discontinuity throughout their lifespans, this is unrelated to the actual result of the GD in elections. A logistic regression using the 2012 results as the only independent variable shows that it is not a good predictor of branch discontinuity ($p = 0.393$). Second, the electoral performance of the GD in these municipalities does not have an effect on how long the branches last. The correlation between the 2012 results and the age of the branches is non-existent ($r = 0.03$, $p = 0.825$). Electoral performance has a negligible effect on branch activism, as well. The seventy-four branches display wide variation in how active they are but these differences are unrelated to their electoral standing in the municipality where they are hosted. The correlations between electoral performance and the intensity and consistency of branch activism are non-existent ($r = 0.00$, $p = 1$ for intensity; $r = 0.07$, $p = 0.54$ for consistency).

---

[3] The analysis does not take into account the January and September 2015 elections because they followed the local organizational development of the GD.

Overall, the evidence shows that local party branches develop independently of the electoral standing of the GD in the local community where they are established. As shown before, local party presence boosts the electoral standing of the party but the opposite does not seem to hold. At least when measured as percentage of votes, electoral context does not determine the evolution of local party branches.

The electoral context a local party branch faces does not simply come down to its percentage of the votes but also depends on a number of other electoral parameters that need to be taken into account when analyzing electoral effects on organizational development. Going beyond electoral results, it is important to examine the electoral characteristics of the municipalities where the GD set up its local branches. The most important of these characteristics is the size of the district measured by the number of seats allocated. One can expect that the larger the district, the more likely that the local branch in the district will stay alive and remain active. The central party might be more reluctant to give up larger districts, where it has larger chances of winning seats. Moreover, local functionaries might be incentivized to sustain their activism in settings where the local unit might have some realistic chance of winning a seat in the next election. To the contrary, subnational units in smaller districts, where the chances of winning a seat are non-existent or very slim, might be easier to shut down either by the central party or by the local functionaries. Once the early enthusiasm of national electoral victory dissipates, it can be expected that local party functionaries will find it harder to sustain units in settings with no realistic prospect of being awarded a seat for hard activist effort.

To analyze the effect of district size, Greek districts with GD presence are divided into those awarding one or two seats and the rest. In the former, the GD has no chance of winning a seat, whereas in the latter there is a possibility of parliamentary representation. Although imperfect, the division of the districts in these two groups allows a strong test of how party branches develop when party functionaries have no chance and when they have some realistic possibility of winning parliamentary representation. The results are positive for most measures of organizational development and provide considerable evidence showing how the size of the district – and, more specifically, the prospect of winning a seat – can affect the organizational development of a local branch. First, local branches in larger districts are significantly more active than branches in smaller districts. Whereas the sixty-six branches in the larger districts averaged an intensity score of 0.75, the eight branches in the single or two-member districts averaged an intensity score of 0.15. A two-sample t-test of the two means shows that the difference is statistically significant ($t(72)$ = −4.86, p < 0.001). Similarly, branches in larger districts tend to be active with higher levels of consistency than the branches in smaller districts, organizing activities throughout the year rather than solely prior to elections. The average consistency score of the sixty-six branches is 0.37 compared with 0.14 for the eight branches in smaller districts. A two-sample t-test of the means shows, again, that the differences are statistically significant ($t(19)$ = −4.44, p < 0.001). Second, branches in larger districts tend to last longer than those in smaller districts. Throughout the period under study, branches in larger districts were open for 1,318 days (a little more than 3.5 years) and branches in smaller districts for 800 days (a bit more than 2 years). A two-sample t-test of the means shows that the differences are statistically significant ($t(11)$ = −2.48, p = 0.03). Although district size affects a number of organizational patterns, it has no effect on branch continuity. In larger districts about 42 percent of the branches displayed some discontinuity during this period compared to 50 percent of branches in the smaller districts. A chi-square test shows that district size and branch discontinuity are unrelated ($X^2(1)$ = 0.001, p = 0.72). Overall, then, the prospect of parliamentary representation has some effect on the level of activism a branch develops and on its overall lifespan but not on the actual decision to shut the branch down.

A more direct way of examining how electoral context affects the organizational evolution of subnational party units is looking at actual seats won. Given the complicated method of seat allocation in Greece, one can expect local party functionaries to get the strongest signals about the prospects of winning seats by the allocation of seats in the past election, especially the landmark election of June 2012. One can expect that in settings where the party won seats, the local branch can evolve differently than in settings where no seats are won. On the one hand, the access to an incumbent might give local functionaries an extra incentive to undertake party activity and might yield extra resources to the local branch. On the other hand, incumbency might make MPs less willing to devote time to the local branch due to busy parliamentary schedules and commitments. The vast discrepancy in the benefits accrued for incumbents and for local party volunteers might also become a source of internal friction that undermines the organizational development of local branches.

To examine the effect of incumbency on the organizational development of local party branches, the seventy-four are divided into two groups. The first group includes the thirty-five branches in districts where the GD won one or more of its eighteen seats. The second group includes thirty-nine branches in districts where the GD did not win a seat. The two groups display important differences in local activism but no differences in their longevity or continuity. First, incumbency is shown to have a significant effect on the intensity and consistency of political activities organized by local branches. The branches with an incumbent organized an average of 0.97 activities per quarter and the branches without an incumbent put together 0.43 activities. A two-sample t-test of the two means shows that they are statistically significant ($t(46)$ = 2.56, p = 0.013). Similarly, those braches in districts where the GD won a seat had an average consistency score of 0.42 compared with 0.27. A two sample t-test of the two means shows that the difference is statistically significant ($t(66)$ = 2.40, p = 0.019). Although incumbency seems to energize local branch activity, it does not seem to have a significant effect on fate of the local structures. In fact, incumbency is associated with higher levels of branch discontinuity than non-incumbency. In branches set up in districts that won a seat in 2012, nineteen out of thirty-five branches (54 percent) displayed some discontinuity throughout this period. In branches without incumbents, there was discontinuity in thirteen of thirty-nine branches (33 percent). A chi-square test shows that incumbency and branch discontinuity are not related ($X^2(1)$ = 2.501, p = 0.114). Similarly, having an incumbent does not get to affect how long a branch lasts. Branches with an incumbent stayed open on average for 1,301 days and the rest for 1,227 days. A two-sample t-test of the two means shows that the difference is not statistically significant ($t(51)$ = 0.43, p = 0.673). Overall, then, having a member of parliament in the district where the branch is based can help mobilize local functionaries into action but it does not affect the longevity or continuity of the local party structures.

Conclusion

The link between party organization and electoral outcomes is one of the most important lines of inquiry in the broader literature on political parties (Kitschelt 1994; Grzymala-Busse 2002; Levitsky 2003; Samuels 2004) and in the extant literature on far right parties (Kitschelt and McGann 1995; Lubbers et al. 2002; Carter 2005; Art 2008). This chapter engages with and departs from these works by turning organization into a dependent variable. The analysis here shows how electoral dynamics can shape both organizational *choices* and *outcomes*. With regards to choices, the analysis here shows that the local organizational expansion of the GD was only partly driven by electoral considerations. Limiting organizational expansion to the confines of its small network of party devotees, the party made organizational choices that were electorally suboptimal, like opening multiple branches in neighboring or small areas. Moreover, this chapter has systematically traced how electoral context shapes organizational *outcomes*. The most important element of the electoral environment is the prospect of winning a seat and not the actual votes won in the locality where a branch is located. Having an incumbent in the district where the branch is located seems to energize local functionaries into action: branches in districts where the GD won a seat in 2012 were significantly more active than branches without incumbents. Similarly, branches in districts with multiple seats, which stood a better chance of electing an MP, were twice more active than branches in single- or two-member districts, where the party had no realistic prospect of winning a seat. This is consistent with findings from research on party activism in majoritarian electoral systems, which shows that the electoral competitiveness of an electoral setting (e.g., battleground states in the United States or marginal constituencies in the United Kingdom) might incentivize local activists or the central party to undertake more local work (Seyd and Whiteley 1992; Beck and Heidemann 2014). Whereas the possibility of winning a seat seems to have a strong effect on the degree of mobilization of local party branches, it has a smaller effect on the overall longevity of these branches. In fact, incumbency seems to be associated with higher discontinuity rates, a result that the qualitative evidence produced in Chapter 6 might help explain. Branch fatalities in Larissa, Evia and Kalamata suggest that incumbency exacerbates the inherent friction between militants and moderates, resulting in organizational failure.

CHAPTER 8

The State and Local Organizational Development

This chapter examines how institutional responses to extremist right-wing parties affect their local organizational development. Institutional responses to extremism are usually subsumed in scholarly analyses of how democratic states use "militant democracy" to deal with actors threatening their democratic foundations. The first section of this chapter reviews this work to generate expectations about the effects of militant democracy policies on the organizational development of political parties. Whereas scholarly work on militant democracy tends to focus on outright bans of political parties by judicial authorities, this book adopts a broader definition to include a wider range of institutional responses and to examine how these responses affect central party organizations and then trickle down to party subunits. The second section examines the responses of the Greek state to the Golden Dawn (GD). It naturally focuses on the years before and after the arrest and criminal prosecution of the party leadership in 2013. Going beyond this judicial process, it also examines the varying responses of other institutional actors – police and municipal authorities – to the GD. The third section examines how state intervention affected the local organizational development of the GD.

Militant Democracy and Organizational Development

State responses to extremist right-wing parties have gained significant scholarly traction because they drive to the heart of democratic politics. Through their rhetoric and activity, extremist right-wing parties raise questions about the limits of widely accepted democratic freedoms, such as those of association, assembly and expression. At a normative level, these questions revolve around the justifiability of curbing such freedoms to defend democracy. Although few normative analyses would fully adopt Karl Lowenstein's dictum that "fire is fought with fire" (1937b: 656), they tend to acknowledge the need for some degree of militancy to defend democracy (Issacharoff 2006; Kirshner 2014). The range of justifications for curbing freedoms ranges considerably in the literature on militant democracy but the basic idea is that democratic agents have a right to defend the system from its opponents. Identifying these agents poses additional normative challenges, in part because judicial processes involve, at some point, political input or because they revolve around laws enacted by political agents. Similar challenges exist in the determination of the degree of input international or supranational institutions can have in defending democracy (Müller 2016).

At an empirical level, the challenges posed by extremist right-wing parties are two-fold: first, the identification of the range of available legal and policy tools to curb extremism, and second, the assessment of their effectiveness. In the postwar period, the push to protect democracy from extremism came at both the international and the national level, in part as a response to interwar atrocities and the Holocaust. At the United Nations level, the 1969 International Convention on the Elimination of All Forms of Racial Discrimination set the basis for the formulation of legal instruments for the elimination of hate speech. The European Union started taking a more active stance on these issues after the 1980s, with a set of declarations and measures to combat and criminalize certain forms of extremism (e.g., Fennema 2000; CFR-CDF 2005; Council Framework Decision 2008/913/JHA). Despite the common push to address issues such as hate speech and Holocaust denial, established democracies display wide variation in how they go about balancing between the protection and regulation of fundamental rights such as free speech (Rosenfeld 2002; Knechtle 2008; Thiel 2009). The arsenal of democracy defenders varies considerably across both time and space, from outright bans of political parties to curbs in what parties can say and do. The one measure that has received most attention is the ban of extremist organizations, especially political parties, which are considered necessary for well-functioning democracies and which, unlike other organizations, often enjoy special constitutional protection (Thiel 2009: 403). By one count, party bans have been used in more than twenty occasions in postwar Europe, especially after the 1990s (Bourne 2012), when fragile democracies were exposed to different forms of extremism (Tyulkina 2015). The most watched country for militant democracy policies, Germany, has employed bans twice, for the Reich Party in 1952 and for the Communist Party in 1956 (Issacharoff 2006). Since then, the Constitutional Court has twice rejected requests to ban the NPD (for the first request, Minkenberg 2006). This admittedly "exceptional" or "extreme" measure (Venice Commission 2000) to ban a party has been undertaken in Austria in 1988, the Netherlands in 1998, Belgium in 2004, Slovakia in 2006 and the Czech Republic in 2010.

Apart from parties, legislation set in place at both the national and supranational level has led to the disbandment of hundreds of extremist associations, some of which had ties with political parties. One of the best known recent examples is that of the Hungarian Guard, which was thought to be affiliated with Jobbik. It was banned by national courts, a decision upheld by the European Court of Human Rights (ECHR 2013). Laws against racism have also set the basis for prosecuting far right politicians such as Nick Griffin of the British National Party, Jean-Marie Le Pen of the French National Front and Geert Wilders of the Dutch Party for Freedom (van Spanje and de Vreese 2015). The existence of such legislation is thought to have deterred or moderated extremism, compelling the extremists to change their behavior. A policy tool used to curb racism is legislation like the one passed in Belgium which links eligibility for public funding with party programs (Rummens and Abts 2010).

The assessment of the effectiveness of militant democracy policies is intrinsically difficult because there are only a few cases of targeted parties and because of the difficulty in systematically gathering empirical evidence about such parties. The effects of state intervention on extremism can be broadly categorized into those affecting political demand for and, more importantly for this study, the political supply of extremism. With regards to political demand, attempts to regulate constitutionally protected freedoms can be assessed by examining whether militant democracy policies affect voter behavior. One the one hand, militant policies can undermine the legitimacy of extremist ideas, thereby sending a strong signal to voters against the desirability of these ideas. On the other hand, militant democracy policies risk reinforcing the anti-system or anti-immigrant image these parties seek to capitalize on. The empirical evidence on the effects of militant democracy policies on voter behavior is mostly indirect and tends to suggest that voters do not desert the parties after the initiation of such policies against them (Fennema 2000; Brems 2006; Minkenberg 2006; Bale 2007; van Spanje and de Vreese 2015). That being said, the emphasis on electoral results risks viewing militant democracy as an electoral strategy and thereby subsuming it in the broader political game. Unlike party tactics and strategies for dealing with far right parties like the *cordon sanitaire* (Mudde 2007; Art 2011; Downs 2012), militant democracy involves the regulation of freedom and involves not only political but also administrative agents. It is important then to go beyond voter behavior to fully assess the effects of militant policies against extremists.

This turns attention to how militant democracy policies affect the supply of extremism. One set of effects relates to the very ideas these parties propagate. It can be hypothesized that targeted organizations or individuals will moderate their behavior by toning down their extremist programs and rhetoric. Extremists might have to soften their views to avoid the legal ramifications of the militant democracy policies or, when banned, they will form more moderate organizations that will avoid the legal fate of their previous political engagement. The basic idea is that militant democracy policies provide the impetus for change in the behavior of extremists. Actors stop behaving as they did before and *learn* from the institutional measures against them that they have to change course (Bermeo 1992). Alternatively, it can be expected that militant policies reinforce the targeted behavior, thereby exacerbating the problem they seek to solve. Rather than being convinced to abandon or hide their ideological beliefs, staunch ideologues might turn to even more radical tactics to help realize their ideological goals. If they cannot freely express their ideas in the political arena, they might resort to other means of political expression, not least by undertaking violent political action (Tilly 2005; Minkenberg 2006). In this sense, militant democracy policies might encourage staunch believers to change tactics but in the opposite direction than the one expected, thereby having perverse effects (Bale 2007).

Despite a notable strain of literature on the programmatic maneuvering of far right parties in the competitive space (e.g., Kitschelt and McGann 1995; Meguid 2005; van der Brug et al. 2005; de Lange 2007; Mudde 2007), systematic analyses of how far right parties change their ideas in the face of militant measures against them are scant and mostly rely on accounts of individual cases. One of the most analyzed cases, the Vlaams Blok, is suggestive of the moderating effect of militant democracy policies on political ideas. The successor party, Vlaams Belang, adopted new statutes and program, dropping some of its more radical demands such as the blanket call for the repatriation of all immigrants. Although some consider the changes merely cosmetic or already under way as the party sought to broaden its electorate, they were substantial enough for the party to avoid being cut off from state funding, which would otherwise be jeopardized due to recently passed legislation against racism (Erk 2005; Brems 2006; Bale 2007). In the controversial case of the German NPD, the attempt to ban it in the 2000s did not seem to bring about a programmatic change in the expected direction. To the contrary, the hard core of the NPD is thought to have become more committed to its extremist views (Minkenberg 2006: 41). Rather than moderating the ideological platform of the party, militant democracy policies exposed the German secret services, which had infiltrated the party with informants leading to the dismissal of the court case by the Federal Constitutional Court (Chapter 10).

Militant democracy policies can be expected to affect not only party discourses but party organizations as well. The effects of repressive policies can be expected to take a toll on party structures, setting in motion various organizational processes that eventually affect not only party programmatic development but, more importantly for the purposes of this book, party organizational evolution. The social movement literature is particularly relevant in the understanding of these processes. The emphasis this literature places on processes rather than variables (e.g., McAdam et al. 2001); on political action instead of ideas; and on the analysis of mechanisms, tactics and consequences of institutional repression can help provide a useful starting point for the understanding of how institutional hostility gets to affect organizational development. Because of their movement nature, extremist right-wing parties are targeted not only for their ideas but also for their contentious and often violent political activity. It is thus reasonable to go beyond their programmatic responses to repression and to disaggregate the mechanisms set in motion when institutional actors apply varying degrees of repression against them.

Given the complexity of the processes set in motion by state repression, the range of repressive mechanisms and actors and the interaction between the state and the targeted organizations (Davenport 2005), one cannot easily foretell the outcome of institutional efforts to curb extremism. Borrowing from Tilly (2005), one can expect extremist right-wing organizations to increase or decrease their mobilization in response to state repression. Once targeted by militant democracy policies, extremist right-wing parties can be expected to increase their mobilization efforts in order to expose and benefit from the repressive policies of the state. Alternatively, they might be compelled to decrease mobilization either due to lack of resources or for tactical reasons (e.g., to avoid further repression). At the organizational level, this can be observed by tracking the organizational evolution of the party before, during and after the period of institutional hostility. The level of mobilization can also be gauged by taking into account the activism patterns of the party. Targeted organizations can also be expected to adjust to different levels and types of repression by changing their repertoire of action (e.g., Tilly 1978; Tarrow 1994; della Porta 1995; della Porta and Diani 2006). It is plausible that, when faced with the prospect of repression, movement parties might withdraw from the streets and focus on more conventional types of political action.

Alternatively, they might seek to reinforce their street – and violent – activism, in anticipation that this will increase their leverage with institutional actors exercising repression.

Empirical evidence gauging the effects of militant democracy policies on party organizational development is limited. It mostly comes from broader sketches of the organizational evolution of these parties or their successors. The first of relatively recent bans of extremist right-wing parties in Europe offers very little to the understanding of the effects of militant democracy on organizational development. The ban of the National Democratic Party of Austria took place at a time when another far right party, the Freedom Party, witnessed a spectacular electoral ascendance under Jörg Haider. Norbert Burger, the leader of the National Democratic Party, subsequently founded a little-known association, *Bürger-Rechts-Bewegung*, but died a few years after the ban, in 1992.[1] In the case of the Dutch Center Party '86, the legal process to ban the party in the late 1990s, amplified internal dissent about its strategic direction. The extremists in the party won the internal feud but by 1998, when the party was banned, they ended up heading an empty vessel as many key people defected to the other extremist right-wing party, the Center Party (Mudde 2000: 145–148; de Witte and Klandermans 2000: 705). The case of the failed attempt to ban the German NPD is also interesting. After the attempt to ban it in 2001, the party suffered a substantial loss in party members but its inner core is thought to have become more committed. During the same time, there was a spurt in smaller and even more extreme neo-Nazi groupings, the *Kameradschaften*, to which some former NPD members sought refuge (Minkenberg 2006; see also Chapter 10). The ban of the Vlaams Blok seems to have been inconsequential for its subsequent organizational development. An analysis of the organizational evolution of the party shows a spurt in party membership after 2004 (van Haute and Pauwels 2016). In Slovakia, the ban of Slovak Togetherness in 2006 set the stage for the founding of the LSNS. The party sustained its controversial street-level activism through protests and demonstrations, partly focusing on generating and capitalizing on anti-Roma sentiment (Nociar 2012). Similarly, the Czech Worker's Party was reconstituted to the Workers' Party of Social Justice (Downs 2012). Some people deserted the new party but, like its Slovak counterpart, the new party retained its activist profile. It "renewed its vigilance units, although with weakened paramilitary traits, calling them now Civic patrols of the Workers' Party"

[1] Dokumentationsarchiv des österreichischen Widerstandes (Hrsg.), Handbuch, S. 131 f.

(Mares 2011: 45). Overall, the evidence on the effect of repressive policies on the organizational development of extremist right-wing parties is too limited and not consistent enough to allow firm conclusions. Targeted parties seem to follow divergent organizational paths, often associated with broader sociopolitical developments as well as with specific institutional environments rather than with attempts to repress them.

Empirical attempts to assess the effectiveness of militant democracy policies can benefit from the consideration of a broader range of repressive measures, not only at the national but also at the subnational level. The first analytical step requires the expansion of the range of repressive measures under study. Just as resistance takes a wide variety of forms (Scott 1985; Davenport 2005), so does repression. When it comes to institutional forms of repression, outright bans of extremist right-wing parties are the most controversial, and thus the most studied, measures. But militant measures against extremists are not confined to what courts decide but also involve a broader range of institutional actors, both political and administrative. Arguably, much of the institutional "everyday hostility" against extremist right-wing parties takes place in this nexus between political and administrative institutions. Decisions to decline requests for the use of public buildings for meetings, city squares for demonstrations and busy roads for marches constitute militant measures against extremism that cannot be adequately captured by analyses of court decisions and judicial processes. These can be thought of as "softer" forms of repression. "Soft measures would leave a party in existence but officially limit its possibilities for political participation, or de facto make its life difficult" (Müller 2016). Some of these measures bring attention to administrative agents, such as the police, which are known to be particularly important for understanding the street-level mobilization (della Porta and Reiter 1998; Earl 2006) often employed by extremist right-wing parties. The second analytical step is the examination of how militant democracy plays out not only at the national but also at the subnational level. Centrally directed militant democracy measures are still the key to understanding the effects of repression but the subnational differences in the application of repression point to the need to cast a wider explanatory net and incorporate the subnational level in accounts of the effectiveness of militant democracy. Rather than focusing on broad sketches of organizational effects at the national level, the incorporation of the subnational level into the analysis provides the basis for understanding how and why even centralized policies of repression yield different organizational outcomes.

The State and the GD

Having briefly sketched the European empirical terrain, this section focuses on how Greek authorities have dealt with the GD since 1993, when it became a political party, until the arrests of its leadership and functionaries in 2013. It then focuses on the criminal investigation against the party leadership and ends with a consideration of the varied responses of other state actors, such as police enforcement agents and municipal authorities.

Throughout the 1990s, the GD has been implicated in a number of violent or criminal acts involving its activists, primarily in Athens and Piraeus. The incidents sometimes occurred after major outdoor events of the GD in Athens, like its annual Imia commemoration or anti-immigrant marches. The main targets in these incidents were leftist activists, antifascist groups and random immigrants. The incidents mostly involved beatings and stabbings, sometimes by prominent activists of the party, giving rise to calls to ban the party. Throughout the years leftist MPs filed a number of parliamentary questions asking the government about the legality of the party. The government deflected such calls by pointing to the protection of freedom of expression in Greece and the judicial approval of the party. For example, in 1995 the Minister for Public Order responded to a parliamentary question of a communist MP by stating that "ideas are free and only illegal acts can be prosecuted." The minister added that although the GD is an extreme right organization it is approved by the Supreme Civil and Criminal Court of Greece.[2] The relative tolerance of Greek authorities to the GD was also due to a general consensus among Greek constitutional experts against party bans (Psarras 2014; Anthopoulos 2015).

Pressure on Greek authorities to take action against the GD intensified after the near killing of a leftist student by a prominent member of the party in the late 1990s. The incident occurred in June 1998, when a group of GD members violently assaulted and nearly killed Dimitris Kousouris and seriously injured two other leftists. The leader of the group was Antonis Androutsopoulos, nicknamed Periandros, who at the time was considered the number two of the party and was a member of the Political Council. This was not the first incident involving prominent party members. When the Periandros incident occurred, Dimitris Zafiropoulos and Charilaos Kousoumvris, prominent members of the party in the

---

[2] "Parliamentary question about the GD," *Golden Dawn* [newspaper], March 10, 1995, p. 2. For this point, see also Psarras 2014.

1990s, were tried for an assault on a leftist group in 1996.[3] But the Periandros incident was much more serious due to the near death of Kousouris. Due to its seriousness, the incident attracted considerable media publicity and increased pressure on Greek authorities to take action against the party. As in the 1996 case involving Zafiropoulos and Kousoumvris, the Greek authorities followed the well-ploughed judicial path of criminally prosecuting the individuals involved but not directly involving the party in the prosecution of some of its top members. Greek prosecutors charged Androutsopoulos with attempted homicides and, after fleeing trial for seven years, he was convicted in 2006 to twenty-one years in prison.[4] When the issue of the legality of the party came back to the Greek parliament in late 1998, the Greek government had not changed its stance on how it dealt with the GD. The communist MP who raised the issue received the same response from the Greek government as his predecessors – that the GD is a legal political party and that ideas are free.[5] In essence, Greek authorities avoided linking the violent activity of individual members of the GD with the political party, even when these members were prominent figures of the party.

The response of the GD to the 1998 incident is instructive into the tactics the party would adopt whenever its top members were prosecuted and its legality came under scrutiny. First, the party would deny any involvement in the violent incidents and try to present judicial processes as a plot by the political establishment to silence its nationalist ideas. Moreover, the party would use the prosecution of its top members to close ranks and mobilize support in their defense. After the Periandros incident the party set up a "committee for the support of persecuted nationalists" asking its activists to stand by the party in these difficult moments.[6] In line with this approach, the party would turn scheduled court hearings into political events and mobilize its activists to bolster the defenses of the party against its political opponents. Scheduled court

---

[3] Details about this trial were published throughout time in the *Golden Dawn* newspaper. See, for example, "A trial with sole evidence an anonymous call," *Golden Dawn* [newspaper], September 22, 2000, pp. 1, 3. Zafiropoulos, a member of the Political Council of the GD and the subsequent leader of Patriotic Alliance, which was set up in the mid-2000s to contest elections, was also tried for another violent incident, this time in a demonstration that took place in 2000 against Turkey. See "Intercontinental 2000: Prosecutions for an event against 'Greco-Turkish friendship' after three years," *Golden Dawn* [newspaper], February 6, 2003.

[4] An appeals court subsequently reduced his sentence to twelve years and he was released in 2011, bitter about the way he was treated by his comrades in the party (Psarras 2012).

[5] "The GD is a legal political party, according to the Minister of Public Order," *Golden Dawn* [newspaper], November 20, 1998, p. 1.

[6] "No prisons for nationalists," *Golden Dawn* [newspaper], September 25, 1998, p. 1.

proceedings would occasionally set the stage for violent confrontations between GD activists and their opponents.[7]

In the next few years, the GD used similar tactics when its members became implicated in a number of violent incidents against political opponents. Its usual tactics became more difficult to sustain after an incident in November 2005 that involved firing a gun from the offices of the GD against political opponents who were out in the street and assaulted its offices in Athens.[8] The incident came at a time of growing – sometimes violent – counter-mobilization against the GD, which was increasingly more active in the streets by organizing various outdoor events, including a controversial gathering of other European extremist right-wing parties. Since the incident occurred in the party offices, the firing of a gun from the offices led to a police investigation against the party leader. The change in the way the police approached this violent incident did not go unnoticed by Michaloliakos who noted at the time: "For 11 entire years, respecting the fact that I am the leader of a small legal political party, they have never called me for not even a single [police] testimony. The New Democracy is in government for nineteen months and I have already been called [for a testimony] and, from what I understand, they are preparing an indictment."[9] In the next issue of the party newspaper, Michaloliakos used the assault against the party offices as a pretext for "the suspension of every political activity of the party."[10]

After officially resuming its operations in 2007, the GD would continue its street-level activism and its members would continue to be implicated in a number of violent incidents. After 2008, much of the street action concentrated in the Agios Panteleimonas and Attica squares in central Athens. The influx of a large number of immigrants in these areas and the reactions of local residents against deteriorating social conditions provided the background for a number of localized protests. GD members would participate in such protests and seek to capitalize on local resentment (Dinas et al. 2013). GD mobilization in the area would lead to counter-mobilization by antifascist and pro-immigrant groups that would occasionally turn

---

[7] "The omissions from a postponed trial," *Golden Dawn* [newspaper], January 19, 2001, p. 4.

[8] Discussion with several GD activists who are aware of the incident. See also Psarras 2012: 162; and "Bomb attack against the old offices of the Golden Dawn in 74 Solomou Avenue," *Golden Dawn* [newspaper], August 3, 2006, p. 7.

[9] Nikos Michaloliakos, "The Golden Dawn sent to the firing squad," *Golden Dawn* [newspaper], November 24, 2005, p. 16.

[10] Nikos Michaloliakos, "Announcement of the Secretary General of GD," *Golden Dawn* [newspaper], December 1, 2005, p. 3.

violent.[11] During this period, GD members were accused of undertaking "cleansing operations" in the Agios Panteleimonas and Attica squares against immigrants and their shops.[12] They would also be involved or implicated in an increasing number of physical assaults against leftists and immigrants alike. In areas such as Agios Panteleimonas, racist attacks against immigrants started becoming very common, prompting international monitoring organizations to investigate the role of both the GD as well as local police in the growth of hate crimes (Human Rights Watch 2012). Since 2011, when a number of human rights groups formed the Racist Violence Recording Network to begin recording incidents of racist violence, there have been hundreds of such attacks against asylum seekers and refugees, primarily in Athens. The number of such attacks grew rapidly between 2011 and 2013, especially after the electoral breakthroughs of the GD in 2012. The leadership of the party would signal the permissibility of violent assaults by using forms of demonstrative violence against political opponents and immigrants. The most serious incidents involved hate crimes committed by GD functionaries or supporters against immigrants. For example, a party candidate in the 2012 elections stood trial for the 2011 stabbing of an Afghan asylum seeker. And the head of the party in Perama was charged for the attempted homicide of Egyptian fishermen, attacked in their homes by a group of alleged GD members in June 2012. In January 2013, a Pakistani immigrant, Shehzad Luqman, was stabbed to death by two members of the GD.

The frequency and magnitude of criminal attacks put the Greek police under considerable national and international pressure, reigniting a long-held discussion in Greek public discourse about the links between the Greek state and the extreme right (Christopoulos 2014). The scrutiny of the police gathered momentum after the 2012 elections, when it became apparent that in special voting centers, where thousands of on-duty police officers voted, the party received significantly higher results than in the regular voting centers (Papanicolaou and Papageorgiou 2016).[13] Critics of

---

[11] See, for example, "The first repentant voters made their appearance," *Golden Dawn* [newspaper], June 12, 2009, p. 3; "Mad against the GD by Syriza's newspaper and the TVXS of Kouloglou," *Golden Dawn* [newspaper], July 22, 2009, p. 7.

[12] See, for example, "Newspaper Ethnos on the mobilization against the illegal immigration law," *Golden Dawn* [newspaper], March 3, 2009, p. 3; "Sign of the times," *Golden Dawn* [newspaper], October 20, 2010, p. 5.

[13] The voting patterns of Greek officers on duty were first reported in the Greek press after the 2012 election. They were also observed after the September 2015 election. See, for example, Vasilis Lampropoulos, "One in two police officers voted Golden Dawn," *To Vima*, May 11, 2012 (https://goo.gl/L6v1uG); "Police officers are the most fanatic supporters of the Golden Dawn," *To Vima*, September 21, 2015 (https://goo.gl/KNFjkF).

the police pointed to possible complicity between police officers and the GD, especially in areas such as Agios Panteleimonas, where the vigilante-type activities of the party substituted for the law and order function of the local police. The police were accused of tolerating the violent tactics of the party and of discouraging the reporting of hate crimes by the victims (Human Rights Watch 2012; Amnesty International 2014). The Greek police force also found itself on the defensive for the policing of various GD events. Moreover, the police received criticism for the way they handled various violent incidents involving GD MPs. Video footage of the MP Christos Pappas dragging a GD demonstrator away from a police detention coach right in front of police officers helped reinforce perceptions of excessive police tolerance or, even, collusion between the police and the GD.[14]

The September 2013 murder of antifascist musician Pavlos Fyssas in Keratsini drastically changed the stance of the Greek police toward the GD, compelling it to target the party itself instead of individual perpetrators of violent or criminal acts. A day after the Fyssas murder, the Ministry of Public Order and Citizen Protection sent a police report to the Supreme Court that included thirty-two incidents that took place in 2012 and 2013 that the police associated with the GD. Some of the most serious incidents on the list were the murders of Fyssas and Luqman; the attempted homicides of Egyptian fishermen in 2012 and of communist (PAME) unionists in 2013; and various other physical assaults against immigrants and leftists. The majority of incidents included some form of physical violence exercised by individuals affiliated with the GD. The police list also included some of the best-known events involving members of parliament, such as the destruction of immigrants' stalls in an open market and the assault against the mayor of Athens (Ellinas 2013; 2015). The Ministry argued that these were not isolated crimes perpetrated by the individuals involved but part of a systematic pattern of criminal violence organized by the GD. After a preliminary inspection of the evidence, the prosecutor of the Supreme Civil and Criminal Court decided that there was sufficient evidence for criminal prosecution, in accordance with Article 187 of the Penal Code for criminal organizations.[15]

---

[14] The video footage is available here: https://goo.gl/zvHkNF. The MP later stated on TV that "the state is illegal. The law at this time is the people who protest." The police subsequently charged Pappas.

[15] This is the article used to prosecute the terrorist organization 17 November.

On the basis of a preliminary investigation by the prosecutor, the main leadership and dozens of functionaries or supporters of the GD were arrested in late September 2013.[16] In February 2015, a council of the Court of Appeals sitting with three judges decided by majority that there was enough evidence to send sixty-nine individuals before the three-member Criminal Appeals Court of Athens and one individual before a Minors' Court. The leader of the party, all other MPs and other party functionaries or members were charged for joining and running a criminal organization from 2008 until the arrests of 2013. Some were additionally charged for the illegal possession of weapons. Most of the other defendants sent for criminal trial are party functionaries, members or supporters accused for direct involvement or for being accessories to various criminal acts. The list of defendants includes the murderers of Fyssas and Luqman, as well as key functionaries of the local branch of Nikaia, such as the branch head, George Patelis. The vast majority of crimes were committed in the Attica region. Some of the defendants are implicated in more than one criminal act. An additional number of twelve defendants were removed from the indictment and the subsequent criminal trial. By February 2015 when the case was sent to a criminal trial, most of those arrested, including the leader and top party MPs, had stayed in prison for more than a year. They started being released in March 2015, after nearly eighteen months of imprisonment without trial. According to Article 6 of the Greek Constitution, this is the maximum period that, under "absolutely extraordinary cases," someone can be imprisoned without trial.[17]

The decision of the Criminal Appeals Court of Athens notes that the GD had a hierarchical structure and that, hence, all orders for criminal actions were given by the leadership of the party. The judges accepted the public prosecutor's report, which noted that the operation of the GD aimed to violently confront immigrants, dissidents and, more generally, ideological adversaries with the ultimate goal of imposing its political ideas. The local organizations of the party were in charge of undertaking violent actions, through an organized plan, executed by "security squads" (*tagmata*

---

[16] Joining and running a criminal organization was interpreted by the Greek authorities as an ongoing crime, and hence, the leader and other members of the party arrested on the spot (flagrante delicto), without a need for a court order or, in the case of members of parliament, for a vote in the parliament to lift their parliamentary immunity. For those MPs not arrested on the spot, the investigators filed a request to the Greek parliament and achieved the lifting of their parliamentary immunity for their prosecution.

[17] Greek Constitution, downloaded from www.hellenicparliament.gr/Vouli-ton-Ellinon/To-Politevma/Syntagma/.

efodou, τάγματα εφόδου) made up of people with special physical characteristics and training similar to that of men in Greek special forces.[18] These "security squads" were accused of being involved in the two murders, a number of attempted murders, physical attacks, thefts, arsons and other crimes committed between 2008 and 2013. The two judges in the Criminal Appeals Court were convinced that the affiliation of the perpetrators of the crimes to the GD proved that they were members of a criminal organization run by the MPs of the party. The organization was accused of always operating with an organized action plan, allocation of roles and a strictly set schedule and being involved in dozens of criminal offences. The dissenting judge noted in his opinion that the GD cannot be characterized as a criminal organization because there is no evidence that the criminal activity was undertaken for material profit. The trial began in April 2015 amid expectations that it will take a number of years to be completed due to the large number of defendants and witnesses. By February 2018, the court had more than 225 daily sessions to examine the 131 witnesses and it had not gotten yet to the most important defendants.

In addition to the criminal prosecution of the defendants by the Greek state, there was also a civil suit against them by the private Initiative of Lawyers for the Civil Suit of the Antifascist Movement. The lawyers are representing the Fyssas family, the Egyptian fishermen and communist (PAME) unionists. In their own filing to the court, the antifascist lawyers who undertook the initiative for the civil suit differentiate their claims from those of the state prosecutors in two important ways. First, the antifascist lawyers want the court to take into account evidence showing that the criminal activity of the party started long before 2008. Whereas the state prosecutors examine incidents that took place after 2008, the civil suit lists ninety incidents dating back to 1996.[19] Second, the civil suit asks for further investigation into the relationship between the GD and other state and political actors. The antifascist lawyers want the state to delve deeper into the bonds between the GD and the police or other officials.

---

[18] The term "security squads" is used repeatedly in the legal documents, in quotation marks. It is a Greek translation of Hitler's Storm Troops (*Sturmabteilung,* SA).

[19] The memorandum submitted to the court for the criminal trial includes a number of cases for which there are final court decisions, such as the 1998 Periandros case described above; the 1996 incident involving prominent GD members Zafiropoulos and Kousoumvris; a 2001 case involving a member of the GD, Dimitris Papageorgiou; and a 2002 incident of injuring students, in which Kousoumvris was involved. The memorandum includes excerpts from the court decisions which mention the GD. The memorandum of the civil suit against the GD is available here: https://goo.gl/biwWzg.

The criminal prosecution of the GD helped bring to the surface some evidence linking individual police officers to the party and its activities. The preliminary investigation by the prosecutor in September 2013 noted that "in some cases, which is plausible that their number is higher, Greek police officers contributed or, in the best of cases, tolerated the members of the [GD] organization to committing criminally reprehensible acts, a point that must be further examined."[20] At around the time of the GD arrests a number of high ranking police officers in various departments and units either were transferred away from their positions or resigned.[21] After the arrests, the minister of Public Order and Citizen Protection ordered an investigation to "clarify exactly what sort of structures Golden Dawn has within the police."[22] The preliminary findings of this investigation were included in the Special Report on the "Extensive Investigation into the active involvement of police officers in the illegal activity of the Golden Dawn and possible participation in committing offenses of racist violence or corruption." Prepared by an internal directorate of the police, the report was hastily presented in October 2013, only a month after the arrests. Having investigated 319 police officers and 104 police units, the investigation identified 10 police officers with direct or indirect involvement with the GD and instantly arrested some of them. A number of these officers served as security guards for GD MPs and were arrested for the illegal possession of weapons. Disappointing the political opponents of the GD, the report concluded that "it could not be established that there are structured groups of active police officers, with a common criminal aim who have such relationship among them so that they can consider themselves a compact group, in relation to others."[23]

---

[20] The preliminary report of the prosecutor was published in the Greek press. Yianna Papadakou, "The entire report with which the prosecutor 'bound' the Golden Dawn," *To Vima*, September 29, 2013 (downloaded from https://goo.gl/1m4TUh; last accessed June 2017).

[21] A number of newspaper reports linked the transfers or resignations of high ranking police officers with the ongoing investigations regarding the GD. See, for example, "The negligence of the police in Chalkida [Evia] and the resignations," *Kathimerini*, September 24, 2013 (downloaded from https://goo.gl/WH7Amj); "Massacre in Greek Police for the Golden Dawn," *Ethnos*, September 23, 2013; Yiannis Souliotis, "Internal turmoil in Greek Police]," *Kathimerini*, September 25, 2013 (downloaded from https://goo.gl/A6mnYn); Yiannis Souliotis, "Investigation in Athens police," *Kathimerini*, October 2, 2013 (downloaded from https://goo.gl/izowtB).

[22] Kerin Hope, "Greek police 'infiltrated' by Golden Dawn," *Financial Times*, October 11, 2013; downloaded from https://goo.gl/jGn123.

[23] The presentation of the findings of the Special Report was published here: https://goo.gl/kbJWco. A full 110-page report, which includes the findings for each of the officers, was submitted to the prosecutor who ordered it in February 2014.

The "Institutional Diffusion" of State Intervention

The criminal prosecution of the top members of the GD by the Greek state set in motion a process of "institutional diffusion," galvanizing an entire set of political and institutional reactions against the party, at both the national and at the subnational levels. Initially after the 2012 election the rest of the political parties expressed varying degrees of opposition against the GD but their stance toward the party was merely political – denouncing its ideas and actions. Although the rest of the political parties – especially those of the Left – condemned the GD, they stopped short of using their legislative authority against it, in part due to a concern about the political ramifications of exercising such militant democracy policies. The Fyssas murder and the prosecution of the GD leadership helped solidify a political consensus to push beyond this embryonic, unstated and awkward *cordon sanitaire*, by using institutional authority against the GD. This consensus was particularly strong in the immediate aftermath of the murder and the arrests.

The first and most important legislative measure against the GD was the suspension of state funding, which curbed the financial resources the party had available for its organizational development. After the arrests, the Greek parliament passed an amendment to a 2002 law about the funding of political parties, which stated that in case of criminal prosecution of the leader or more than a fifth of the central leadership of a party, in accordance with articles 187 of the criminal code, state funding is suspended by an absolute majority in parliament. The suspension can be imposed if the acts of these individuals were committed as part of the activity of the party. The funds can be returned to the party if its leadership is acquitted. In December 2013, the Greek parliament decided by a majority of 239 out of 271 voting members of parliament to suspend public funding to the GD,[24] a decision that was subsequently affirmed by the Greek Council of State (the highest administrative court).[25]

A second legislative measure that also targeted the GD, albeit less directly, sought to impose stricter penalties for the incitement of hatred or violence against vulnerable minorities. In 2014, Law 4285 sought to amend a 1979 anti-racism law, which, according to critics of the Greek justice system, was rarely and lightly used by Greek courts (Papapantoleon

---

[24] Minutes of the Greek Parliament, 8 December 18, 2013, p. 4985 (downloaded from: https://goo .gl/Df4Hb1). See also https://goo.gl/cwcCGs.
[25] Council of State, Plenary Session, 518/2015, the decision was published on February 16, 2015.

2014). The law sought to impose harsher criminal convictions against anyone who publicly incites, causes or stimulates acts that can cause discrimination, hatred or violence against individuals or groups of people, based on their race, color, religion, descent, national or ethnic origin, sexual orientation, gender or handicap. The law also sought to criminalize the approval or denial of crimes, including but not limited to the Holocaust.[26] The latter clause proved controversial, as its breadth was thought to curb freedom of expression and to risk criminalizing historical research. Unlike the law for the suspension of state funding, the new anti-racism law passed with the support of the New Democracy-led government coalition but not the rest of the parties.[27] Moreover, in 2015, the Greek parliament passed amendments to the criminal code (Law 4356; articles 81A and 361B of the criminal code) to impose harsher penalties for racist crimes and to prohibit the exclusion of minorities from the supply of goods and services.[28] The latter specifically targeted the food, clothing and blood donations organized by the GD in major public squares "for Greeks only."

In addition to legislative measures targeting the GD, the Greek government also instituted a number of administrative measures. The most important of such measures involved the reorganization of the Greek police to address the rising number of racist assaults. With a presidential decree issued in December 2012, and in response to national and international criticism that it did not thoroughly investigate incidents of racist violence, the police established two departments and sixty-eight offices dedicated to dealing with racist violence across the entire country. The purpose of these new administrative units was to prevent and contain criminal acts against people of different backgrounds, including ethnic origin. The establishment of the units signaled a change in the approach of the Greek police, which had previously treated racist violence like any other.[29] As part of its now systematic efforts to address radicalization and extremism of all hues, in 2016 the Greek police started educating first-line officers on how to identify and deal with such phenomena at the local

---

[26] Law number 4285, *Government Gazette of the Greek Republic*, issue 191, September 10, 2014, pp. 6441–6444.

[27] Minutes of the Greek Parliament, September 2 and 9, 2014 (downloaded from: https://goo.gl/gxUHhq and https://goo.gl/QH7CVt).

[28] Written response of Greek Police to author's request for information, protocol number 1519/17/2377446, November 27, 2017.

[29] Presidential decree 132/2012, "Establishment of Departments and Offices to Address Racist Violence – Amendments to presidential decree 14/2001 (A' 12)," https://goo.gl/t4pQN3.

level. The handbook prepared for the purposes of this education includes a large list of symbols – like the swastika or the Celtic cross – associated with right-wing extremism. Spotting such symbols in local communities is the first step to identifying the existence of possible extremist cells.

Besides the central administrative reorganization to combat racist violence and extremism, there were instances of special administrative measures taken at the subnational level to deal with the GD. The Greek police became a notable player in attempts to curb the capacity of the party to use public spaces for its outdoor events. According to Article 11.2 of the Greek constitution, the right to freely associate can be restricted and outdoor gatherings can be banned in a specific area if there is a threat to "socioeconomic life."[30] Unlike elsewhere, in Greece, such executive decisions are not normally subjected to judicial review. The police used this executive authority to restrict or ban GD events even before the arrests, usually claiming threats to the public order by the organization of counterdemonstrations by anarchists and antifascists. On some occasions, as in the case of Athens, the intervention of police was requested by the municipal authorities – in some instances, at the top political level.[31] After the Fyssas murder, the police banned a planned distribution of food and clothes "by Greeks only" in the Nikaia region, amid fears of violence due to sizable counter-demonstrations.[32] In January 2014 the police banned the planned march of the GD after its annual Imia commemoration as well as the two counterdemonstrations planned against it.[33] In June 2015 the Thessaloniki police banned the other major event of the party, the commemoration of Alexander the Great, fearing violent incidents due to antifascist counterdemonstrations.[34] In January 2016 the Attica police restricted the annual Imia event of the party to the area around its offices, prohibiting both the march and the countermarch in the center of Athens.[35] To these executive decisions one must add a number of instances in which the police can exercise their discretion to either block

---

[30] Greek Constitution, downloaded from http://www.hellenicparliament.gr/Vouli-ton-Ellinon/To-Politevma/Syntagma/.

[31] In May 2013 the mayor of Athens had asked the minister of Public Order for police help to prevent the distribution of food from the GD in the Constitution Square. George Kaminis, interview with author, Athens, July 2016.

[32] Decision of the General Police Director of Attica, September 20, 2013, protocol number 3017/1/16.

[33] Decision of the General Police Director of Attica, January 31, 2014, protocol number 3017/1/21.

[34] Decision of the General Police Director of Thessaloniki, June 25, 2015, protocol number 3560/15/1136069.

[35] Decision of the General Police Director of Attica, January 29, 2016, 3017/1/27.

the access of GD supporters to a specific protest location or disrupt outdoor activities, such as canvassing or motorcading, by taking participants to the closest police station for questioning.[36]

Besides the Greek legislature and police, attempts to curb the presence of the GD diffused into other institutional arenas as well, bringing to the fore new actors and different approaches. One set of such actors were local Greek authorities, which were already troubled by the activism of the GD in their localities. After the Fyssas murder, the Central Union of Greek Municipalities asked "municipal councils to isolate the GD with their decisions and to declare it unwanted in their cities."[37] Dozens of municipal councils, especially those in which Left-wing parties had majorities, subsequently passed numerous resolutions condemning the GD and its presence in local communities. More importantly, some municipalities started exercising their institutional authority to deny the GD public spaces for their events. A number of municipalities, such as those in Nikaia and Volos, would deny GD requests for the use public spaces for outdoor events, like the distribution of food and clothes, or for indoor meetings of party supporters.[38] The most known case was the communist mayor of Patra, Kostas Peletides, who was taken to court by the GD for denying giving the party public spaces prior to the 2015 elections.

> Our stance against the GD begins with the character of this organization. We characterize it as a criminal organization ... So the stance of the municipality is that we do not facilitate their activities because they are against the people of Patra ... One example is that before elections they should have some space in public squares. Another example is the exercise of legislative audit or some permit that they might need. We do not intend to facilitate any of these. This is a unanimous decision of the municipal council. The decision of the municipal council goes back to 2014, when the council decided not to give the St. George square to the GD prior to the January 2015 election ... The tools we have at our disposal are political.[39]

---

[36] Whereas executive decisions to ban a protest need to be publicly documented, there is no administrative record for the use of police discretion to disrupt – but not ban – party activities. GD members claimed the disruption of outdoor party activities or events in interviews #10, #28 and #43.

[37] "Resolution of the board of the Central Union of Greek Municipalities for the murder of P. Fyssas and for dealing with Nazism in our country," *CUGM*, September 26, 2013 (downloaded from https://goo.gl/QtDvcM).

[38] For examples, see the decisions of the Nikaia municipal council on September 17, 2013, October 2, 2013 and January 19, 2016, as well as that of the Volos municipal council on November 18, 2015 (downloaded from https://goo.gl/U69obE, https://goo.gl/chyJrr, https://goo.gl/7H6YnK and https://goo.gl/Np24tC, respectively).

[39] Kostas Peletides, interview with author, Patra, July 2016.

The trial received considerable media attention and generated broader support for the mayor of Patra by other municipalities. In February 2017, the court decided to acquit the mayor because he was implementing the unanimous decision of the municipal council.

Another known example of exercising institutional authority to restrict access to public resources was in Athens, one of few municipalities where the GD has presence in the municipal council. Even before the Fyssas murder, the mayor, George Kaminis, started taking a more militant stance toward the party. In May 2013, the mayor intervened to block a food distribution event in one of the best-known public squares in Greece, the Constitution Square, compelling the police to prohibit the gathering. The GD went on with the gathering but was stopped by the police. The confrontation eventually led to an attempted assault by one of its MPs, George Germenis, on the mayor (Ellinas 2015), which subsequently became part of the legal case made by prosecutors against the party leadership. According to the mayor, this event sent a significant signal on how to handle such food distributions across the country. "I believe that what we did then with the prohibition of the use of the Constitution Square was very important. Because if they had taken the Constitution Square to distribute food, then they would have such events across the country, with this unacceptable reasoning, 'for Greeks only,' which constitutes an insult to the value of human beings." Moreover, the mayor excluded GD councilors from various ad hoc municipal committees and, as a matter of political principle, walks out of the municipal council whenever Elias Kasidiaris, the GD spokesperson and MP, talks. But the former constitutional law professor and Greek ombudsman also stresses that legality is the limit to how far one must go to block the GD and disagrees with the breadth of measures taken in Patra – we should "shake them with legality," he says.[40]

The Effects of Militant Democracy

The way the Greek state chose to deal with the GD after September 2013 presents a rare opportunity to examine the efficacy of militant democracy policies. Having stopped short of banning the party, the protracted nature of state intervention provides a natural experimental condition (Dunning 2012) for testing how militant democracy affects organizational development. In essence, the arrest and imprisonment of GD leaders constitute an exogenous shock to the organization, generating the possibility of examining the internal evolution of the party, before and

[40] George Kaminis, interview with the author, Athens, July 2016.

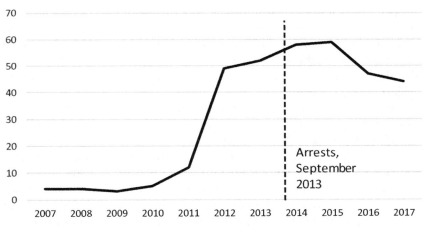

Figure 8.1   Number of GD branches (end of year).

after this shock. This section marshals qualitative and quantitative evidence to empirically assess the effects of state intervention on the national and subnational organizational development of GD.

Despite official party proclamations about operational continuity, demonstrated with the opening of new branches and mobilization against the imprisonment of the party leadership, the arrests took a toll on the organizational development of the party. First, the criminal prosecution initially slowed down and then reversed the local organizational expansion of the GD. The number of local party branches grew from 52 in September 2013 to 60 in May 2014 but since then it started shrinking, dropping to 48 in September 2016. As Figure 8.1 shows, after 2014, the party stopped opening new branches and in the last two years of the period under study it only set up branches in Ampelokipi and Florina. GD branches started shutting down before the arrests but they gathered pace afterwards, especially in 2016, when twelve branches shut down. Some of the branch closures are directly linked to the criminal prosecution of local party functionaries. The prime example is the Nikaia branch, which was one of the most active branches of the party during its nearly two years of operation. At some point in its short lifespan, the branch would organize two or three weekly events, such as speeches, motorcades, food distributions and self-defense training sessions for women, before it shut down. The closure was directly associated with the arrest of some of its leading functionaries, including its head Patelis, for their complicity in the Fyssas murder or other crimes. Similarly, the dismantling of the

Ierapetra branch in Crete seems to be associated with the criminal prosecution of its top functionaries for assaulting immigrants in February 2013.[41] In addition, the prosecution of GD members gave rise to internal feuds, as some of the accused sought to shift the blame on others. There is some evidence that the branch closures in Larissa and Evia are related to the judicial process against the GD (Chapter 6).

The most important effect of the criminal prosecution on the organizational development of the party was indirect. Asked about the life of local branches, dozens of GD local functionaries make a distinction between the periods before and after the arrests. The criminal prosecution of the party functionaries and the subsequent murders of two of its activists reduced the number of attendees in GD events, which had peaked in the previous year. The recollection of a leading party member is similar to that of many others: "Up until 2013, in all local branches you would see lots of people. There was a spirit of enthusiasm. After the prosecutions, this was reduced, but it did not go away entirely, as the plotters aimed. In the [anonymized] branch, I remember that by 2013, the regular office hours of the branch were not enough to see all those coming to the office."[42] The head of one of the most popular and active branches described a similar process: "In our indoor events, we usually have about 100 people. There has been some variation. After the prosecutions, people were scared. The plotters against the party would basically say that whoever is involved in GD activism is a member of a terrorist organization and must be imprisoned."[43]

Moreover, the criminal prosecutions seem to have taken a higher toll on smaller branches, which tended to rely on the financial contributions of its loyal supporters to stay afloat (pay for rent, outdoor activities, transportation to centrally organized events, etc.). In branches relying on few individual contributors, the drop in the number of those attending the branches and their activities led to the closure of these branches.

> The reasons for the closure of the branch are financial. Those instrumenting the imprisonments, to some degree, achieved their aim. They scared people away, so they are less willing to contribute financially. When the police started doing searches in the local branches, people became afraid. Those of us who had nationalist conscience became more determined. But [anonymized] is a small society and people are afraid.[44]

---

[41] This case was tied to the dozens of other cases for which the GD leadership is charged for running a criminal organization.

[42] Interview #29, August 2016.   [43] Interview #42, September 2016.

[44] Interview #24, July 2016.

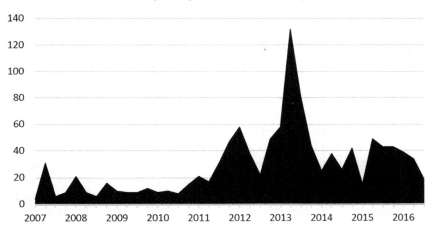

Figure 8.2   Number of GD local activities, per quarter (2007–2016).

The central party would financially support local branches to keep them from closing, fearing the signal this would send to the local society. But the suspension of state funding made it more difficult for the central party to support local branches. "At some point the Chief said if a local branch cannot collect €200 per month to stay afloat, then it must shut down. What this means is that the local branch could not find ten people in the local society. It is myopic to keep a branch when you do not have even this small number of people supporting it."[45]

Second, the criminal prosecutions affected not only the organizational structures of the party but also its activism. The effect of the prosecutions on activism was mostly felt at the local level. Despite the imprisonment of key party members, the central party continued to organize some of its key events, primarily commemorations like Imia, demonstrations against immigration and protests against the criminal prosecutions. The latter became very frequent during the imprisonment of the party leadership, causing organizational introversion at a time when the party desperately needed to capitalize on new opportunities (e.g. the refugee crisis) in its broader environment. At the subnational level, the closure of a number of branches meant that local activism became less frequent. As Figure 8.2 shows, the number of activities organized by the various local branches of the GD peaked in 2013. During the second quarter of 2013, the party

[45] Interview #44, September 2016.

newspaper recorded 132 events organized by the subnational units of the GD – more than quadruple the average number of the quarterly activities reported throughout the decade under study. The number dropped sharply after the arrests and for the next three years local party activism stayed at the levels the party had reached prior to its 2012 electoral breakthroughs.

The effect of institutional hostility on the organizational development of the party becomes even more evident when one takes into account activism data for each branch. By generating measures for the intensity and consistency of branch activism before and after the arrests, it is plausible to explore how the changed institutional environment affected patterns of local activism. For the purpose of this analysis, only those branches with measures both before and after the arrests can be included – a total of 53 out of the 74 branches in the dataset. The 21 branches left out of the analysis had either shut down before the arrests or were founded afterwards. The first measure examines how active each of these 53 branches were before and after the arrests. The average intensity scores of the branches for the periods display substantial differences. On average, each branch organized 1.17 activities each quarter prior to the arrests and 0.51 activities afterward. A two-sample t-test of the two means shows that they are statistically significant ($t(109) = 3.6199$, $p < 0.001$). The second measure examines how consistently the 53 branches organized their activities before and after the arrests. Again, the consistency scores differ substantially. The branches were twice as consistent before the arrests (0.54) than they were afterwards (0.28). A two-sample t-test of the two means shows that they are statistically significant ($t(117) = 4.6628$, $p < 0.001$). Overall, then, the analysis of patterns of activism before and after the arrests shows a sharp drop in both the intensity and the consistency of branch activism. This drop is not simply due to the reduction of the total number of local branches but, more importantly, it is evident at the level of each branch.

Third, the dramatic change in the institutional environment also affected the nature of local activism. As discussed in Chapter 5, since 2007 the GD started intermittently engaging in symbolic forms of social activism, disseminating food and clothes to people in need. Public funding allowed the party to turn these symbolic into substantive events involving hundreds, and sometimes thousands, of people lining up to get groceries or clothes. Local organizations in some of the major urban and suburban settings became key organizers of social activism and used it as means to gain legitimacy in local societies. As noted in Chapter 5, the party newspaper reported 114 such activities, most of them in the brief period after the electoral success of the party. After the suspension of party funding, the capacity of local party branches to sustain this type of activism dropped

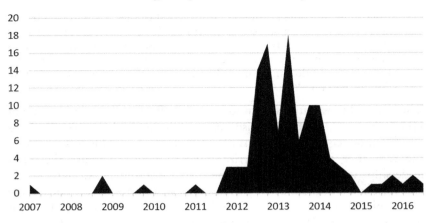

Figure 8.3   Number of GD local social activities, per quarter (2007–2016).

sharply (Figure 8.3). Although local party functionaries suggest that the party continues to engage in social activism, the scope of these activities is much smaller. They mostly involve handing out a few bags of groceries and some clothes directly to the homes of people the party identifies rather than handing them out in public squares.

> From December 2012 until the prosecutions we used to have an open event for handing out food. In some instances, we would give out as many as 200 kilograms of fish. Five or six of us would go down to the fish market and get fish for these events. Since the prosecutions, we have limited the distribution to 20–25 people, to which we send food every once in a while. [Name, anonymized] finds some Greek families facing economic problems, I inform the local branch and, once I have enough food, I call them. If they cannot come to the branch, I take the food to their homes. Because many people are afraid to come to the offices, we take them the food directly. We do not care if they vote for the GD but we do tell them our positions.[46]

In the absence of state funding, some of the big local branches that organized food rationing on a more regular basis started viewing this type of activity as a liability, because people started expecting regular support from the party that it could not give. Moreover, the new anti-racist law (4356/2015) added to the restrictions imposed by municipal authorities to the distribution of food "to Greeks only." After the law, the GD could no longer publicly state that it was distributing food to Greeks only without risking new judicial action against it.

---

[46] Interview #32, August 2016.

After some time, the distribution of food and clothes was restricted by the law. The distribution of food "to Greeks only" is considered racist. This was the final blow to this type of activism. The distribution of food "to Greeks only" started being restricted even earlier but this was the final blow. We looked for a window that would allow us to continue these activities but we did not find one.[47]

The criminal prosecutions seem to have also affected the violent nature of GD activism. After the imprisonment of its leadership, the party has avoided more contentious forms of political activism. This was especially the case after 2015, when Syriza came to power, because the party leadership was convinced that the new government would protect anarchist and antifascist activity in the streets. "From 2015 onwards, there was a political decision for withdrawal ... There was a general decision for outdoor activities. We would restrict ourselves to offices, hotels, etc. In terms of activism, there would be dissemination of the party newspaper and material in the street and in toll booths."[48] "We still undertake street activism but not so much as before ... There are guidelines from the center to do fewer outdoor activities because there is reaction [from anarchists], and it is not beneficial for us."[49] In the absence of official of data, it is difficult to accurately gauge changes in levels of violence associated with GD activism. The party newspaper, however, provides a useful proxy for violent incidents because it systematically aggregates media reports associating the GD with violence, and then refutes them. Figure 8.4 displays the distribution of 204 newspaper reports of different incidents of violence from 1993 to 2016.[50] As the figure shows, the number of violent incidents mentioned in the newspaper increased sharply in the mid-2000s, before the official suspension of party activities, then dropped, and reached new levels in the late 2000s when the party started its vigilantism in the Agios Panteleimonas area. More interestingly, and in line with the qualitative evidence, the number of reported violent incidents dropped considerably after 2013. Data from the Racist Violence Reporting Network, which sought to fill the official gap in the reporting of racist violence, show a similar trend. The number of incidents involving racist

[47] Interview #33, August 2016.   [48] Interview #47, May 2017.   [49] Interview #28, July 2016.
[50] All newspaper reports from 937 newspaper issues were coded for references of violence from the GD or its members. In nearly all the reports the newspaper refutes publications in other media outlets linking the GD with violence. Overall, there were 204 reports mentioning an equivalent number of incidents involving the GD or GD members. An additional number of reports not explicitly mentioning the GD were left out.

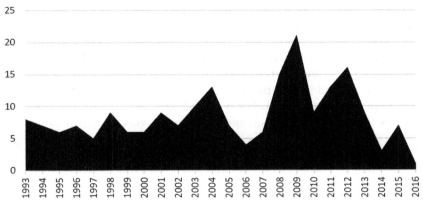

Figure 8.4 Violence from GD, incidents reported in party newspaper (n = 204).

violence was considerably high in 2012 and 2013, and then sharply dropped.[51]

Conclusion

Modern democracies occasionally resort to "militant" policies to defend themselves from those seeking to harm them. Although a growing literature examines the range and need of such measures in different settings and times, the systematic investigation of their effectiveness remains scant. This chapter investigated the range of judicial, legislative and administrative measures taken against the GD after 2013, which marked a major change in how the Greek state handled right-wing extremism. Although the ultimate outcome of the militant measures against the GD is yet to be determined, the systematic analysis of quantitative and qualitative data has shown that the *process* itself has taken a considerable toll on its local organizational development. The criminal prosecution of party leaders and functionaries stopped and, subsequently, reversed the expansion of the local organizational network of the GD. The arrests led to the closure of a number of party branches either because the local functionaries were criminally prosecuted or because the rest were scared away. One major effect of the judicial and legislative measures against the GD was to deprive it of human and financial resources necessary to sustain its local organizational presence. Without such resources, the GD had to curb its local

[51] Annual reports of the Racist Violence Recording Network.

activism, which had reached unprecedented levels prior to the arrests. An analysis of the intensity and consistency of activism before and after the arrests yielded significant statistical differences, demonstrating the substantial effect they had on the mobilization capacity of local branches. Moreover, the criminal prosecution of the party members, along with the legislative and administrative changes that followed, helped change the nature of its street activism. For both financial and legal reasons the party had to curb its social activism and moderate its violent activist profile.

CHAPTER 9

Societal Responses and Local Organizational Development

Attempts by extremist right-wing parties to grow organizational roots in local societies mobilize a diverse array of societal groups against them. The organizational effect of this mobilization has received some scholarly attention but, for the most part, it has defied systematic empirical investigation. This chapter seeks to bring together an array of evidence to systematically trace societal mobilization against extremist right-wing parties and to assess the effects of these societal responses on their local organizational development. The first part of the chapter examines how the literature treats societal reactions to extremism to generate various hypotheses about how such reactions shape organizational outcomes. The second section provides an overview of societal responses to the Golden Dawn (GD) in the past decade. It focuses on the diverse array of antifascist actors; their varied organizational resources; and their wide range of tactics. The third section seeks to provide a systematic examination of the effects of societal reactions on the organizational evolution of various local branches of the GD.

Societal Responses to Organizational Development

Societal responses to extremist right-wing parties are the least studied of the various factors examined in this book. Although there are a number of works directly or indirectly examining how the electoral or institutional environment affects the organizational development of far right parties, much less attention has been paid to the social environment in which these parties seek to grow roots. In some of the works incorporating the social environment into analyses of far right trajectories, attention is usually directed to societal facilitators, such as the presence of local nationalist networks, regional subcultures or, more generally, societal rootedness (de Witte and Klandermans 2000; Mudde 2007; Bolleyer 2013). Societal impediments to organizational development are usually overlooked or subsumed in accounts of political responses to extremism, like the strategy of isolation or inclusion (e.g. Mudde 2007; van Spanje and van der Brug 2007; Art 2007; Downs 2012). To some degree this is a reasonable analytical strategy because many of the groups countering the far right are directly or indirectly linked to political parties. In most settings, antifascist activity is partly undertaken by groups directly associated with parties of the Left. In postwar Italy, for example, it was the communists who sought to counter the violent activism of the Movimento Sociale Italiano in the streets (Caciagli 1988). In Britain, the Anti-Nazi League formed to counter the National Front included a considerable number of Labour MPs (Taylor 1982). Despite ties to political parties, though, many of these actors are autonomous enough to merit distinct analytical treatment. Some of the most notable actors against far right parties are anarchist groups that usually dissociate themselves from political parties. Moreover, their resources and tactics sharply differ from those of mainstream political actors and, hence, need to be analyzed separately. Some of the groups are primarily involved in the battle of ideas, countering extremism through intellectual publications, monitoring every move of right-wing extremists and documenting a wide range of far right activities, especially those involving violence. Other groups are primarily involved in either conventional or more contentious street-level action, through disruptive counterdemonstrations that sometimes turn violent. Violent tactics include the destruction of far right party branches or physical attacks against members of far right parties.

Although the analysis of this diverse array of actors, resources and tactics poses significant empirical obstacles, a number of works highlight the analytical utility of unpacking this "black box" of societal impediments to organizational development. Some of the most important insights into the effectiveness of societal responses to extremism come from the individual experiences of far right activists. Interviews with these activists help bring to the surface the range of obstacles they face in their private, professional and political lives. Experiences of social, professional and political stigmatization and marginalization are common among those involved in far right parties and movements (e.g., Milesi et al. 2006; Linden and Klandermans 2006). But their actual effects on activism are not straightforward. According to the one of the most comprehensive studies of far right activists in Europe, "stigmatization may deter people from activism, as suggested by our comparison of the relative strength of extreme right in the five countries, but once they are in it it becomes the cement that holds them together because of the feeling of injustice and discrimination it generates" (Klandermans and Mayer 2006: 273).

A socially hostile environment shapes not only the trajectory of individual activists within a party but also the trajectories of the organizations themselves. Societal impediments to organizational growth include frequent and systematic counter-mobilization against extremist right-wing parties, which complicates their organizational efforts. On some occasions, social reactions to extremism include physical attacks against party offices, the destruction of party material and the violent disruption of party-organized events. Even if far right activists remain committed to the cause, their capacity to engage in organizational activities can be limited in settings where the scale and intensity of societal reactions effectively prohibits public events. In the Netherlands, for example, it is thought that violent antifascist action "makes it difficult for the [extreme right activists] safely now to hold any public meetings" (Husbands 2002: 64). The organizational effects of societal reactions to the far right parties go beyond the ability to exercise the right to assemble. Socially hostile environments affect key organizational functions by influencing the type of activists parties recruit. A very difficult societal environment might take a toll on the organizational development of a far right party, if it discourages more moderate individuals from joining. Moderates are thought to bring into parties politically useful skills that parties can use to enhance their organizational development. "Repressive environments thus 'work' by selecting for the types of activists that undermine radical right party development: they discourage the recruitment of moderates with significant human capital, leaving radical right parties with an extremist or opportunist composition that is politically unsustainable" (Art 2011: 48–49). The basic idea, then, is that social sanctions ultimately affect party organizational development by affecting the quality of activists parties can recruit and keep in their ranks.

The main idea of the few works examining societal reactions to far right parties is that organizational development varies depending on the societal environment. The social context in which far right parties develop is mostly examined at the national level. It is thought that social actors in some countries are less tolerant of the far right than those in other countries. A number of works tend to agree that the Netherlands is one of the least favorable of such environments. Especially in the 1980s, the failure of various far right parties is associated with the activity of Dutch antifascists (Husbands 2002; Linden and Klandermans 2006). There is also considerable evidence suggesting the effect British antifascism has had on the development of far right parties in Britain from the 1970s onwards (e.g., Taylor 1982; Copsey 2011). Similarly, the failure of the German far right is associated with the intensity and scope of antifascism, which, interestingly for our purposes, is less prevalent in the east (Art 2011). And in post-communist Hungary, the Democratic Charter is thought to have been successful in its campaign against the far right (Szôcs 1998). In other national settings, societal reactions to the far right seem to have been less effective or, simply, weaker. Some of the most successful parties, such as the French National Front and the Vlaams Blok, witnessed organizational growth despite societal impediments to their development. There is also evidence that in Austria, Denmark, Italy, Norway and Switzerland far right activists seem to have faced far fewer obstacles than those in the rest of Europe (Art 2011). Overall, then, there are some strong indications that the varied societal responses to the far right have brought about different developmental outcomes.

The examination of societal reactions to extremism opens new venues for the analysis of organizational development. To fully explore these venues, it is necessary to further refine the theoretical and empirical analysis. First, it is important to better incorporate specific characteristics of the far right parties into the investigation of societal reactions to the far right. As discussed in Chapter 2, there are notable differences between radical and extremist right-wing parties. The latter are usually movement parties, which seek to mobilize support through both conventional and unconventional means. Their street-level action, along with their extreme ideology, is more likely to mobilize social actors against them. The very threat these parties pose to the street dominance of some of these otherwise distinct or loosely connected actors is also likely to set the basis for coordination or, even, alliances amongst them. The nature of far right mobilization might also determine the tactics the opposition uses against it. Arguably, the plight of extremist right-wing parties for street-level dominance is more likely to generate violent reactions. Overall, then, societal reactions to far right parties can vary depending on the nature of these parties themselves: the more extreme the parties, the more intense the opposition.

Second, the investigation of societal impediments to organizational development can gain analytical leverage if it takes into account how state responses to extremism shape the behavior of societal actors. One of the difficulties confronting inquiries of societal responses is that they are sometimes endogenous to the institutional environment. In line with literature on repression, it is plausible that there is an interaction between institutional and social hostility (e.g., Earl 2006). Arguably, the capacity of societal actors to curb extremism depends on the degree to which institutional actors allow them a room to maneuver. For instance, Dutch police are thought to have permitted antifascist groups to confront the far right, taking a less protective role toward its demonstrations than British or German police (Husbands 2002: 63–64). In this sense, the impact of antifascism in the Netherlands was probably bigger than elsewhere, not necessarily because antifascism was stronger but because the institutional environment was more conducive to antifascist counter-movements.

Third, the analysis of societal reactions to extremism needs to go below the national level for scholars to better appreciate how local dynamics shape the outcome of confrontations between right-wing extremists and their opponents. Even in those cases of widely spread or institutionally induced social repression, one cannot expect that it is evenly applied across a country. In antifascist strongholds, such as Hamburg or Berlin, one can expect right-wing extremism to face bigger resistance than in most parts of eastern Germany which are either less urban or, more generally, have no antifascist networks or infrastructure. Even in local settings where antifascism is strong, the outcome of confrontations with right-wing extremists cannot be predetermined by the mere presence of the former. These confrontations are dynamic and their outcomes are determined by the organizational resources each side might have at its disposal at a given point in time as well as by the tactical choices they make. The resources and tactics of social actors and their opponents vary considerably within countries, necessitating an approach that goes beyond analyses of societal responses at the national level.

Societal Responses to the GD

Societal opposition to right-wing extremism in Greece has been based on a diverse array of actors, with different resources and a wide range of tactics. Most of the actors originate in various segments of the radical or revolutionary Left as well as in the highly fragmented and disconnected anarchist or autonomist networks. The distinctions between the various groups, networks and organizations comprising the antifascist front are not always easy to identify because there is often a considerable degree of overlap between them. The transformation of the GD into a political party in the early 1990s triggered the mobilization of a number of *actors* against it. One of the organizations that confronted the GD in the 1990s was the Youth against Racism in Europe (YRE), which opened a chapter in Greece in

Societal Responses and Local Organizational Development

1994. YRE institutionalized annual antiracist festivals and camps in the 1990s and it subsequently evolved into the Anti-Nazi Zone – YRE, which specifically targets the "neo-Nazi gang of the GD."[1] The early 1990s also witnessed a number of militant and, at times, violent confrontations between the GD and the Socialist Revolution Organization (OSE, Οργά-νωση Σοσιαλιστική Επανάσταση), which later became the Socialist Workers' Party (SEK, Σοσιαλιστικό Εργατικό Κόμμα). The mosaic of leftist organizations and collectivities that sought to oppose the GD also included the New Left Current (NAR, Νέο Αριστερό Ρεύμα); the Renewing Communist and Ecological Left (AKOA, Ανανεωτική Κομμου-νιστική και Οικολογική Αριστερά); the Consistent Left Movement of Greece (SAKE, Συνεπής Αριστερή Κίνηση Ελλάδας); the Internationalist Workers' Left (DEA, Διεθνιστική Εργατική Αριστερά) and the Movement of Solidarity for Refugees. The various leftist groups opposing the GD would occasionally join forces with trade unions, especially for major mobilizations, such as the one that took place after the 1998 Periandros incident. "The incident led to enormous antifascist mobilization. OSE had a major role here. The trade unions also had a central role against fascism, unions like the Center of Athens Labor Unions and the Federation of Secondary Education State School Teachers, along with antiracists and antifascists."[2] Opposition to the GD was also organized by various anarchist or autonomous groups in major urban centers, like Athens and Thessaloniki. In the next decade, opposition to the GD took the form of the various organizational entities that strived for the representation of the radical and revolutionary Left. Their confrontation with the GD remained part of a broader agenda against neoliberalism, imperialism and war. "Between 2001 until around 2006 there were two committees which took charge of antifascist activity. The first one is the Initiative Genova 2001 and, from 2003, the Alliance for Stopping the War. The two put forth a defensive shield for immigrants who were assaulted by the fascists. The European Social Forum also contributed in this effort."[3]

The end of the 2000s witnessed the appearance of a set of new actors and more systematic attempts to counter the organizational development of the GD. Renewed efforts to oppose the activity of the party largely reflected the facts on the ground. Toward the end of the decade, the GD

---

[1] Takis Giannopoulos, member of Anti-Nazi Zone – YRE, interview with the author, July 2016.
[2] Petros Constantinou, member of Antarsya, municipal councilor of Athens, coordinator of the Movement United Against Racism and the Fascist Threat, interview with the author, July 2016.
[3] Constantinou, ibid.

started undertaking vigilante-type activities in the center of Athens and sought to infiltrate various urban centers through violence-prone, street-level activism. In areas such as Agios Panteleimonas, the forceful presence of the GD and the attacks it prompted against the increasing number of immigrants became the impetus for increased counter-mobilization by various leftist groups, pro-immigrant associations and anarchists. The mobilization against the GD took place amidst a broader wave of protest in Greece, which preceded but was subsequently boosted by reactions to austerity (Andronikidou and Kovras 2012; Rüdig and Karyotis 2014; Lamprianou and Ellinas 2017b). This new wave of protest created the space for the mobilization of existing and new actors against the GD. One of the most important new actors was the Movement United Against Racism and the Fascist Threat (KEERFA, Κίνηση Ενωμένοι Ενάντια στον Ρατσισμό και τη Φασιστική Απειλή). Founded in 2009 by people associated with groups that opposed the GD in the 1990s, such as SEK, KEERFA brought together a wide alliance of trade unionists, leftist activists, immigrant associations, immigrant advocacy groups, human rights organizations and academics. One of its main aims was to take the opposition to racism and fascist at the local level and "get rid of fascists from all neighborhoods."[4] Initially KEERFA concentrated its activity in the broader Attica region but over time it managed to mobilize support across Greece. Another actor that acquired a prominent role during these years was the Anti-Nazi Zone – YRE, which sought to coordinate the dozens of local antifascist initiatives that sprung up in various urban and suburban centers, especially in Athens and Piraeus.[5] The need for coordination was also recognized by various pro-immigrant NGOs, which founded the Racist Violence Reporting Network to facilitate the recording of racist violence by victims who feared deportation in case they reported such incidents to official authorities (see also Chapter 8). In addition to these actors, the renewed street-level mobilization and electoral rise of the GD also witnessed the counter-mobilization of hundreds of anarchist or autonomous groups against it across Greece.

This diverse set of actors opposing the GD had different *resources* at their disposal. First, societal opposition to the GD relied on the involvement of hundreds of volunteers in dozens of networks, organizations, groups and other collectivities who engaged in the various organizational

---

[4] KEERFA, Movement Proclamation, October 24, 2009 [downloaded from https://goo.gl/pNUfzJ].
[5] Officially, this was the Antifascist Coordination of Committees – Initiatives – Collectivities of Athens – Piraeus.

tasks associated with combatting the GD. Their numbers grew considerably in the late 2000s and grew even further after 2012. "In the 1990s antifascism was just an embryo. Very few of us were involved."[6] After 2012, dozens of local antifascist and antiracist organizations sprung up across Greece, providing the human resources necessary for antifascist activity. The degree of fragmentation constituted an organizational impediment for effective collective action. To overcome the problem of fragmentation, KEERFA and the Anti-Nazi Zone sought to provide the necessary coordination among the various societal actors that sought to confront right-wing extremism. Some of the founders of these groups have been involved in various forms of antifascist activity since the 1990s and brought to the broader antifascist movement considerable organizational experience. These are individuals with high levels of ideological and moral engagement with the antifascist cause, whose prior involvement allowed them to quickly capitalize on the opportunity the rise of the GD generated and extend their organizational reach. The peak of their organizational efforts was 2013, especially after the Fyssas murder, when antifascism temporarily acquired a much wider social base. The organizational resources available to the various groups opposing the GD depended on their profile and tactics. More violent actors benefited from the existence of squats, especially those in major urban centers, such as Exarcheia, or major universities, such as those in Athens and Thessaloniki. Squats in Greek universities enjoy a degree of protection from police intervention and provided a relatively safe haven and a certain degree of anonymity for violent confrontations with the GD in neighboring areas. The Technical University of Athens has also helped provide a relatively safe haven for the operation of the Athens Indymedia, which since the early 2000s served as a forum for the exchange of information, ideas and, occasionally, spite among the various groups opposing the GD.

Second, the societal opposition to the GD relied on communicative and intellectual resources. A significant segment of the Greek press amplified the messages of the various groups opposing the GD, published their press releases and mobilization calls and helped spread the way they framed GD-related issues. Moreover, some Greek newspapers systematically reported on the ideological lineage and violent activism of the GD, thereby amplifying its neo-Nazi roots and associating it with criminal activity. One of the most systematic and known opponents of the party was the column *Ios* (Virus), written by an autonomous group of journalists in the subsequently

---

[6] Giannopoulos, ibid.

defunct *Eleftherotypia*. One of the journalists of *Ios*, Dimitris Psarras, is one of the arch-enemies of the GD for his systematic framing of the GD as a neo-Nazi criminal organization and his reporting of crimes committed by its members. Psarras has written the most comprehensive book on the history of the party (2012) and, as a close observer of its trajectory, has become a witness in the GD trial. In more recent years, the systematic reporting of such newspapers as *Efimerida ton Syntakton* has been supplemented by a number of research, documentation and support initiatives and networks. The Racist Violence Recording Network was founded in 2011 by dozens of NGOs seeking to fill the gap in official statistics regarding racist violence (see above). Some of the most important initiatives were undertaken as part of the legal efforts to document the association of the party with criminal activities. Founded in October 2013, JailGoldenDawn is an initiative of the volunteer lawyers assisting the civil action against the GD. It systematically reproduces legal documents related to criminal activities of its members; reports on developments during the criminal trial; and analyzes various developments associated with the party. Golden Dawn Watch is an initiative undertaken and supported by human rights organizations, immigrant associations, antiracist and antifascist groups, citizen networks and journalist unions to monitor all developments associated with the trial. This network of NGOs has reporters following the hundreds of court sessions and trial hours, documenting major developments and interpreting incoming testimonies and facts.[7]

Third, many of these antifascist groups had access to political and institutional authority. Some of the leftist groups and networks that led the street confrontations against the GD were directly or indirectly associated with the Coalition of the Radical Left, Syriza, and its progenitor, the Coalition of Left and Progress. A loose association of many radical and revolutionary leftist factions, Syriza had at the time a small but persistent presence in the Greek parliament (e.g., Vernardakis 2011; Spourdalakis 2013; Tsakatika and Eleftheriou 2013; Katsourides 2016). The involvement of some of the Syriza factions, such as AKOA, and later DEA and Start (Ξεκίνημα), in the mobilization against the GD helped put the issue on the parliamentary agenda. Even during the period when the GD had an insignificant electoral presence, Syriza would occasionally raise the issue of its legality in parliament.[8] Toward the late 2000s, some of the leading

---

[7] Given the international significance of the trial, the group translates the reports into English, as well.
[8] For example, see "Organized attack against the GD," *Golden Dawn* [newspaper], February 20, 1998, p. 3.

members of leftist factions, like those of SEK and NAR, which led the street opposition against the GD, joined a new radical or revolutionary left party, Antarsya (ΑΝΤΑΡΣΥΑ, Anti-capitalist Leftist Cooperation for the Overthrow).[9] KEERFA, which undertook to eradicate fascism from all neighborhoods, was essentially the front movement of Antarsya (Loudos 2014). Founded in 2009, the party remains electorally insignificant, receiving between 0.33 percent and 1.19 percent in the five national elections held between 2009 and 2015. The militant activism of KEERFA, though, helped elect one of its best known activists, Petros Constantinou, to the municipal board of Athens in 2010, the same year Michaloliakos was also elected. The lawyers voluntarily involved in the initiative for the Civil Suit of the Antifascist Movement against the GD also come from KEERFA and Antarsya.

The wide range of actors and resources opposing the GD has generated an equally distinct set of *tactics* ranging from confronting the party in the institutional arena to violent assaults against party members. Those actors who seek to confront the GD in the institutional arena often resort to Greek courts, hoping to harm the party and its leadership through convictions for criminal acts committed by party members. Since the early 1990s, lawyers with ties to the various antifascist groups have taken numerous cases to courts seeking to link the criminal activities of various members with their party affiliation. Using their communicative resources, they have managed to put the GD in the spotlight for these crimes. They have also managed to use these trials as opportunities to mobilize activists who would regularly attend the trial sessions to offer their support, counter the activism of the GD and serve as witnesses for some of the incidents. Not surprisingly, the gathering of activists from both sides during court sessions would often lead to violent confrontations between them (see Chapter 8). The institutional tactic of the antifascist opposition is not accepted by all actors who oppose the GD. Some anarchist groups refuse to take violent assaults by members of the GD before the police or, ultimately, before justice, due to their mistrust of the Greek state.[10] Mistrust of the Greek state is deeply rooted among the societal actors opposing the GD, who blame the police or the courts for excessive tolerance to the behavior of the party. A good example of this mistrust is the civil action

---

[9] In Greek, "antarsia" means revolt.
[10] An interesting contrast is the approach of two well-known anarchist squats, Resalto and Antipnoia. The former chose not to involve the Greek police after an attack on their squat whereas the latter took a similar attack to court and it is now part of the overall case against members of the GD.

brought by antifascist lawyers against the GD. The lawyers who are representing some of the main plaintiffs in the civil action do not hide their deep mistrust of the state prosecution. "The civil action will grant the antifascist movement independent access to court documents, exposure to the wider public of the crimes committed by the gang, examination of witnesses and the accused persons, ultimately, the final conviction of the perpetrators and moral accomplices of the crimes of the Nazi Golden Dawn."[11]

Another tactic of societal actors opposing the GD was the involvement of the widest possible segments of society in their cause to convince power holders to take action against the party and to limit the capacity of the party for organizational development. Since the 1990s some of the groups involved in antifascism organized dozens and, after the 2010s, hundreds of talks, festivals, camps and all sorts of other events seeking to attract broader social support. These activities aimed to bring to the surface the ideological roots of the GD and to highlight its violent activity. They would also serve as a forum discussing the ideological approaches and tactical dilemmas of the various actors. These discussions would often bring to the surface the differences between some orthodox Marxists who see the rise of parties like the GD as an epiphenomenon of deeper structural problems caused by capitalism and some radical or revolutionary leftists who identify the GD as an enemy in itself that requires action against it. The groups seeking to widen the social front against the GD would take this confrontation to the street but, generally, refrain from violent forms of protest. Throughout the 1990s and, subsequently, in the 2010s, the opening of new local branches by the party would set the occasion for protest marches demanding the closure of its offices. Major incidents, such as the 1998 almost deadly attack on leftists, would turn such protest marches into major events, bringing together much wider segments of civil society, such as trade unions. The attempt to expand the social base of the antifascist movement gained momentum after the murder of Fyssas in 2013, which set the stage for massive demonstrations in major urban centers.

A small set of actors is systematically involved not only in attempts to mobilize wider segments of society in antifascism but also in more militant efforts to block the organizational development of the GD. These attempts often bring the participants in direct confrontation with GD activists. They are generally riskier and hence involve smaller and usually younger

---

[11] "Declaration: For the Civil Action of the Antifascist Movement in the Golden Dawn trial," October 24, 2013 [downloaded from https://goo.gl/qrJY7W].

crowds. Militant activism is primarily disruptive. A key mechanism of disruption is the organization of demonstrations in areas where the GD has scheduled events. Due to their militant nature, these demonstrations serve as a deterrent for people to attend the GD events or, more generally, help to cancel the events.

> We managed to cancel two or three speeches of the GD, for which they had made an open call. Whenever they would make an open call for a meeting, we would have a counter-meeting . . . This is the main benefit of the bigger counterdemonstrations. Even if there is a crypto-fascist in neighborhood that would otherwise attend a GD event, when there is a counterdemonstration, he will not. People do not go because they fear the booing from those gathered. It is not that they fear that something will happen to them but that they will be personally hated, at work or elsewhere.[12]

The disruption is caused because the counterdemonstrators might block access to an indoor event or because they will increase the risk of clashes during an outdoor event. As discussed in Chapter 8, the latter might compel the police to cancel the outdoor event or to restrict it so that the GD cannot march or demonstrate anywhere but in the area surrounding its offices. Besides counterdemonstrations, militant activism can also disrupt even routine activities of the party, such as street canvassing. In major urban centers, the view of groups of GD members distributing party material would occasionally cause instant mobilization of antifascist activists seeking to counter their efforts. As mentioned earlier, militant action occasionally takes place even in Greek courts. One of the most notable instances of such action was in November 2016 when a group of antifascists challenged the GD militants attending the trial. "This was the day of their annual commemoration and we sought to break their morale. By entering the court with our fists up, we let them attack us and, in defense, we responded."[13]

A small segment of the societal opposition to the GD resorted to violence. Rejecting non-violent means of protest as ineffective, small anarchist or autonomous groups or terrorist networks undertook dozens of attacks against the party. The rationale behind the embrace of violence as a tactic against right-wing extremism is aptly put by a member of one of the many Leftist militant groups combatting the GD in the streets.

---

[12] Local activist of KEERFA, interviewed by author, Patra, July 2016.
[13] Member of Organization Militant Antifascism (ORMA, Οργάνωση Μαχητικού Αντιφασισμού), Athens, February 2018. ORMA was founded in 2014 to undertake militant action in Athens and Piraeus.

"As Marx said, violence is the midwife of history. Big struggles have been
won through violence . . . In this specific field, the Left has chosen the
peaceful way. 'We will educate people, we will confront their arguments.'
But the peaceful way alone cannot change things."[14] Most of the attacks
against the GD involved physical damages to party offices, sometimes
through explosives. The party newspaper lists dozens of such attacks since
the early 1990s, undertaken usually by anarchist groups and occasionally
by terrorist organizations. One of the most serious of such attacks was
undertaken in 2010 by the "Conspiracy of Fire Nuclei" causing the total
destruction of main headquarters of the party in Athens.[15] Attacks were
also undertaken against hotels or other buildings that would host events of
the GD, as a message to the owners to refrain from doing so. Violent
tactics against the GD would also include assaults against party members
or functionaries. In November 2013, in retaliation to the Fyssas murder, a
newly appearing terrorist organization killed two party members, George
Fountoulis and Manolis Kapelonis, and seriously injured a third one,
Alexander Gerontas. The three were guarding the local party branch in
the northern suburbs of Athens. Moreover, throughout the past years,
there have been dozens of violent encounters between antifascist groups
and GD activists and a number of physical assaults of individual party
members and vice versa. Since the commencement of the GD trial in
2015, there have been a number of such encounters outside – and, in a few
cases – inside the court house among small groups of activists.[16]

The use of violence by some of the groups involved in the antifascist
movement is a constant source of tension and division between them. The
more moderate groups – who engage in what they call "democratic antifascism" – believe that violence undermines their attempts to attract broader
social support for the antifascist cause. By contrast, the more radical ones
believe that violence is the only effective answer to violence. Although both
types of actors agree on the need to deny the GD the role of a legitimate
political actor in the system, they tend to disagree on the way to do it.

> The role of an antifascist organization, which is a minority organization,
> constitutes a major source of division regarding the activity of the various
> actors – how they understand the role of the minority. Some aim to
> mobilize the wider majority of the people who are generally negative against

[14] Ibid.
[15] Yiannis Souliotis, "The 'Nuclei' behind the last three attacks," *Kathimerini*, March 23, 2010
(downloaded from https://goo.gl/7FELgi). "The walls fall, our hearts do not" *Golden Dawn*
[newspaper], March 31, 2010, pp. 1, 9.
[16] The author observed one such encounter during one of the sessions of the trial in September 2016.

fascism. That is, to mobilize the democratic majority of people, who are not necessarily activists, for the antifascist cause. Others aim to clash with the GD in a physical fashion. This is a dividing issue for the antifascist movement.[17]

The violent groups fighting the GD in the streets are usually very small in size but their effects are thought to be wider, in part because their actions deter more people from participating in the movement and because they are thought to legitimate the violent activity of the GD.

> Obviously, we cannot generate a repulsive image of the antifascist movement. Ultimately, [these violent groups] help both the fascists and the police in their own unacceptable acts. These groups are not the entirety of the autonomous space, there are serious collectivities in this space who participate in the Antifascist Coordination of Committees – Initiatives – Collectivities of Athens – Piraeus, work with us and have a very different approach. Those teams which understand the issue as a gang, beating the fascists and nothing else, obviously do not help.[18]

Measuring Antifascist Mobilization

The wide array of actors mobilizing against right-wing extremists, the different resources they have at their disposal and the distinct tactics they employ complicate efforts to systematically record antifascist mobilization. Not surprisingly, references to the effects of such mobilization tend to rely on broad sketches of the social environment rather than on efforts to empirically trace and measure antifascism. To overcome the intrinsic complications of analyzing antifascist activity, this chapter relies on a dataset of activities recorded on the Athens Indymedia. The Greek version of Indymedia was founded in 2001 and belongs to the global network of Independent Media Centers.[19] As a relatively open medium based on user-generated content, Indymedia constitutes a wide-ranging source of information for the thousands of activities organized by the many self-proclaimed antifascist collectivities across both space and time. These collectivities include some of the best known and organized antifascist organizations such as KEERFA; some of the best known anarchist

---

[17] Thanasis Kampagiannis, Lawyer, plaintiff in the Golden Dawn trial and member of the JailGoldenDawn initiative and KEERFA, interview with the author, July 2016.
[18] Giannopoulos, ibid.
[19] The first Independent Media Center was founded in Seattle in 1999 to provide coverage of the protests against the World Trade Organization. In the next decades it became a network of over seventy autonomous media centers across the world.

collectivities such as Resalto; and hundreds of small local collectivities across Greece. Most of these collectivities use their own media (e.g., blogs, websites) to disseminate information about their activity, making it difficult to systematically aggregate the information. The difficulty lies not only in the large number of these collectivities but also in the fluidity and volatility of their existence. Indymedia helps overcome this difficulty by keeping a record of thousands of posts about activities organized or undertaken by antifascists since 2002. Although this is not a record of all events and activities, since some collectivities might choose other means to publicize their activity, it is the most comprehensive source of information on antifascist events and activities. The "radical" and "passionate" posts of Indymedia users might conflict with its aimed "accuracy," often yielding a wide range of recollections of what actually happened.[20] Once used carefully, though, Indymedia reports of antifascist events and activities can offer a rare glimpse of the level of antifascist mobilization across time.

The dataset consists of 2,966 antifascist activities manually coded through the careful reading of the 8,640 posts in the thematic category "antifascism" of Athens Indymedia.[21] Each post has a date of publication and this date was the one included in the analysis. The analysis counts each activity only once, excluding multiple posts on the same event. In other words, this is a count of activities, not posts. The period under study is March 2007, when the GD officially resumed its operations, to September 2016 – the same period used for the analysis of GD activities reported in its newspaper. The analysis of the type of antifascist activities highlights the action repertoire of the hundreds of antifascist groups organizing them. The most common of these activities are organized or spontaneous gatherings of antifascists in various outdoor locations. These activities are organized by antifascists to counter events planned by the GD, commemorate events such as the Fyssas assassination and support their cause during court proceedings. There is a total number of 1,058 activities or 35.7 percent of all activities broadly categorized as gatherings or other outdoor activities (Table 9.1). These activities often lead to direct and, on some occasions, violent encounters with the GD and the police. Another major category in the Indymedia data involves protest marches. Some are major events attracting thousands or hundreds of people but most are minor

---

[20] https://indymedia.org/or/static/about.shtml.
[21] Most of the posts in the thematic category "antifascism" include commentary of current affairs in Greece and abroad as well as ideological and historical analyses, which are not relevant for, and excluded from, this analysis.

Table 9.1 *Antifascist events organized in Greece, 2007–2016 (n = 2966)*

Type of event	Number	% of total
Speech (lecture, discussion; usually held indoors)	107	3.6
Informational activity (street canvassing, leafleting, graffiti)	561	18.9
Protest march	663	22.4
Demonstrations (outdoor gatherings, music festivals, solidarity in courts)	1058	35.7
Blockade	51	1.7
Video projection	100	3.4
Patrol (of squatts, antifa organizational infrastructure)	80	2.7
Organizational meeting (e.g., of Indymedia operators, neighborhood assembly)	229	7.7
Other (athletic and theatrical events, social activism, cleaning graffiti)	117	3.9
Total	**2966**	**100.0**

gatherings of a few dozens. The number of reported protest marches in the dataset totals 663 or 22.4 percent of all activities. The action repertoire of the antifascist groups naturally includes the dissemination of information about the antifascist cause. There is a total of 561 activities or 18.9 percent of the total in the dataset involving the distribution of pamphlets by the various collectivities, the placement of banners and graffiti. Antifascist groups also organized hundreds of other events, such as speeches, book presentations and film screenings, usually propagating the positions of the antifascist movement and mobilizing support for its cause. The dataset also includes many calls made by local antifascist collectivities for gatherings to discuss strategies, tactics and resources.

The analysis of antifascist activities across time reveals interesting patterns that merit more attention. Each month throughout this ten-year period an average of twenty-five activities were reported across Greece – almost one per day. Antifascist mobilization was very low in 2007 and witnessed a spurt after 2008, when a notable confrontation between the GD and antifascists took place in the January Imia commemoration. The vigilantism of the GD in the Agios Panteleimonas area in central Athens helped sustain these levels of mobilization, with short peaks at the beginning of each year due to the Imia event. During this period, antifascist activity did not solely target the GD but also LAOS, the radical right-wing parliamentary party. Antifascist mobilization increased significantly in 2012 and peaked in 2013, with more than fifty activities per month.

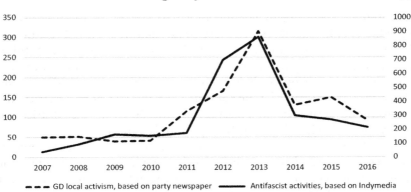

Figure 9.1   Antifascist and GD activities, 2007–2016.

The Fyssas murder provided the impetus for massive antifascist mobilization with 250 activities organized in September 2013 and 158 activities in October. Antifascist mobilization subsequently subsided but remained higher than the pre-2012 levels, peaking in September of each year, primarily because of the activities organized to commemorate the murder.

Figure 9.1 shows the 2,966 antifascist activities reported on Indymedia and 1,249 local GD activities reported in the party newspaper between 2007 and 2016. Although the data comes from two distinct datasets, the graph suggests that antifascist and GD mobilization follow similar patterns. First, both types of mobilization witness a sharp rise in the period 2011 and 2013, with antifascist mobilization tailing GD activism. Second, antifascist and GD activism drop sharply after 2013, following the cyclical patterns documented in social movement studies (Koopmans 2004; della Porta and Diani 2006). It seems that, to the extent that the arrests affected GD activism, there was also a spillover on antifascist mobilization. Third, although antifascist and GD mobilization subsided after 2013, it remained at higher levels than those recorded in the previous decade.

Apart from the development of antifascist mobilization across time, the Indymedia data also allow gauging of the geographical distribution of the antifascist activities. For nearly all activities reported on Indymedia, it was possible to assign a code for the electoral district where they took place, allowing a breakdown of the activities for each of the fifty-six districts. The analysis of this breakdown shows that, with few exceptions, antifascism is more prevalent in the more populous parts of the country. About a third of all activities (35.6% or 1,055 activities) took place in the city of Athens and its suburbs. There is also notable antifascist activity in the first district of Thessaloniki (6.3% or 188 activities) and the second district of Piraeus (4% or 120 activities). The analysis of the geographical distribution of the activities shows there is a positive and strong correlation ($r = 0.68$, $p < 0.001$) between the total count of activities in each district and the size of the district.[22] Once adjusted for the size of the district, the intensity of antifascist mobilization is *also* high in the districts of Rethymno, Chania, Magnesia, Rodopi, Kavala and Achaia.

In addition to providing a comprehensive picture of antifascist mobilization across space and time, Indymedia also allows an exploration into the degree of violence involved in the various encounters between antifascist actors and the GD. Indymedia posts usually describe incidents of violence occurring from either side, as various antifascist actors rush to proclaim victory over their opponents or report the incidents of physical violence used against them by members of the GD. Violent incidents reported by Indymedia range from assaults by or against individual members of the various groups to fatal or serious injuries such as the Fyssas assassination.[23] Although most incidents of violence occur during planned activities of the various groups, some randomly occur on other occasions. The dataset includes 329 incidents of reported antifascist violence against GD premises or people and 263 – mostly different – incidents of violence by people affiliated with the GD against antifascist groups. The number of violent incidents reported on Indymedia suggests that violence is the exception rather than the rule in antifascist mobilization and that most antifascist activities are non-violent. The pattern of violent incidents from and against antifascist groups displays patterns similar to those observed for antifascist and GD mobilization. Mostly subdued in the latter half of the 2000s, violence peaked between 2011 and 2013 and then subsided. Interestingly, here, the drop is much sharper for the GD after the arrests than it was for the antifascists. Antifascist violence remained at relatively high levels for another year before it dropped to lower levels in 2016 (Figure 9.2).

The geographical distribution of antifascist violence is similar to that of antifascist activities. This is not surprising as most violent incidents occur during planned events of either side. Interestingly, violent incidents

---

[22] The size of each district is calculated by the number of seats allocated to each district in the September 2015 national legislative election. For example, Athens B is awarded 44 seats and Athens A 14 seats.

[23] To verify the reliability of the posts containing information about incidents of violence, I randomly checked whether the incidents were also reported in some of Greece's major newspapers. I found confirmatory reports for 82 percent of the sample posts I checked.

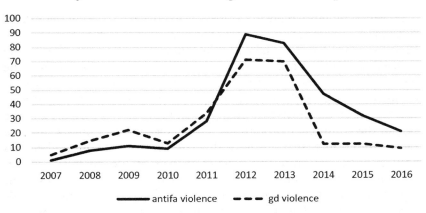

Figure 9.2   Incidents of antifascist and GD violence, 2007–2016.

primarily take place in some of the major Greek cities and in densely populated areas such as Athens A and B. Out of the 329 violent incidents claimed by antifascist groups, more than one hundred occurred in Athens. In Thessaloniki, a total of twenty-one incidents were reported throughout this decade and in Achaia another twenty-three incidents. Antifascist violence is also more frequent in Magnesia (especially in Volos) and in the city of Ioannina. Rethymno and Chania in Crete also have a relatively high frequency of violent incidents. The one feature nearly all these locations share is the presence of a major university and strong anarchist or autonomous associations.

Antifascist Mobilization and Organizational Development

How does antifascist mobilization relate to the local organizational development of extremist right-wing parties? The reports of antifascist activity on Indymedia can help gauge the intensity and consistency of antifascist mobilization, and hence, its association with the local organizational development of the GD. It can be expected that the more intense and consistent the mobilization by antifascist groups, the harder it is for right-wing extremists to develop their organizational presence in local settings. Alternatively, one can hypothesize that antifascist mobilization enhances the organizational development of extremist right-wing parties. The intensity of antifascist activity is calculated by counting all activities reported by all antifascist groups in the decade under study, in each of the forty-five electoral districts where the GD set up organizational structures.

The average intensity score of the forty-five districts is 1.52. In the Athens A district an average of 17.1 activities were organized each quarter, by far a larger number than anywhere else in Greece. In the Kilkis district the average was merely 0.1, as there were only seven antifascist activities in the nearly ten years under study. The consistency of antifascist activity is counted by dividing the number of quarters for which there was at least one activity by the thirty-nine quarters that make up this period. As in the case of the consistency measure for GD branches, this number can take values from 0 to 1. In a district with a consistency score of 0.5 there has been at least one antifascist activity in half of the quarters between 2007 and 2016. Again, the Athens A district is the most consistent, organizing an activity in every one of the thirty-nine quarters of this period. The Thessaloniki A and Athens B districts are also almost perfectly consistent with scores close to 0.9. Kastoria is one of the least consistent districts, organizing antifascist activities in only one out of the 39 districts (0.03).

Since the Indymedia data are at the district level, the local organizational development of the GD is calculated in a similar way as before but at the district level. For each district, there are measures for branch intensity and consistency as well as for branch longevity and continuity. The intensity and consistency scores for GD activism in each district are calculated using the GD newspaper. The branch age and continuity scores are also drawn from the newspaper, which, as discussed in Chapter 5, systematically reports the list of all GD branches. In districts hosting more than one branch of the party, the organizational development of the GD is measured as an average of the scores received by each branch. For example, the Attica district had seven GD branches throughout this period. Whereas Artemida and Aspropyrgos have been intensely and consistently active since their founding, Saronikos and Mandra were considerably less active before they shut down. The intensity and consistency scores of the Attica district are calculated as an average of the respective scores of each branch (0.8 and 0.4, respectively). The age of GD branches in the Attica district is measured as the average of the number of days the seven branches were open (985 days). The discontinuity of GD branches in Attica is measured as a percentage of the number of branches that at some point shut down (57% or 4 out 7 branches).

The analysis of the two datasets shows that antifascist mobilization is positively correlated with local GD activity but does not seem to affect the longevity of local GD structures. Intense antifascist activity across the forty-five districts is positively and strongly correlated with the average intensity of GD branch activism in each district (r = 0.52, p < 0.001). There is a similar association between the consistency of antifascist activism during this decade and the consistency of local GD mobilization in each district (r = 0.48, p < 0.001).[24] These two findings show that, to a considerable extent, antifascist mobilization goes in tandem with local GD activism. The more intense or consistent the mobilization of antifascist groups, the more intense or consistent the local activism displayed by GD branches. By contrast, antifascist mobilization does not seem to have any meaningful effect on the development of local GD structures. The associations between the intensity (r = 0.20) and consistency (r = 0.17) of antifascist mobilization and the longevity of GD branches are weak and not statistically significant. In addition, there is no association between the intensity and consistency of antifascist activities organized in the forty-five districts and the survival rates of the local GD branches. At least at the district level, antifascist mobilization does not seem to have an observable effect on the longevity of local organizational infrastructure.

The Indymedia data also allow the exploration of the association between antifascist violence and the organizational development of the GD. As before, this association is examined for the forty-five districts in which the party set up brick-and-mortar presence by calculating how the intensity and consistency of antifascist violence in each district affects various indicators of party organizational development. Antifascist violence seems to have a similar effect on organizational development as antifascist mobilization. There is a strong, positive and statistically significant association between the intensity of antifascist violence in each district and the average intensity of GD activism (r = 0.50, p < 0.001); and between the consistency of antifascist violence and the average consistency of GD activism (r = 0.54, p < 0.001). As before, the evidence from the two distinct datasets suggests that GD activism is more intense and more consistent where there is intense and consistent violent antifascist mobilization. Again, the two types of mobilization seem to thrive on each other. Violent antifascism, though, does not seem to affect the organizational evolution of local party structures. The correlations between the intensity and consistency of antifascist violence in the forty-five districts and the average life span of party branches are positive but weak and non-significant (r = 0.21, p = 0.21; r = 0.25, p = 0.09, respectively). Similarly, violence is not associated with the survival rate of local party branches.

---

[24] These are Spearman's rank correlations. Pearson correlations are higher than 0.7 and statistically significant, primarily due to the scores of a few districts such as Athens A and Thessaloniki A.

184 Societal Responses and Local Organizational Development

The association between the intensity and consistency of antifascist violence and the average continuity rate of the branches in each district is in the expected direction but weak and not statistically significant ($r = -0.08$, $p = 0.58$; $r = -0.12$, $p = 0.41$). Overall, antifascist violence correlates with local GD mobilization but does not seem to affect subnational GD structures.

The Effects of Societal Opposition to the GD

The probabilistic associations reported above between antifascist mobilization and the organizational development of the GD cannot adequately capture the notable variation in organizational outcomes and the range of processes set in motion by societal hostility to right-wing extremism. Besides these associations, then, it is necessary to delve deeper into particular cases to understand the dynamics and outcomes of societal opposition to extremist right-wing parties. The use of qualitative evidence on the organizational development of individual GD branches will illuminate the processes set in motion in settings with varying degrees of antifascist activity and will allow the identification of various factors affecting the different responses of the party.

The Piraeus Branch

The organizational development of one of the oldest GD branches, in Piraeus, can serve as exemplary case of the association between antifascist efforts to curb right-wing extremism and organizational outcomes. The party set up a branch in this populous port city in early 1996 despite strong societal reactions to its organizational presence. On its inaugural event and in subsequent years, the Piraeus branch became the focus of unprecedented, at the time, antifascist mobilization and it experienced a number of physical assaults.[25] After the GD resumed its official operations in 2007 the branch went through a period of reorganization and by 2009 it emerged as one of the most active branches of the party.[26] The branch started systematically organizing events in various Piraeus neighborhoods and surrounding localities, generating reactions by organized

---

[25] "Incidents at the inauguration of our offices in Piraeus," *Golden Dawn* [newspaper], January 31, 1996, p. 1.

[26] For the reorganization of the party, see "Strong presence in Piraeus," *Golden Dawn* [newspaper], November 25, 2009, p. 3.

leftists, who saw the street presence of the GD as a threat to their organizational dominance and electoral traction in areas such as Perama and Keratsini. The strong and frequent reactions to the presence of the GD in Piraeus, especially in areas where the communists have a relatively strong street presence, encouraged the central party to respond by investing more resources in the area and purposefully seeking to dominate the street in communist strongholds. Under the leadership of Ioannis Lagos the Piraeus branch became a regional stronghold with ties to the branches set up in neighboring areas such as Nikaia, Perama and Salamina. The branch sustained strong organizational ties with the Athens branch, with which it shared organizational resources and militant tactics. Before the arrests of 2013, the street militancy included orderly marches of dozens of Piraeus branch members in military camouflage, army boots and flag-bearing sticks across various neighborhoods as demonstration of street dominance. After the arrests, the remaining branch members dropped the camouflage, boots and sticks but continued leafleting marches in Piraeus and neighboring streets. They also continued their noisy motorcades, "a type of action that helps attract a younger crowd because, by nature, it demonstrates power."[27] During the period under study, the party newspaper published reports for ninety-seven activities of the Piraeus branch. Averaging 2.5 activities every quarter, the branch had a consistency score of 0.8, meaning that it organized at least one activity in 80 percent of the quarters. The arrests took a toll on the branch because a number of its key people were implicated in the crimes listed by Greek authorities as evidence against the party leadership. Apart from the many Nikaia members, the list of defendants also includes some of the top functionaries of the Piraeus and Perama branches. More importantly, the events of September 2013 led to massive mobilization against the party and some of the biggest antifascist demonstrations in Greece. It also led to a number of physical assaults against the branch premises and functionaries. This strong societal pressure, though, did not curb the organizational activity of the Piraeus branch. In fact, Piraeus is one of the few branches with increased intensity and consistency scores after the 2013 events. The mere size of the Piraeus electoral constituency and its centrality to the messages the GD wants to signal through street dominance have helped sustain its levels of activity, even in the face of antifascist pressure.

---

[27] Interview #42, September 2016.

The Kavala Branch

The organizational development of the Kavala branch can also help illustrate the dynamics between GD and antifascist activism. Since its founding in 2012, the local GD branch ranks as one of the most intensely and consistently active. Based on the Indymedia data, the district of Kavala is also a hub of notable antifascist activity. Under the leadership of Dimitris Voyiatzis, the local GD branch has been regularly organizing lectures and leafleting. Perhaps due to the small size of this city of sixty thousand inhabitants – which compromises the anonymity enjoyed by militant activists in large urban centers – violent confrontations between GD and antifascists are relatively rare. But antifascist activity is relatively high and involves protests, marches and demonstrations from small anarchist or autonomous groups as well as from a relatively small group of KEERFA activists. Antifascist groups in the town benefit from the existence of squats – some of the oldest in Greece – utilized to bring the various antifascist groups together and organize action against the GD and other far right groups in the city. Antifascist pressure partly explains why much of the outdoor activity of the local branch takes place outside the city center, in surrounding villages where antifascism is very weak or non-existent. Even in these settings, the outdoor party activism undertaken by the small network of ten to fifteen GD loyalists is not publicized *a priori* to avoid antifascist protests. Rather than being deterred by antifascism, local party functionaries tend to use it as a tool to mobilize their own loyalists for action. Local party functionaries are convinced that high levels of activism are necessary to signal to their opponents that they are not yielding to pressure:

> It is a matter of strategy. An important part of what we do is propaganda. It is important for the enemy to know that something is going on in the local branch; that you are doing things. When you organize an event and outsiders see people coming to the office, they know that you are there and that you are strong. Some local branches that did not organize events displayed weakness. This encouraged assaults against them and eventually the branches shut down. It is important for the enemy to know that you are strong.[28]

The difficult environment faced by the Kavala branch not only enhanced its capacity to mobilize its loyalists but also helped local functionaries

---

[28] Interview #31, member of local branch council, August 2016.

convince the national party to allocate more resources to the local branch. In the past years, the central leadership of the party in Thessaloniki invested considerable human and financial resources to support the activities of the branch and to help it sustain its mobilization potential.[29] As in the case of the Northern Suburbs, analyzed below, environmental difficulties helped the local branch extract more resources from the central party to confront them.

The Northern Suburbs Branch

The branch in the Northern Suburbs of Athens constitutes an illustration not only of the link between GD and antifascist mobilization but also of the association between violence and organizational outcomes. The branch was established in late 2012 as part of the rapid organizational expansion of the party in local communities. The branch organized forty-five activities throughout the period under study, averaging 2.8 activities per quarter – the highest intensity score after the Athens and Thessaloniki branches. The forty-five activities have been organized with remarkable consistency, at least one in every quarter – the highest consistency score a branch can receive. In November 2013, two of its members were killed and a third was seriously injured by a terrorist group while guarding the branch. The branch and some of its key members were subsequently assaulted in a number of occasions, mostly by people protesting its presence in the northern Athenian suburbs. Based on GD newspaper reports, the branch witnessed the highest number of assaults by opponents, after those of Athens and Thessaloniki.[30] Despite this very hostile environment, the branch managed to sustain very high levels of political activity – in fact, improving the intensity and sustaining the consistency of its political activism after the November 2013 events. As in the case of Piraeus, the branch became emblematic for the purported resilience of the GD to violent attacks against it. Given its importance for the overall image of the party, the central party leadership sought to sustain its local presence by sending its top functionaries to give lectures and encouraging activists from neighboring branches to participate in party events. In this sense, the use of violence had the opposite effect: instead of undermining the local presence of the party in the northern suburbs of Athens, it encouraged the

---

[29] Interview #29, member of political council, August 2016.
[30] Apart from the deadly attack on November 1, 2013, the party newspaper reports four additional assaults on the branch itself and against branch functionaries.

national party to divert organizational resources to the local branch to deflect antifascist pressure and sustain its presence.

The Patra Branch

Despite the positive and strong association between GD and antifascist activism, there are a number of local organizational outcomes that significantly deviate from this pattern and are worth analyzing in some detail. The branch life of Patra contrasts with the organizational development of the branches described above. Located in third biggest city and in one of the most notable antifascist – and, more broadly, leftist – strongholds, the branch had trouble sustaining high levels of mobilization and witnessed several instances of discontinuity. The Patra branch shut down shortly after it was opened and then a new attempt to set up a branch came to fruition after a long period of discontinuity, in late 2015, before the branch shut down again in 2017. The organizational discontinuity of the local branch occurred amidst significant and violent resistance to its presence. The troubled organizational trajectory of the local branch contrasts with its relatively long history. The Patra branch was one of the first the party set up in the early 1990s, relying on a local group of activists who are still active in the party. Based on the listing of party branches by the party newspaper, the Patra branch was active until August 1999.

> We set up an office in 1992, one of the first local party branches. It was just about fifteen of us back then, mostly university students. We would give out leaflets, organize ideological and historical speeches, post pamphlets, etc. Back then there were no anarchists, just the Communist Youth of Greece. This started changing towards the late 1990s. The role of the local university is important here. It provides an asylum for anarchists. The branch closed down in the following years due to lack of funds.[31]

The Patra cell became active again towards the late 2000s as it sought to capitalize on the influx of immigrants in the city port. Party activists started taking part in various events organized against the presence of immigrants in various city squats and, on some occasions, they were implicated in violent clashes with immigrants, leftists or anarchists.[32]

---

[31] Interview #22, July 2016.
[32] "Gathering against illegal immigrants in Patra with participation of the Golden Dawn," *Golden Dawn* [newspaper], issue 727, June 15, 2011, p. 9; "New mud attack from Patra," *Golden Dawn* [newspaper], issue 656, December 10, 2008, p. 13; "Serious incidents again in Patra with Afghans," *Golden Dawn* [newspaper], issue 663, March 18, 2009, p. 6.

Their activity helped bring together a number of antifascists to establish a local cell of KEERFA and to start taking militant action against the GD. When they set up their local office in March 2012 it was quickly destroyed by violent antifascists and the branch had to move to a new office, which they also subsequently abandoned.

> For some time after 2012 we had no office. No one would lent office space because they were afraid it would have the fate of the previous one, it would be burned. There were also reactions from neighboring shops and businesses. There was a climate of terror among people about the presence of our party. We eventually moved into the political office of [former GD MP] Michael Arvanites, on the second floor.[33]

Societal reactions to the GD in settings such as Patra not only brought about organizational discontinuity but also affected the type of organizational activity the local branch was able to undertake. Operating in a hostile social environment, local activists restricted themselves to indoor events, mostly speeches to a limited number of activists held in the branch office. In a setting like Patra, outdoor activism was much rarer than the indoor branch activity. It would primarily involve disseminating pamphlets in areas outside the city center and, preferably, at a time when antifascist activists would be caught off guard. As one of the more seasoned local activists recalls: "The other day we threw five thousand pamphlets for Cyprus, using our cars. We went really early in the morning. We had to be careful to throw the pamphlets after the garbage collection tracks."[34] Whereas local GD activists strongly believe that they do the best they can in a socially hostile environment, their opponents attribute their organizational troubles to antifascist activity:

> The closure of their offices in Patra was due to the fact that they could not go out to give out their pamphlets, they could not distribute food, they could not undertake much outdoor activity. Then they opened an office again. They have to shut it down! As a matter of fact, though, their activities are non-existent. Whatever they do, it is outside the city center. They throw a large number of pamphlets, they do it at night, in haste. They throw their pamphlets at 4 or 5 in the morning.[35]

Antifascist activity complicated the organizational development of the GD in Patra but antifascism did not occur in an institutional vacuum. Antifascist groups operated in an institutional environment that was

---

[33] Interview #23, July 2016. [34] Interview #22, July 2016.
[35] Interview with Patra antifascist, July 2016.

particularly sympathetic to their cause. As discussed in the previous chapter, the communist mayor of Patra went out of his way to avoid giving the GD any public resources, including the space authorities are obliged to provide for the campaign activities of all political parties. The combination and social and institutional pressure might explain why the organizational development of the GD in Patra defied the broader pattern described above.

The Case of Ioannina

Antifascist activity not only affects the development of the GD in settings where it has established brick-and-mortar presence but also is related to the failure of the party to set up branches in other districts. Whereas the GD managed to set foot in most major cities and municipalities in Greece, in a number of local settings the third biggest Greek party is strikingly absent. The most notable absence is from one of the most populous cities of Greece, Ioannina. Located in the northwestern region of Epirus, Ioannina hosted a number of activists with a strong interest in securing the rights of Greek-speaking populations in parts of southern Albania. In the 2000s, some of these activists sought to establish a local cell to propagate nationalist ideas, demanding that northern Epirus (southern Albania) is Greek. Their first activities are recorded in the party newspaper as early as 2004.[36]

> I am in the GD from 2004 until today. Back then, I stayed in the city of Ioannina and, along with others, I started to propagate nationalist ideas and sought to establish a local branch. We started with about fifteen people. Our first activity was throwing leaflets stating that "northern Epirus is Greek" in the night before the parade of 28 October. In 2007, we organized a march for the autonomy of northern Epirus, always facing significant pressure from various leftists.[37]

The attempt to reach local society intensified in the subsequent years. Local organizational efforts reached their highest level in 2009, when the few dozen activists sought to organize a major event for northern Epirus.[38] Joined by the daughter of the party leader, Ourania Michaloliakou, who attended the local university, the activists "sought to take over the main

[36] "Continuous nationalist activity in Ioannina," *Golden Dawn* [newspaper], issue 543, November 4, 2004, p. 2.
[37] Interview #37 with two former Ioannina activists, September 2016.
[38] "Ioannina: Anarchists assault nationalists," *Golden Dawn* [newspaper], issue 663, March 18, 2009, p. 11.

square, in the heart of the city."³⁹ GD activists were met with fierce and violent resistance from a various antifascist groups. After nearly two hours of fighting in the city center, the activists were joined by reinforcements from Thessaloniki who helped end the skirmish with only minor injuries for the two sides. Although the GD activists claimed to have won the day, their organizational attempt to set up a branch did not materialize. Life in Ioannina became unbearable for most activists who eventually either stopped being active or simply left the city.

> The antifascists knew the GD activists and started targeting them at a personal level. The students left the city and [the leader of the cell, anonymized] left the city for this reason. He could not get around. Wherever he would go, at home, in his work, on the street, in the university, he would face a lot of pressure. A number of activists were beaten up at least once, sometimes more. The cell leader had to flee one night when sixty or seventy people went into the university and started looking for him. Eventually, the party gave up its effort to set up a local branch. The chief did not want the city to turn into battlefield.⁴⁰

Even in 2012, when the national party started gaining electoral traction and legitimacy, the GD found considerable resistance in Ioannina. This resistance did not stop with the party activists but, more broadly, it spread to anyone who sought to legitimize the presence of the GD in the city. For example, in April 2012, a television host who dared to allow a party spokesperson to make an audio statement for a story related to the party was subsequently showered with yogurt by a group of anarchists who entered the studio during his news broadcast. Overall, the societal reaction to the GD prevented the establishment of a local branch in one of the most populous Greek cities. Despite persistent attempts to set foot in Ioannina, GD activists met so much social resistance that they eventually deserted their local organizational efforts.

Conclusion

This chapter traced societal reactions to the GD and examined the effects of societal pressure on its local organizational development. Using a diverse array of qualitative and quantitative evidence, the chapter has analyzed the various antifascist actors, resources and tactics involved in the struggle to prevent right-wing extremists from growing roots in local societies and gauged how antifascist mobilization affected the evolution of local party

---

³⁹ Ibid. ⁴⁰ Interview #33, member of central committee, August 2016.

units. The increased local mobilization of the GD in the late 2000s and early 2010s brought to the surface hundreds of distinct actors opposing it – from parliamentary political parties to anarchist groups. Apart from the human resources at their disposal, these actors utilized their communicative capacity, intellectual means and spatial assets to counter the electoral ascendance and, more importantly, the local expansion of the GD. Their tactics ranged from countering the GD through institutional means (e.g., in courts) to criminal violence. The most common and widely used tactic against the GD was the mobilization of as many people as possible to confront the party in the streets.

Using thousands of Indymedia posts, the analysis here sketched geographical and temporal variation in antifascist mobilization and compared it with the mobilization of the GD. Antifascism is an urban phenomenon concentrated primarily in Athens and a few other, albeit not all, major cities. It seems to thrive in settings close to Greek universities, which provide a considerable range of resources to antifascist groups including spatial assets and protection from police intervention. Antifascist mobilization started growing in the late 2000s, when the GD started its vigilante activism in Athens. It witnessed a multi-fold increase in 2012 and 2013, after electoral ascendance of the party and its subsequent rapid local expansion. Antifascist activism dropped sharply afterwards but stayed at higher levels than in the late 2000s. Comparing GD activism with antifascist mobilization has shown a strong association between the two. The spikes and drops in antifascist mobilization mirror those of GD activism. Similarly, antifascist violence displays similar temporal patterns with GD violence.

The close association between GD and antifascist mobilization can also be observed at the local level. Combining two distinct datasets for antifascist and GD activism reveals a strong association between antifascist and GD mobilization. Intense and consistent antifascist activity is positively correlated with intense and consistent GD activism. In other words, right-wing extremism and antifascism seem to unharmoniously co-exist.

Despite the strong probabilistic association between antifascist and extremist right-wing mobilization, the causal story is a lot more complicated. As the brief micro-cases presented in this chapter suggested, in a number of settings, such as Piraeus, Kavala and the Northern Suburbs, antifascist mobilization has seriously complicated but it has not shortened or discontinued local party life. In other important settings, such as Patra and Ioannina, antifascist mobilization dealt a major or fatal blow to efforts to grow roots in local societies. Although cursory, the analysis of party life in branches confronting notable antifascist pressure has outlined some plausible explanations for these divergent organizational outcomes. In part, the reasons for the endurance or failure of local branches are endogenous: local party success relates to the capacity of local militants to extract resources from the central party to confront the local pressure. Notable exceptions to this pattern can be observed where local antifascists have broader institutional or social support or in settings where they established a stronghold long before right-wing extremists formed the organizational infrastructure to combat them. In such settings, the GD shut down its local branches or, aware of the environmental difficulties, it deserted efforts to set up a brick-and-mortar presence.

CHAPTER 10

The Local Development of Extremist Right-Wing Parties in Germany and Slovakia

This chapter seeks to probe the generalizability of the findings outside the Greek context by examining the organizational development of extremist right-wing parties in Germany and Slovakia. Utilizing the analytical framework developed and tested in the previous chapters, this chapter investigates the process of organizational development of two relatively similar parties in two distinct settings. As Chapter 2 shows, the German National Democratic Party of Germany (*Nationaldemokratische Partei Deutschlands*, NPD) and the Kotleba – People's Party Our Slovakia (*Ľudová strana – Naše Slovensko*, LSNS) belong to the category of extremist right-wing parties because, like the Greek GD, they share a racial or biological conception of nationalism; they have extra-parliamentary and extremist origins; they share international links; and they are known for their street-level activism. The postwar and postcommunist contexts in which the NPD and the LSNS have developed are different from the postauthoritarian setting in which the GD evolved. The three countries have different political, electoral and party systems and the three extremist right-wing parties face a different set of sociopolitical and socioeconomic conditions.

The main purpose of this chapter is to show that, despite these notable contextual differences, the organizational development of the NPD and LSNS is affected by endogenous and environmental factors similar to those analyzed in Greece. The first section of the chapter briefly describes the basic characteristics of the two parties, highlighting their similarities to and differences from the GD. The second section utilizes interviews with the party leadership, organizational data from official and party documents, and the secondary literature to sketch the organizational development of the German and Slovak parties. In line with the emphasis on subnational patterns of organizational development, most of the field work on the NPD was done in its regional stronghold in Saxony and on the LSNS in Prešov. The section examines in turn the endogenous, electoral, institutional and societal factors affecting the development of the two parties.

The NPD and LSNS in the Universe of Far Right Parties

Like the GD, the NPD and the LSNS are among the most extreme parties in Europe. The NPD was founded in 1964 and it is one of the oldest far right parties. It had notable electoral success in state parliaments in the 1960s but narrowly failed to win national parliamentary representation in 1969 (Nagle 1970; Stöss 1991). The party stayed on the margins of electoral competition for decades (Kitschelt and McGann 1995: 209–211), even in the late 1980s and 1990s, when other far right parties, such as the Republikaner and the German People's Party (*Deutsche Volksunion*, DVU), managed to stage breakthroughs in a number of state parliaments (Backes and Mudde 2000). After a failed attempt to ban it between 2001 and 2003, the party witnessed electoral breakthroughs in two state parliaments in the 2000s, most notably in Saxony where it received 9.2 percent in 2004 and 5.6 percent in 2009 (Art 2004; Backes 2006). Following the initiation of a new attempt to ban it in 2012 and its narrow failure to stay in the Saxon parliament in 2014, the party received a mere 0.4 percent of the vote in the 2017 federal election, compared to 1.3 percent in 2013. Electorally insignificant across Germany, the NPD performs much better in eastern than in western Germany (Decker and Miliopoulos 2009), despite the squeeze of its already small electoral base by the Alternative for Germany (*Alternative für Deutschland*, AfD). In Saxony alone the NPD has 68 seats in local councils out of the more than 300 it has in the entire country.[1]

The LSNS has a much more recent history than the NPD and the GD. It was founded in 2010 by people previously involved in Slovak Togetherness, a party banned by the Slovak Supreme Court in 2006 because of its extremist rhetoric and anti-democratic program. As the name of the party suggests, the leading figure of the party is Marian Kotleba, the leader of Slovak Togetherness and a key figure in nationalist Slovak politics since the early 2000s. The party received 1.3 percent of the vote in the 2010, and 1.6 percent in the 2012 national legislative election, missing the 5 percent threshold for parliamentary representation. As is often the case with far right parties (Kitschelt and McGann 1995; Dinas et al. 2013), the major breakthrough for LSNS came in the regional elections of 2013. Kotleba received 21.3 percent in the Banská Bystrica

---

[1] Interview with Jens Baur (Regional chair, Saxony) and Peter Schreiber (member of party board), Saxony, October 2017. See also "Karlsruhe prüft Kriterien für mögliches NPD-Verbot," *Spiegel*, March 2, 2016, https://goo.gl/z4dJMX.

region, which was enough for him to advance to the second round and become the regional governor. The electoral breakthrough in this secondary election became the impetus for a national breakthrough in the 2016 legislative election. The party received 8 percent of the vote and elected 14 representatives in the 150-member parliament. In the 2017 regional elections Kotleba lost the governorship but by that time the party had managed to establish a local presence in most Slovak districts. In May 2017 the prosecutor general asked the Constitutional Court to ban the party.

In terms of ideology, the NPD and LSNS have consistently adopted a biological form of nationalism reminiscent of the National Socialist emphasis on race. Due to the restrictive environment for extremist right-wing parties, which are systematically monitored by the German Ministry of Interior, the NPD avoids direct biological references (Art 2011: 191) but emphasizes the importance of the people's community (*Volksgemeinschaft*) – a concept also emphasized by the Nazis (Welch 2004; Rensmann 2006: 71).[2] According to the NPD, personal freedom is derived and guaranteed in the *Volksgemeinschaft*, which should therefore be protected from immigration and immigrants. Like most far right parties, then, the NPD calls for an end to the "foreign infiltration" of Germany, which undermines German identity. It states that "Germany belongs to the Germans" and advocates the return of foreigners to their countries of origin (NPD 2013: 8). In the past decades, the party has also incorporated a number of social themes in its program, especially after attempts of the Social Democratic government in the 2000s to introduce reforms to the social welfare system (Art 2011).

Operating in a less restrictive environment, the LSNS makes direct references to racial inequality. As in many eastern European countries, identity politics in Slovakia revolves around the presence of minorities, especially the Roma, who officially make up only 2 percent of the population. The LSNS seeks to capitalize on negative public sentiments toward the Roma by linking their predicament with failed government policies, especially those of the Left (Bustikova 2014). In its 2016 program, the party repeatedly refers to the Roma as "parasites," condemning the government for failing to act against "the terror of the gypsies." The party

---

[2] Interestingly, the program published by the NPD in Greek for the European elections makes more direct references to the biological conception of nationalism the party adopts than the program in German. For example, it states that "as nationalists we feel we are responsible for sustaining and continuing our state and racial existence against various threats" (NPD 2014b, p. 13). It also warns against the "racial death" of Europe in 20–50 years.

seeks to eliminate the injustice against "decent people" who work all their lives but have lower income "than the gypsy thief who never works." Known for its militant marches and street activism, Kotleba aspires to establish domestic militia to enforce the law in Roma "colonies" and introduce tougher punishment for "politicians and parasites" alike (LSNS 2016).

One of the main characteristics that sets extremist and radical right-wing parties apart is their association with the past. Extremist right-wing parties are rooted in past conflicts, usually side with the losers of these conflicts and advocate for the ancien régime. Like most extremist right-wing parties, then, and unlike the Alternative for Germany, the NPD is rooted in Germany's Nazi past. A few years after its founding, twelve out of eighteen members of the federal NPD board were former members of the NSDAP. Moreover, a significant segment of its membership base and an even larger portion of its functionaries were former members of the Nazi party or one of its successor organizations (Gnad 2005: 669–670). Although time has limited the direct association of the party with the Nazis, the party continues to signal this association by the way it chooses to commemorate the past (Art 2005). The NPD organizes a relatively large gathering of its members to commemorate the bombing of Dresden by the allies and has been at the forefront of street protests contesting the commemoration of *Wehrmacht* crimes.

The LSNS is also associated with the Slovakia's Nazi past. Although the party was founded in 2010, it seeks to associate itself with the legacy of the First Slovak Republic, which collaborated with Hitler between 1939 and 1945. The first independent Slovak state was headed by Josef Tiso, a Catholic priest who was executed in 1947 for treason. Modern historiographers blame Tiso for the deportation and execution of the Jewish population of Slovakia by the Nazis. In its pamphlets, the party generously gives Tiso the title of a national hero and pledges to continue his legacy. He is systematically commemorated in various events organized by the party and praised for his contribution to founding an independent Slovak state based on Christian values. While heading Slovak Togetherness, Kotleba would clearly signal his association with the legacy of the wartime Slovak state by wearing a uniform that resembled that of the paramilitary Hlinka Guard during commemorations of Tiso. The Guard was known for dominating the Slovak street, terrorizing political opponents and targeting the Jews (Jelinek 1971).

The international links of extremist right-wing parties are also important to better appreciate their differences with radical right-wing parties.

The two subcategories of far right parties have distinct associations with parties in other countries. The NPD has been at the forefront of attempts to create a European association of far right parties separate from that created by radical right-wing parties in the European Parliament (Chapter 2). In February 2015, extremist right-wing parties formed the Alliance for Peace and Freedom (APF) as a European party that stands for a confederate Europe of sovereign nations. Since the founding of the APF, NPD functionaries, such as its former chairman and member of European Parliament Udo Voigt and its former board member Jens Pühse, have been actively trying to establish international links among the various extremist right-wing parties. Pühse has been trying to bring together European far rightists since the 1990s and throughout most of this time he has established firm connections with many far right groups across Europe, including the GD. In recent years, NPD functionaries have been utilizing the organizational experience of the NPD to put together a number of international events and gatherings. The initial members of the APF included the GD as well as the Italian Forza Nuova, the Czech Workers' Party and the Spanish National Democracy. In 2016, Kotleba People's Party – Our Slovakia joined the APF but, by that time, the GD dropped out.

One of the most notable characteristics of extremist right-wing parties is the way they practice politics. As Chapter 2 suggests, their political praxis is what makes them movement parties, mostly known for their contentious, disruptive and violence-prone forms of political activity rather than for their involvement in the institutional arenas of politics. The NPD is probably the best example of this dual track of politics. The party strategically focuses on dominating in the streets (Art 2011) and systematically organizes various forms of contentious actions such as street marches, demonstrations and provocations. The movement-type activity of the party, analyzed in the next section, often leads to violent encounters with antifascist protestors, which reinforce the image of a violence-prone party that is more active in the streets than involved in conventional politics.

The LSNS also relies on the street presence of its local activists to infiltrate local societies and make its positions known. Its repertoire of local activism, also analyzed in the next section, includes conventional forms of party activity, such as speeches and leafleting, but it also involves more contentious activities, such as protest marches and petition drives. Like the GD, the LSNS seeks to legitimize itself in local communities by publicizing social types of activism, such as financial handouts to individuals or families. Since 2016 the party has gained international spotlights by systematically organizing train patrols targeting Roma passengers. Even after a law passed in late 2016 to stop these vigilante-type activities, the LSNS continued to organize such patrols.

The Organizational Development of the Far Right in Germany and Slovakia

The organizational structures of the NPD and LSNS display notable similarities to that of the GD, especially in the emphasis they place on establishing and maintaining local branches. But the three parties also display differences in how they are set up, in part because of the different ways in which the three states are administratively organized and in part because of the different institutional environments the parties confront. The NPD has the more elaborate organizational structure due to the size and federal structure of Germany but also due to strict regulation of parties and the systematic monitoring of extremism. The highest organ of the party is the party congress, which meets every other year to choose the nineteen elected members of the party board (*Parteivorstand*). The everyday organizational and operational matters are undertaken by the presidium (*Parteipräsidium*), which includes the party chairman and other members of the board. The party has sixteen state associations (*Landesverbände*) for each German state, with their own congresses and boards. The party statutes also provide for regional associations (*Bezirksverbände*), which are supposed to be formed within states but tend to be much rarer (e.g., in Bayern).

The smallest financially autonomous units of the party are the district associations (*Kreisverbände*), which are supposed to represent the NPD in one or more of Germany's 402 rural and urban districts. District associations have at least seven members but the numbers vary considerably. According to the NPD, some of its largest district associations, with more than sixty members, include München (Bavaria), Nürnberg-Fürth (Bavaria), Neu-Ulm (Bavaria), Havel-Nuthe (Brandenburg), Oberhavel (Brandenburg), Ostvorpommern (Mecklenburg-Vorpommern), Westmecklenburg (Mecklenburg-Vorpommern) and Sächsische Schweiz/Ostergebirge (Saxony). Whereas in the GD the councils of these local branches are appointed, in the NPD they are elected by the members of each district association. The assemblies of district associations also elect the delegates sent to the federal party congress. District associations with seven to thirty members send one delegate and for every thirtieth additional member, they can send a second delegate.[3] The district associations of the NPD have an important role in the overall organizational workings of the party. They can file proposals to the party congress and nominate people for the various party positions.

The district associations are at the forefront of party efforts to infiltrate local communities. Like the GD, the NPD lacks organizational presence in the entire country. The density of NPD district branches varies considerably across Germany. The NPD has presence in 32 percent of the districts in the eleven western states and in 70 percent of the districts in the five eastern states.[4] Figure 10.1 highlights the higher density of NPD district associations in the eastern states. A similar picture emerges from the analysis of the membership figures reported by the sixteen *Bundesverfassungsschutz* (BfV) offices. Overall, in 2018 the NPD had about 4,500 members in all sixteen German states. About a third of these members are in the five eastern states, almost twice as many one would expect based on population size. At the thirty-sixth party congress in Saarbrücken in March 2017, the NPD claimed to have 155 district associations entitled to send 219 delegates.[5] Unlike the GD, which prides itself for its brick-and-mortar branches in city squares and major avenues, the NPD does not have many offices. The few NPD offices are usually outside major urban centers, in smaller towns such as Köpenick (Berlin), where the party has its headquarters, or in Riesa (Saxony), where the publishing company affiliated with the NPD, the *Deutsche Stimme Verlag*, is based.[6] The regular newspaper listings in the monthly party mouthpiece Deutsche Stimme provide some insights into the internal workings of these district associations. Life in these district associations involves periodical meetings – usually once or twice a month – in a pub or a room in a larger facility to discuss current affairs, organizational issues and upcoming activities.

As in the case of the GD, the analysis of the activities undertaken by NPD district associations provides rare insights into the internal life of the party. In Germany, these activities are meticulously monitored by German intelligence authorities and, in some regions, thoroughly reported to

[3] The information is based on responses to a questionnaire sent to the Press Office of the NPD, July 2016. According to the party statutes, district associations might choose to establish smaller local units (*Ortsbereiche*). These are rarer and lack financial autonomy.

[4] Figures based on the analysis of online listings of district branches by the sixteen state associations of the NPD in 2017.

[5] Satzung der Nationaldemokratische Partei Deutschelands, Berlin, 2015. Information about the voting rights of district associations and the proceedings of the 2017 congress is also based on written responses to questions sent by the author to the press department of the NPD.

[6] Although Riesa is thought to be one of the main strongholds of the party, the NPD office is located in an industrial center in a remote part of the city.

Figure 10.1   NPD district associations in Germany, 2017.

parliament. The analysis of 1,440 activities reported to the Saxon parliament between 2000 and 2016 provides a rare glimpse of what some of the best-organized district associations of the NPD do.[7] The internal life of

[7] Given the special weight Saxony has in the overall workings of the party, with a relatively high concentration of district associations, the presence of *Deutsche Stimme Verlag* and nearly a quarter of

Table 10.1 *Activities Organized by the NPD in Saxony, 2000–2016*

Type	Number	% of total
Speech/lecture/meeting	309	21.46
Demonstration/protest/march	414	28.75
Canvassing/information stands	380	26.39
Commemorations	124	8.61
Organizational meetings	82	5.69
Other	66	4.58
Festivals	40	2.78
Social activism/community work	4	0.28
Founding of new district branch	21	1.46
Total	**1440**	**100**

district associations revolves around the organization of lectures, speeches and informational gatherings. The Saxon BfV reported to the state parliament 309 such activities between 2000 and 2016, or 21.5 percent of the total (Table 10.1). The most frequent type of party activity undertaken by NPD district associations takes place in Saxon streets. The action repertoire of local party members involves the organization of or participation in demonstrations, protests, marches, blockades, provocations and signature drives. The number of participants in these events varies substantially from a few dozens to hundreds, and, on rarer occasions, thousands. The few hundred NPD members in Saxony put together 414 protest activities throughout this period or 28.8 percent of the total. Another set of activities involves the distribution of party leaflets and information by party activists. As in the case of the GD, NPD canvassing usually involves a small number of activists distributing party material to particular localities. The hundreds of pages of official filings to the Saxon parliament include 380 canvassing and informational activities between 2000 and 2016 or 26.4 percent of the total. Local NPD activism also involves the organization of various commemorative gatherings, marches or events. For example, the NPD commemorates the bombing of Dresden every February and *Volkstrauentag* every November. Most of these events usually bring together a few dozen activists and on some occasions a few hundreds. The BfV reported 124 commemorative events or 8.4 percent of the 1,440 events reported during this period. Although in the 2000s the NPD sought

all its elected officials in local councils, the internal workings of its district associations are key to understanding the local development of the NPD.

to legitimate itself in local communities through social activism, the BfV reports only record a handful of such activities, like garbage collection.

The formal structures of the LSNS are less elaborate than those of the NPD in part due to differences in the administrative division of the country and the degree of party regulation. The party statutes are only a few pages long, missing key details on the specific role of major party organs in the overall workings of the party. Based on these statutes, the supreme party organ is the party congress, which regularly meets every four years to elect the president, secretary and three vice presidents of the LSNS and determine its overall strategic direction. The party executive includes these five officials as well as the eight heads of the regional organizations of the LSNS – appointed by the five-member executive. All members of the party executive – the president, Marian Kotleba, the party secretary, Ratislav Schlosár, and three vice presidents, Martin Beluský, Ján Mora and Milan Uhrík – and four of the regional chairs were also elected in the national parliament in 2016. The regional organizations of the LSNS correspond to the administrative division of Slovakia into eight regions. Their work in local communities is achieved through the establishment of district organizations in major localities. Whereas the NPD grants a formal role to the district party associations in the party structure and statutes, the LSNS does not. Moreover, neither the regional nor the district associations have financial autonomy, which is centrally managed by the executive.[8] Overall, then, the formal party institutions point to a highly centralized party, which is managed from the very top, despite the presence of notable regional and local structures.

Although the LSNS grants no formal role to its district associations, they are at the heart of party efforts to grow roots in local communities. Party executives stress the importance of subnational units for spreading the message of the party to Slovak districts by undertaking conventional and contentious forms of local activism. Whereas most new Slovak parties lack elaborate territorial structures and avoid building a membership base (Dolný and Malová 2016), the LSNS has sought to systematically expand its local branch network. In early 2015 the LSNS boasted 30 district associations and by 2018 it listed 60 such associations on its website, covering about three-fourths of the 79 Slovak districts (Figure 10.2). The reach of the LSNS varies substantially across regions: in the densely populated urban region of Bratislava the party set up a local branch in only

---

[8] Statutes of the LSNS, 2009. Also, email communication with Martin Belusky, vice president, LSNS, November 2016.

Figure 10.2   LSNS district associations in Slovakia, 2018.

a third of the districts but in Žilina and Trenčín its subunits cover the entire region. Like the NPD and unlike the GD, the LSNS does not strive to establish brick-and-mortar presence wherever it forms a district association. Actual offices are relatively rare in the universe of district associations and party members have their regular meetings in public or private buildings and locations. Despite this notable local organizational expansion, authority in the party remains highly centralized. The district associations report directly to their regional heads who have ultimate authority over the fate of local branches. The regional chairs appoint the local party heads and closely monitor their membership base. The little green cards of new party members, with pictures of Slovak heroes for each membership year, are handed out during the quarterly regional conferences of the LSNS by the regional head.[9] Despite the emphasis the district associations place on expanding their membership base, the LSNS is far from a mass party. When the party ran for the first time in the national parliamentary elections, it reported having only eleven members. By the 2012 election, it claimed 162 members and, after a sharp drop, its membership base expanded to 796 members by the end of 2016. Although this is a small number compared to the membership base of the more established parties, the upward trend defies the overall decline in party memberships in Slovakia. In 2017 the party claimed to have 1,439 members and its district associations were actively recruiting new members for their activities.[10]

The organizational life of LSNS district associations presents notable similarities to those of GD and NPD local branches. The analysis of all activities reported by the regional associations of the LSNS between 2015 and 2018 provides a useful glimpse of how the party tries to grow roots in local societies (Table 10.2). Much more than the GD and the

[9] Interviews with three members of the thirteen-member party executive body, March and July 2017.
[10] Interview with member of party executive, July 2017.

Table 10.2 *Activities Organized by LSNS Regional Organizations in Slovakia, 2015–2018*

Type	Number	% of total
Speech/lecture/meeting	32	12.9
Protest/patrols/petitions	31	12.4
Commemorations	68	27.3
Social activism/community work	78	31.3
Festivals	8	3.2
Founding of new district branch	9	3.6
Organizational meetings	6	2.4
Other	17	6.8
Total	**249**	**100**

Note: the party started recording these activities on March 15, 2015. The coding ended in April 2018.

NPD, the LSNS eagerly displays its social profile through the organization of various forms of social activism. Some of these activities are strikingly similar to those organized by the GD: the distribution of food, donation of blood and payment of small amounts to vulnerable groups in local communities. Nearly a third (31.3 percent) of the 249 activities reported on the LSNS website involve some form of social activism. In addition to social activism, district associations are also involved in various commemorative activities. Just like the GD and the NPD, the LSNS seeks to appropriate, reinterpret or challenge certain aspects of history by commemorating events associated with Slovak independence and disputing historical narratives generated during the communist era. Commemorations constitute more than a fourth (27.3 percent) of the regional activities the party reported during this three-year period. The action repertoire of the LSNS also includes protests, demonstrations and petitions. In its earlier years, the party gained notoriety for the organization of anti-Roma marches and protests, especially in 2012, when the burning of a major historical site became the impetus for wider anti-Roma mobilization. In more recent years, its local activists have also been putting together petition drives and demonstrations against the relocation of refugees in their localities. These activities make up 12.4 percent of the total activities the party reported. Local organizational life also includes speeches and lectures, which constitute 12.9 percent of all reported activities. The speeches are primarily on current affairs or on historical events. Unlike the NPD and the GD, the LSNS does not devote much attention to ideology.

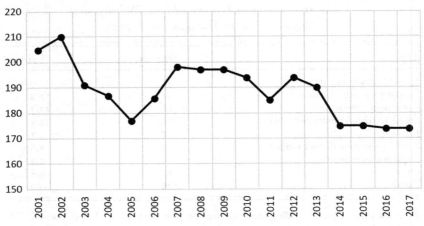

Figure 10.3   NPD district branches (at end-of-year), 2001–2017.

Variation in Local Organizational Development

As in Greece, the local organizational development of extremist right-wing parties in Germany and Slovakia displays notable subnational variation across both time and space. According to the listings of district associations on its various regional websites, since 2000 the NPD managed to sustain local structures in more than 170 out of 402 German districts (Figure 10.3). At some point throughout this period, the NPD neared or topped 200 district associations but, at least on paper, its local organizational network never shrunk below 170 structures. The local organizational life of the NPD, though, is a lot more volatile that these aggregate numbers suggest. Instead of solely looking at the total number of district associations listed on regional websites, a separate analysis investigates the actual addresses of these associations. This second analysis can better capture local organizational discontinuity because it reveals organizational mergers and excludes virtual organizations that do not even have a mailbox. The examination of the listed addresses of various local party organizations shows that, between 2013 and 2018, the addresses of fifty-five organizations disappeared from NPD regional websites. This left the party with only 143 different listed district organizations in 2018, of which 124 had continuous presence since 2013 and 19 were new. Figure 10.4 shows the relatively high rate of discontinuity in local NPD structures, presenting a strikingly similar picture to that observed in Greece.

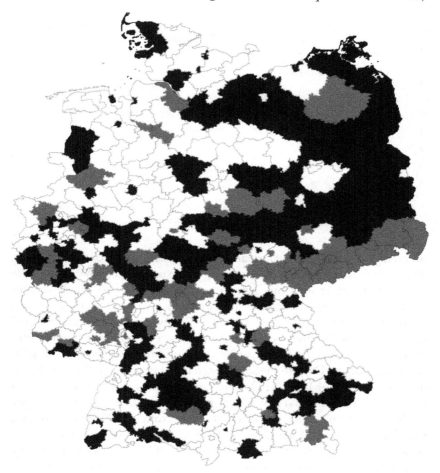

Figure 10.4 NPD district associations in 2018 (black). In gray are discontinued district associations. In the remaining districts (white) the NPD has had no presence.

As in Greece, local NPD structures display variation not only in organizational longevity but also in organizational activity. The analysis of hundreds of local NPD activities organized by its thirteen district associations in Saxony highlights considerable differences in the intensity and consistency of local mobilization.[11] In Dresden, the NPD organized

---

[11] Due to a redistricting that took place in 2008, the analysis here relies on the thirteen district associations set up after this redistricting.

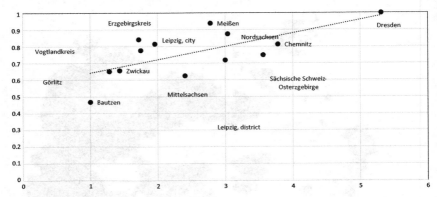

Figure 10.5   The intensity and consistency of local NPD activism in Saxony, 2009–2016 (n = 13 district associations).

on average 5.3 activities each quarter between 2009 and 2016, gaining the highest intensity score in the universe of Saxon districts. Moreover, the NPD organized at least one activity in Dresden in every single quarter since 2009, receiving the maximum consistency score of 1 (Figure 10.5). In Bautzen, the mobilization of the NPD was a lot less intense and consistent. The Bautzen NPD averaged only 1 activity per quarter and, in most quarters, it did not organize anything (intensity score: 1; consistency score: 0.47). Despite the stark differences between the thirteen Saxon districts, the life of local NPD structures is not as varied as that of GD branches. Whereas in Greece a large number of GD branches are empty shells without any noteworthy activity, in Saxony the NPD organized a significant number of activities in all districts throughout most of this period. Bautzen, the least consistent organizer of NPD activities in Saxony (0.47), is much more consistent that the average GD branch (0.34). The median intensity score of the thirteen branches is 2.41 and the median consistency score is 0.78.

The sixty-four district associations the LSNS set up in the past few years across Slovakia also exhibit varied organizational trajectories in terms of both structures and activism. Most of these associations were set up after the 2013 regional electoral success of the party in Banská Bystrica. Evidence for the existence of these structures is harder to find than in Germany or Greece because the LSNS does not provide more than a generic email address and the name of the local head to document their existence. By tracing these names across different points in time, though, one can generate a proxy for the relative continuity of the branches.

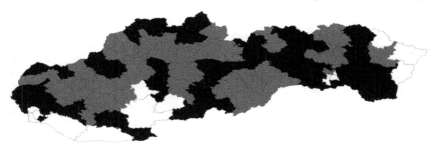

Figure 10.6   LSNS district associations with continued (black) and discontinued (gray)
leadership. In the remaining districts (white) the LSNS had no presence.

The branches without any changes in their local leader in the past years can
be thought to display higher levels of continuity than those with changes.
Since 2015, when the LSNS started publishing the names of its local
leaders, only thirty-four out sixty-four district association have kept the
same leader until 2018. The remainder thirty district branches have
changed their leadership at least once in the previous three years, a sign
of discontinuity in district structures. Figure 10.6 shows the local organizational presence of the LSNS in 2018, distinguishing between branches
with and without discontinuity.

The sixty-four district associations set up by the LSNS since 2015 also
exhibit different levels of local activism. The break-down of the 249 activities reported by the LSNS per district permits the generation of intensity
and consistency scores for all sixty-four district associations. As in the case
of Greece and Germany, the two scores are strongly correlated (r-squared =
0.56 in Slovakia; 0.46 in Germany; 0.71 in Greece). This suggests that the
associations set up by extremist right-wing parties are intensely active not
only shortly before but also in between elections, consistently organizing
and routinizing a number of local party activities.[12] As in Greece and, to a
lesser extent, Germany, the intensity and consistency scores of the activities organized by sixty-four local LSNS organizations vary sharply. In line
with the qualitative information collected from interviews with top LSNS
executives and MPs, district associations in Kežmarok, Poprad and
Ružomberok are among the most active in the entire universe of local
organizations. All organized on average more than one activity per quarter
for more than two-thirds of the quarters. Newer district associations, such
as those in Prievidza and Nové Zámky, are also quite active. By contrast,

[12] Or, relatively inactive both before and after elections.

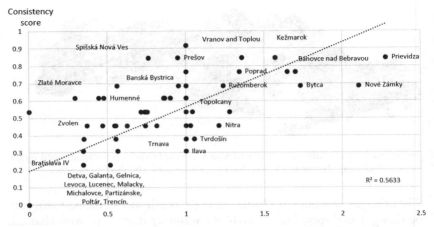

Figure 10.7   The intensity and consistency of local LSNS activism in Slovakia, 2015–2018 (n = 64 district associations).

ten out of the sixty-four local organizations of the LSNS have not reported organizing anything in the previous three years, not even an inaugural event (Figure 10.7). The high frequency of these "empty shells" parallels the local organizational realities in Greece and contrasts with the situation in Saxony, where all district associations were at least moderately active during the period under study.

Factors Affecting Local Organizational Development

The local organizational development of extremism in Germany and Slovakia is driven by endogenous and environmental dynamics similar to those identified in Greece. This section examines, in turn, endogenous, electoral, institutional and societal factors affecting the local organizational development of the NPD and the LSNS.

Endogenous Drivers of Organizational Development

The organizational evolution of extremist right-wing parties is partly shaped by internal party dynamics. In Germany, the emphasis the NPD placed on organizing contentious political activities complicated its local organizational development and shaped its subsequent capacity for environmental adjustment. The organizational goal of the party to dominate in the streets brought it closer to dozens of militant and violent neo-Nazi or nationalist groups. Under the leadership of Udo Voigt, in the late 1990s and early 2000s, the NPD was able to recruit hundreds new members among the *Kameradschaften*, the autonomous nationalists and, subsequently, the *Freie Kräfte*, as foot soldiers for its militant party activism. The neo-Nazi groups would provide manpower for the contentious street activism of the NPD and, in return, the party would make available organizational resources – and the legal protection inherent in being a party instead of an association – to the extremists. The recruitment of militant activists from the neo-Nazi scene helped expand the membership base of the party but the reliance of the NPD on these extremist groups was a liability for its parliamentary strategy. The association of these groups with violence complicated party efforts to reach wider segments of local societies. At the critical moment when it achieved major electoral breakthroughs in Saxony and Mecklenburg – Vorpommern, the NPD could not easily disassociate itself from the neo-Nazi scene. For example, in Mecklenburg – Vorpommern, neo-Nazis managed to hold most of the candidate positions for the 2006 state election and elect two of the six members of the state parliament.[13]

The changed electoral environment and the regional electoral breakthroughs of the party increased calls for a more moderate course, which would require keeping a clearer distance from the neo-Nazi scene and from contentious and violence-prone politics. The calls mostly came from the electorally successful Saxon wing of the party, which appealed to the party leadership to embrace the "Saxon way" – a more moderate course that required less focus on historical revisionism, more parliamentary work and, as the leader of the Saxon NPD, Holger Apfel, put it, "serious radicalism."[14] Initially, the Saxon way failed to gain much traction at the national level but by 2011, and amid growing financial troubles of the national NPD, the growing influence of the Saxon party led to a major leadership change, when Voigt was surprisingly replaced by Apfel as party chairman. Advocating a tactical shift away from "National Socialist ghetto" Apfel found support from deputies of Mecklenburg – Vorpommern, the other electorally successful regional party. The shift aimed to make the party more attractive to wider segments of voters but did not go very far. Caught between street tactics and parliamentary representation, the NPD was

---

[13] *Verfassungsschutzbericht 2006*, Schwerin: Innenministerium Mecklenburg – Vorpommern, p. 81.
[14] *Verfassungsschutzbericht 2009*, Dresden: Innenministerium Sachsen, p. 13; *Verfassungsschutzbericht 2010*, Dresden: Innenministerium Sachsen, p. 11; *Verfassungsschutzbericht 2011*, Dresden: Innenministerium Sachsen, p. 14.

institutionally unprepared to handle the internal feuds generated by the dual emphasis on conventional and contentious politics. The party ended up losing a large segment of its younger, more militant activists without making the electoral inroads necessary to justify this loss. Absent institutional mechanisms to handle the many internal feuds, the intrinsic tension in this dual track of politics eventually destabilized the party. In late 2013, Apfel resigned as chairman and his temporary replacement, Udo Pastörs, the deputy chairman from Mecklenburg – Vorpommern, was soon replaced in the 2014 party congress by Frank Franz.

The leadership change brought about a further push for modernization and professionalization but did not settle the internal tensions between militants and moderates, thereby complicating its subsequent organizational evolution. In the next few years, the party continued to practice its controversial street politics while simultaneously trying to project a more moderate image. The failure to resolve the dilemma between militancy and moderation came at a cost, as the NPD kept losing militants to other extreme right parties such as *Die Rechte* and *Der Dritte Weg*. The continued outflux of militant activists meant that some district associations had to shut down or go into long periods of inactivity. Even in Saxony and Mecklenburg – Vorpommern, where the party had parliamentary representation for a decade, its organizational units lost a significant segment of their membership. There was also a notable deterioration of the local organizational structures. In Saxony, where the party retained dozens of seats in local councils, it had to shut down two of its thirteen district associations, including its major stronghold in Leipzig. The 2015 refugee crisis provided a solid opportunity for anti-asylum demonstrations, protests and marches, which kept the party in the streets, even in the face of organizational deterioration. But, amid these apparent organizational troubles, the political opportunity failed to materialize in electoral rewards because of the sudden rise of the Alternative for Germany (*Alternative für Deutschland*, AfD), which managed to sweep away voters who would otherwise be attracted to the anti-foreigner, anti-system message of the NPD. By 2018, the Saxon NPD only listed its address in Riesa on its website, pointing to the further disarray of its organizational structures. Overall, then, the organizational roots of the party in militant activism doomed its efforts to become more competitive in parliamentary politics, even after some of its more important electoral advances in its recent history. Caught between street and institutional politics, the party ended up losing its militants to more extreme parties and its voters to more moderate alternatives.

The organizational DNA of the LSNS can go a long way to account for its subsequent development, as well. Like the GD and the NPD, the LSNS achieved major electoral breakthroughs while pursuing a dual track of conventional and contentious politics. This was an organizational legacy of the LSNS predecessor, the Slovak Togetherness, which, by the time of its banning in 2006, made an impression with its controversial commemorative marches. The leader of the Slovak Togetherness and the LSNS, Kotleba, became nationally known for leading the uniformed activists and, occasionally, violently clashing with the police. The LSNS continued the legacy of contentious activism and in subsequent years it expanded its repertoire to include protest marches against the Roma, especially in the Banská Bystrica region where the party set up its first organizational stronghold and subsequently won its first electoral breakthrough. After this success, Kotleba sought to establish similar organizational infrastructure in other regions of Slovakia. Given the emphasis the party places on street-level politics, the LSNS expanded its organizational network by primarily recruiting and appointing "biographically available" militants to head its regional and local structures. The appointment of such individuals signaled the continuation of the street mobilization of the LSNS. Lacking an electoral mandate, such individuals were chosen for their capacity to undertake street action as well as their devotion to the party leader – a feature intrinsic to the charismatic nature of the LSNS. For example, in 2015 Kotleba recruited Milan Mazurek to head the eastern Prešov region. The 21-year-old activist became known a year earlier for verbally attacking female immigrants in an anti-Islam protest organized by the party in Bratislava.[15] "I became a member of the party in 2015 when Marian Kotleba came here wanting to give a new life to the regional structures. After a week he gave me an important task. I had to organize a petition against asylum seekers being brought into the region. Kotleba came during the petition and he was very satisfied with my work. At the national party congress, it was decided that I would become the regional chairman."[16] The entry of the LSNS into the national parliament in the 2016 election did not change the emphasis it placed on street-level activism. After the election the LSNS started using its growing activist base not only for protests and demonstrations but also for systematic

---

[15] Mazurek was shown on video directing racial slurs against female immigrants: https://www.youtube.com/watch?v=8eAQp6Doonk.

[16] Interview with Milan Mazurek, head of Prešov region and member of parliament, July 2017, Kežmarok.

patrols of various train routes going through Roma localities. Unlike the GD, the LSNS sought to partly institutionalize its vigilantism to keep the militants under control. Instead of leaving the patrols entirely to the enthusiasm, energy and muscle of its young activists, it used its newly acquired financial resources to pay monthly allowances to those activists regularly involved in the patrols. Many of the activists involved in the patrols, especially at night, were volunteers. But they usually operated alongside activists with more formal responsibilities and commitments.[17]

As in the case of the GD and the NPD, the dual track of politics practiced by the LSNS became a source of some instability in its local structures. The electoral traction of the party in the mid-2010s attracted a group of more moderate functionaries, who were not as committed to the activist profile of the party. The inherent friction between the newcomers and older militants – some with common experiences in the banned Slovak Togetherness – generated significant internal instability. The organizational toll of this instability became evident in the frequent changes of local party leaders in the district associations set up by the LSNS across Slovakia. Lacking a local electoral mandate, local party heads rely entirely on their ties with the regional and national party leaders for their survival. As a result, the career trajectory of local party functionaries in the LSNS is highly uncertain and friction between various party groups takes a toll on personnel continuity. As shown earlier, the analysis of the names of local party heads listed on the party website across different points in time is indicative of the relative discontinuity of local party structures: nearly half of the sixty-four district associations set up in the previous three years experienced discontinuity.

The Electoral Environment and Organizational Development

The way extremist right-wing parties develop depends not only on endogenous but also on environmental factors. Electoral dynamics are the first of three environmental factors affecting local organizational development. Chapter 6 suggested that extremist right-wing parties can yield electoral benefits from the establishment of local party branches but also showed that the reverse association only partly holds. The analysis of the organizational presence and electoral performance of the NPD and the LSNS confirms these earlier findings. The analysis of the 2017 electoral results in districts with and without an NPD branch shows that the party

---

[17] Interviews with a member of the party executive and a head of a local branch, July 2017.

did twice as well where it had some presence as where it had none. In the 157 districts the NPD averaged 0.60 percent of second votes compared to 0.33 percent in the remaining 245 districts ($t(188) = 6.00$, $p<0.001$). In the Slovak case, the LSNS did significantly better (9.37 percent) in the 45 districts where it established a branch before the 2016 breakthrough election than in the 34 districts (7.65 percent) where it had no presence ($t(52) = 2.76$, $p = 0.008$). Overall, then, the picture is the same in all three countries: local organizational presence is strongly associated with better electoral results for extremist right-wing parties.

Although local organizational presence enhances electoral performance, the local organizational development of extremist right-wing parties is only partly shaped by electoral considerations. In the case of the NPD, the electoral environment had a relatively small effect on the organizational development of the party. The electoral stimulus for organizational change was relatively large: the combination of over half million votes and regional parliamentary presence in the mid-2000s constituted the best electoral performance of the party since the 1960s. This positive stimulus, though, did not bring about an equally important change in the structures and activism of the party. During its electoral peak, the number of NPD members in Germany increased significantly from 5,000 in 2003 to 7,200 in 2007, the highest number since 1980 (Figure 10.8). But this was largely because new members joined existing rather than new local NPD structures. The number of district NPD organizations went up from 177 in 2005 to 198 in 2007 (Figure 10.9). The relatively weak association between the electoral environment and local organizational development is also evident in the subsequent years: although the party had a stable electoral standing for a number of years, it witnessed a drop in members and branches.

The analysis of all NPD activities in its stronghold in Saxony is also suggestive of the limited association between electoral performance and organizational development. The analysis of all NPD events organized in Saxony after 2000 shows a marked increase in activism after its major regional breakthrough in the mid-2000s (Figure 10.10). From a few dozens, the annual number of activities averages about one hundred in the years after this breakthrough. Subsequent years, though, show a disjuncture between the electoral environment and the organizational activity of the NPD. In the 2010s the level of party activism seems to be more in tune with changes in the political opportunities available in the environment than with the electoral standing of the party per se. At a time when the party was losing voters, the refugee crisis in Germany increased

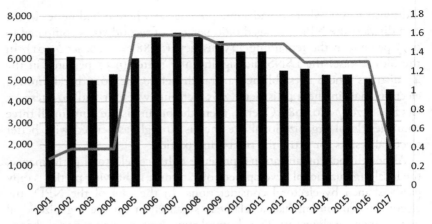

Figure 10.8   NPD members and percent in national elections, 2001–2017.

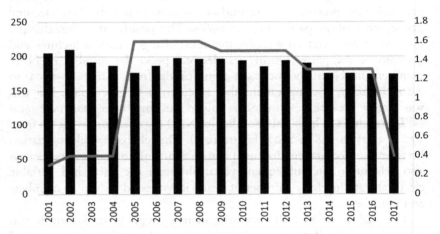

Figure 10.9   NPD district branches and percent in national elections, 2001–2017.

its activism levels to unprecedented levels. In 2015 alone the NPD organized 239 activities in Saxony despite the loss of its regional parliamentary seats in the previous year. Overall, then, the organizational development of the NPD cannot be easily foretold by changes in the electoral environment.

The analysis of the organizational evolution of all NPD district organizations since the 2013 federal elections provides additional evidence regarding the association between electoral results and organizational

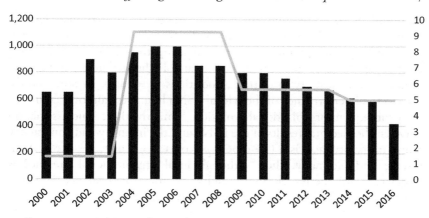

Figure 10.10 NPD members and percent in state elections, Saxony, 2000–2016.

outcomes. According to the addresses provided by regional party associations, between 2013 and 2018, the NPD sustained its organizational presence in 124 out 402 German districts and shut down another 55 district associations. A logistic regression with the 2013 results of these districts as the only independent variable shows that it is not a good predictor of branch discontinuity (p = 0.11). This suggests that, as in the Greek case, the local organizational persistence of the NPD cannot be foretold by its electoral performance. In addition, as in the case of the GD, there is no association between electoral results and local activism. Although the data from Saxony are very thin to allow for even bivariate statistical analysis, since they are drawn from only thirteen districts, the 2013 electoral results of the party in these do not seem to be associated with the intensity or consistency of subsequent NPD activism in these districts. In Dresden, where the party received one of its lowest electoral results in Saxony (2.35 percent), the district association had the highest intensity (6.94) and consistency (1) scores among the thirteen districts. And in Görlitz, where the party received one of its best electoral results (4.24 percent), the district association had the lowest intensity (0.69) and consistency (0.50) scores.

In Slovakia, the sudden change in the electoral environment prompted the rapid organizational expansion of the LSNS and led to a remarkable expansion in its membership base. The LSNS expanded its local party structures from 30 in 2015 to 60 in 2018, covering three-fourths of the 79 Slovak districts. Moreover, its membership base witnessed a multifold expansion from fewer than one hundred members in 2015 to over one thousand in 2017. Despite this national trend, the subnational electoral results of the LSNS cannot reliably predict the development of its structures and activism. A logistic regression using the 2016 LSNS national election results as the only independent variable shows that it is not a good predictor of continuity in district associations (p = 0.42). In other words, the electoral performance of these local LSNS branches cannot account for their subsequent organizational evolution. Similarly, there is no association between the electoral results of the LSNS and the intensity and consistency scores of its local activism (r = 0.065, p = 0.61; r = 0.093, p = 0.46). As in Greece and Germany, then, although local organizational presence is associated with better electoral results, electoral performance is not a reliable yardstick of how local party organizations evolve.

The Institutional Environment and Organizational Development

The organizational development of extremist right-wing parties is affected not only by the electoral but also by the institutional environment. As Chapter 8 has shown, the way institutional actors respond to extremist right-wing parties also affects their capacity to grow roots in local societies. Like the GD, the other two parties examined here have faced the intervention of the state against the way they practice politics but after a varied period of litigation, they are yet to be banned. Their continuity provides an opportunity to examine organizational change during a period of increased institutional hostility.

Due to its Nazi legacy, the postwar German state has developed a number of instruments to curb the political activity of extremist parties. Apart from standard restrictions to some forms of propaganda, they include the systematic surveillance of extremist right-wing associations and parties and the possibility of banning them (Minkenberg 2006: 38–39). The NPD faced the possibility of being outlawed twice. In 2001, after a number of violent incidents by extremist groups, the federal government and the two chambers of the legislature initiated a procedure to ban the NPD because of its association with National Socialism and with violent skinheads and neo-Nazis. In 2003, though, the Federal Constitutional Court dismissed the case when it emerged that a number of witnesses, including "no more than 15%" of the NPD leadership, were actually informants of intelligence services monitoring extremists, the *Bundesverfassungsschutz* (Rensmann 2003: 1121). The public shock caused in 2011 by the discovery of the National Socialist Underground, a small extremist group blamed for the assassination of a number of immigrants, gave rise to new political calls for outlawing the NPD. After deliberations, the regional governments making up the upper house of the German legislature, the Bundesrat, filed a new motion in 2013 to outlaw the party, providing detailed evidence showing how the NPD aims to dismantle the German democratic order. In 2017 the Constitutional Court unanimously rejected the application of the Bundesrat. Its decision accepts that the NPD aspires to establish a non-democratic political system and the party "acts in a systematic manner and with sufficient intensity towards achieving its aims that are directed against the free democratic basic order. However, (currently) there is a lack of specific and weighty indications suggesting that this endeavour will be successful."[18] After the decision, the German government managed to secure a broad majority to change Article 21 of the German constitution denying public funding to parties that are against the democratic order.[19] Relying on the ruling of the Constitutional Court that the NPD is not democratic, in February 2018 the German legislature made a new motion to the Court to withdraw all public funding from the party for six years. The NPD had faced very serious financial problems even before losing all its seats in state parliaments in 2016 and, if the new motion succeeds, it will effectively bankrupt the party. Interestingly, the motion also stated that the prohibition of state funding should also hold for successor parties.

As in the case of Greece, the protracted nature of the attempt to outlaw the NPD provides an opportunity to explore the effects of state intervention on its organizational development. The response of the German state to right-wing extremism is different than that of Greece, where the state criminally prosecuted and temporarily imprisoned the leadership of the party and withheld its state funding. Yet, despite these important differences in the practice of militant democracy, there are notable similarities in the effects these measures have had on the organizational development of the two parties. First, the protracted legal process to outlaw the NPD coincides with a major drop in its membership. Throughout the first attempt to ban it the party lost nearly a quarter of its membership base,

---

[18] Federal Constitutional Court, "No prohibition of the National Democratic Party of Germany as there are no indications that it will succeed in achieving its anti-constitutional aims," January 17, 2017; judgment available at official website, https://goo.gl/zEtQDC.

[19] The amendment was supported by all parties in the lower house except the Greens and some members of the Left Party abstained. It was unanimously supported in the upper house. Archives of the German Bundestag, "Verfassungsfeindliche Parteien von der Finanzierung ausgeschlossen," June 22, 2017; https://goo.gl/dD8UVQ. See also Bundesrat, "Finanzierungsstopp beschlossen - Länder planen nächsten Schritt," July 7, 2017; https://goo.gl/VBZCQa.

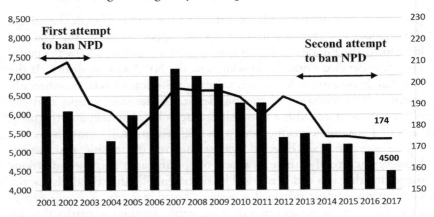

Figure 10.11   NPD members and district branches, 2001–2017.

which shrank from 6,500 members in 2000 to 5,000 members in 2003. There was a similar effect during the second attempt to ban the party, its membership dropping by about a fifth, from 6,300 in 2011 to 4,500 in 2017 (Figure 10.11). Although the drop is associated with internal problems, it is also due to the trouble the party faced sustaining its membership base during this protracted process of litigation.[20] On the one hand, the NPD could not recruit new members during the legal process against it and on the other hand, it witnessed an outflow of hundreds of existing members. As in the early 2000s, the new attempt to ban the party led to the adjustment of relations with various extremist groups, such as the *Freie Kräfte*, but it also coincided with the departure of more militant activists from the party. The latter joined the other major extremist party structures available, *Die Rechte* and *Der Dritte Weg*, which are also monitored by the intelligence services but did not face an imminent threat of being outlawed.

Second, there was a notable retrenchment of local organizational structures. After the first attempt to ban the NPD in 2001, the party witnessed a shrinkage of its district branches, from a high of 210 in 2002 to 186 in 2006. As in the case of the GD, there was some time lag between the judicial process and party organizational retrenchment. During the second and more protracted attempt to ban the party, the organizational retrenchment was also important – the number of district branches listed on the

---

[20] Interviews with two members of the party board, November 2016 and October 2017.

party website dropped from 190 in 2013 to 174 in 2017 (Figure 10.11). Despite official party proclamations of organizational continuity, by the beginning of 2017, when the German Constitutional Court decided against banning the party, the NPD faced significant organizational problems. A significant number of district branches had simply turned into empty shells without any record of notable activity. At the March 2017 party congress, held after the rejection of the NPD ban by the Court, about a fifth of the district associations were not allowed to send delegates to the congress because they had not paid their fees.[21] More importantly, the party had to shut down dozens of district associations. As mentioned earlier, between 2013 and 2018 the party closed fifty-five local organizations and opened only nineteen new ones. As in the case of the GD, the dismantling of local organizational structures cannot solely be attributed to the legal process initiated against it. The organizational disarray of the party was also endogenous: the party faced internal leadership turmoil. But the internal problems are not unrelated to the strategic dilemmas generated by the prospect of being banned and by the subsequent push for modernizational and professionalization. The latter generated friction between the party leadership and local party functionaries. For example, in Leipzig the local branch was dismantled after a feud caused by the links of the district branch with militants.[22]

Third, as the legal process started taking a toll on NPD structures, the party sought refuge in the "movement." During the period of obvious retrenchment in local party structures, the NPD resorted to street-level mobilization. Much of this mobilization effort concentrated in Saxony. Despite the drop in membership and the organizational setbacks, the Saxon regional party managed to sustain the overall capacity for both conventional and contentious types of activism. In fact, there is some evidence that, even with fewer members and structures, the party managed to augment its presence on the street. The analysis of 1,440 activities undertaken in Saxony between 2000 and 2016 clearly shows the rise of NPD activism in the region during the period of the legal process against it. The breakdown of NPD activities indicates notable organizational readjustment: after the onset of the new efforts to ban the party, the regional NPD diverted resources away from conventional party activities, such as speeches, lectures and meetings, and encouraged its members to

---

[21] Responses of NPD press office to emailed questions, July 2017.
[22] *Verfassungsschutzbericht 2016*, Dresden: Innenministerium Sachsen, pp. 62–63

organize more protest, commemorative and canvassing activities. Since the party has fewer members to mobilize, it also had to change its organizational tactics:

> In the past, the emphasis was on putting together large demonstrations. These require considerable organization and resources. We changed this in the last years. Our idea now is to do many smaller manifestations, than a few big ones. We go somewhere with twenty people, we give two or three speeches, and then move on to other locations. We think that in this way, we can spread our message to a larger number of people than with large demonstrations in a single location.[23]

Overall, then, the attempt to outlaw the NPD took a toll on its membership and structures but it also led to organizational adjustment that allowed the party to capitalize on emerging political opportunities and sustain or, even, enhance its capacity to mobilize supporters for conventional and contentious activism.

In Slovakia, right-wing extremism also led to militant democratic responses by institutional and political actors. The first instance of applying militant democracy policies against an extremist right-wing party was in 2006, when the Supreme Court accepted a motion by the Prosecutor General to ban the Slovak Togetherness, the progenitor to the LSNS. Founded in the 1990s as a movement, Slovak Togetherness started gaining significant visibility after 2003, through its commemorative marches and demonstrations. Under Kotleba's leadership, members of the movement would parade in uniforms and insignia reminiscent of the interwar Hlinka Guard and, occasionally, clash with the police. The police would sometimes ban or disrupt their activities because they would incite hatred or racism and, on several occasions, they detained or arrested Kotleba for his actions. Things became more complicated in 2005, when Slovak Togetherness became a political party. As in the case of the NPD and the GD, the murder of a student, Daniel Tupý, by a group of extremists triggered public demonstrations against extremism and eventually led to a motion by the Prosecutor General to ban the party. The Supreme Court decided in March 2006 that the program of the party was undemocratic because it called for the establishment of an Estates System based on national, Christian and social principles that would replace parliamentary democracy. A few months before the 2006 election, Slovak Togetherness became the first party in postcommunist Slovakia to be dissolved

---

[23] Interview with a member of the NPD board, July 2015.

(Mikušovič 2007; 2009).[24] After the dissolution of Slovak Togetherness, some of its leading members took over an existing party, which eventually evolved to the LSNS. Since the Supreme Court primarily focused on the program of the banned party, the new party sought to avoid the fate of its progenitor by avoiding references to a new political order.

> After the first ban of our party we realized we have to change the way we do our work at the official level. That means what is written in our statutes, in our program and so on, because they will try to find any word and use it as basis to ban us. For example, we had written in our program that we wanted to change the constitution, which is something that happens very often in Slovakia. The Supreme Court found this anti-constitutional and banned us.[25]

The LSNS had a different program, symbol and uniform but its political rhetoric and practice retained notable similarities to those of its progenitor. Its program includes racist references to "gypsy terror," "parasites" or "thieves" and the party is still reliant on the mobilization of members and sympathizers for controversial types of activism. Not surprisingly, the LSNS adopted key organizational characteristics of Slovak Togetherness, including the establishment and proliferation of local organizations and the adoption of a repertoire of contentious political action. As discussed earlier, the party sought to sustain or reinforce these basic organizational features even after its national electoral breakthrough in 2016 by rapidly expanding its local organizational network and by initiating train patrols.

By the time the party had become a major political force in Slovak politics, the broader issue of extremism gained prominence on the political agenda. In response to calls for a comprehensive response to extremism, the ministry of interior developed a strategy to combat extremism, which included the development of legal tools to tackle related issues. The strategy was updated several times in subsequent years, amid growing realization by mainstream political parties and actors that some of the views and actions of extremist groups were gaining wider social acceptance (Bodnárová and Vicenová 2013). Much readier to combat extremism than before, the political opponents of LSNS voted for a law in late 2016 to curb vigilantism by only allowing train operators and police officers to

---

[24] The Prosecutor General subsequently filed a motion to dissolve the movement itself but its motion was overruled by the Supreme Court, allowing Slovak Togetherness to exist as an association. Since the banning of the party, Slovak Togertheness has existed intermittently as a movement, taking place in many contentious marches and demonstrations of the LSNS.

[25] Marian Kotleba, communication with author, July 2017.

maintain order on trains. In addition, in early 2017 the government set up a special police unit to combat terrorism and extremism and investigate hate crimes and speech. In April 2017 the police charged two LSNS lawmakers for hate speech, which means that, if found guilty, they could face imprisonment for up to six years. A more decisive step came shortly afterward from the Prosecutor General, who in May 2017 filed a motion to the Supreme Court to outlaw the party because its program and activities violated the Slovak constitution.

Although the militant democracy measures are too recent to allow comprehensive evaluation and are generally milder than those in Greece or Germany, there are some indications of how they are affecting the organizational development of the LSNS. As in Greece and Germany, the initiation of the process to ban the party has arrested the expansion of its local organizational structures. In anticipation and as a result of its electoral success in 2016 the party quickly expanded its local organizational structures from thirty in 2015 to sixty-one in May 2017. Nearly a year after the motion of the Prosecutor General to outlaw the party, the number of district associations stagnated at around sixty. Many of these are empty shells without any activity. Despite the significant growth of party membership, the inflow of members is mostly concentrated in a few organizationally successful local units, such as those in Kežmarok and Ružomberok. A significant number of other district associations lack enough members to justify their existence. As a result, in late 2018 the party was planning a restructuring of its local organizational network, merging some of the smaller units with neighboring ones, to which the central party will start diverting more resources. "There is no reason to copy the official Slovak regions, if we have just a few members in some areas."[26] The party was also preparing for a possible ban by setting up a new party to take over in case the LSNS were outlawed. As Kotleba proclaims, one of the lessons learned from the previous ban is the importance of having an alternative plan to respond to challenges posed by the state. "We realized we always have to have a plan B, which is the reason why we have a second party in the backup."[27] Overall, then, as in Greece and Germany, state intervention curbed the local organizational expansion of the party and its ambition to set up local organizational structures across Slovakia.

Increased institutional hostility in Slovakia took a toll not only on local LSNS structures but on local party activism as well. An analysis of

---

[26] Communication with member of party executive, November 2018.   [27] Marian Kotleba, Ibid.

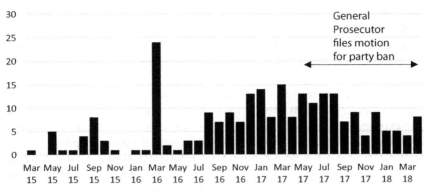

Figure 10.12   Number of local LSNS activities, March 2015–April 2018 (n = 249).

all party activities listed on the party website provides some indication of the effect of the motion to outlaw the party on its local mobilization. As shown on Figure 10.11, party activism witnessed an unusual spurt right before the 2016 election, then dropped, and picked up again during the period of local organizational expansion. Since May 2017, when the government made a motion to ban it, the LSNS witnessed a drop in the activity of its local structures. A comparison of the activism levels of the forty-four district associations that were active a year before and a year after the motion is indicative of the effect of state hostility on local mobilization. The average intensity score of the forty-four branches in the year prior to the intervention of the Prosecutor General was 0.46 and it dropped to 0.32 in the year after the motion. A two-sample t-test between these forty-four yields statistically significant differences in the average intensity of local activities ($t(43)$ = 2.052, p = 0.046). A similar comparison of the average consistency scores of the forty-four branches yields similar results – 0.37 before the motion and 0.22 after the motion. A two-sample t-test among the forty-four branches yields statistically significant differences in the average consistency of local activities ($t(42)$ = −3.267, p = 0.002).

The Societal Environmental and Organizational Development

The organizational development of extremist right-wing parties depends on changes not only in the electoral and institutional, but also in the societal environment. As in Greece, the subnational development of the NPD generated strong societal responses from a large variety of actors, with different resources at their disposal and a relatively large array of tactics. Due to the size and administrative division of Germany, societal responses to extremism depend on a different combination of local and national actors in each setting. A number of these actors, such as trade unions and interest groups, have ties to political parties and a much broader political agenda than antifascism. Another set of actors involves groups or parties of the extra-parliamentary Left, which have anti-capitalist and anti-imperialist agendas and a total membership of about twenty thousand people. They include groups of a few hundred or thousand members, such as the Communist Party of Germany, the Red Help, the Communist Platform of the Party of the Left and various other Marxist and Trotskyist groups. Other antifascist actors, such as autonomous or anarchist groups, do not have direct political ties and antifascism is a significant portion of their political repertoire. Largely rooted in the squatter movements of earlier decades, autonomous and anarchist groups are primarily located in major urban centers and their membership is thought to be around seven thousand people. According to the German Ministry of Interior, which monitors not only right-wing but also left-wing extremism, some of the strongholds of autonomous and anarchist groups are in Hamburg, Berlin and Leipzig. Recent years have witnessed the increased mobilization of such groups, in part due to the rise of the Alternative for Germany, which is sometimes targeted by antifascist groups, in addition to the NPD.

As in Greece, the range of resources the various German antifascist groups have at their disposal varies considerably. Since some groups have ties to political parties, they often try to use institutional authority to monitor or curb NPD activity. In Saxony, for example, MPs of The Left (*Die Linke*) use parliamentary questions to have the Ministry of Interior report all NPD activities in the region. Institutional authority is also brought to bear on the mobilization of civil society groups against the NPD. Elected state or local authorities, like the mayor of Leipzig, Burkhard Jung, would take a public stance against the presence of the NPD as well as against the various offshoots of the anti-Islam movement PEGIDA (*Patriotische Europäer gegen die Islamisierung des Abendlandes*). Antifascist activists acknowledge the importance of having institutional backup: "The political stance of municipal authorities can make a difference in how many people mobilize for the cause."[28] In addition to

[28] Interview with two members of the Antifa Recherche Team (ART) Dresden, Dresden, October 2017.

institutional resources, antifascist activists – like their counterparts in Greece – also have communicative and intellectual resources at their disposal. The communicative resources include the linksunten.indymedia.org, the German version of Indymedia, which posts information about upcoming events and various – sometimes criminal – activities against the NPD.[29] In addition to communicative resources, antifascist groups also have intellectual resources at their disposal. Some groups, such as ART in Dresden and *Chronikle* in Leipzig, are primarily involved in the documentation of racist speech and acts and in the monitoring of right-wing extremist activity. Antifascist networks monitor not just their political opponents but also the actions of the German state, attending trials and documenting police responses. The monitoring of NPD activities prepares the ground for counterdemonstrations, candlelight vigils and peaceful protests. Not surprisingly, this activity mirrors that of the NPD. In 2014, when the NPD was active in the streets because of the elections in Saxony, the regional Ministry of Interior reported a steep rise of street activism by extreme left-wing groups, as well. The level of street mobilization increased further in 2015, mirroring the mobilization of the NPD in Saxony against the influx of refugees.[30] In Saxony, the largest antifascist groups are located in Leipzig, which also has the biggest autonomous and anarchist scene (primarily in the district of Connewitz).

The various antifascist actors use a considerable range of tactics to achieve their ends and, as in Greece, tactical dilemmas are a constant source of tension between them. At one end are those groups that are primarily involved in antifascist activity through some of the institutional and conventional means highlighted above. At the other end are groups who are willing to engage in unlawful activities to counter the NPD and other political opponents. Apart from the destruction of physical property and skirmishes during party events, antifascist tactics also include outing members of the NPD and individually attacking NPD functionaries. The violent tactics of some antifascist networks are highly controversial. Even those who are willing to accept their occasional effectiveness point to the damage these tactics do to the capacity of the antifascist community to build alliances with mainstream political actors.

[29] In 2017, the German government decided to ban the site because of hate speech, raising considerable criticism from users and readers of Indymedia as well as by the police and private detectives who used the site to monitor extreme left activity.

[30] *Verfassungsschutzbericht 2016*, Dresden: Innenministerium Sachsen, p. 216.

There is sometimes violent action against the extremists, like destroying their offices. There has been one prominent case in Saxony of antifascists going to the house of an NPD member and destroying the whole place. I do not condone this and I have nothing to do with such activities. This is certainly a problem with the antifascist movement. Once violence is involved, it is easier for antifascists to be labeled extremists, especially by conservative political actors and parties. Even the SPD, which is generally supportive of antifascist mobilization, wants to have nothing to do with it, if it becomes violent. All parties are quite clear on the violence issue. No violence. So it is harder to build broader alliances against right-wing extremism once violence is involved.[31]

The large number of actors exercising societal pressure against the party, the considerable and varied resources they had at their disposal and the multitude of tactics they employed complicated the organizational development of the NPD. As in Greece, such complications were most evident in settings with strong antifascist activity, which undermined local party structures and activism. The case of Leipzig, where the NPD had to abandon its brick-and-mortar presence amid persistent and strong reactions from institutional and social actors, can serve as an example of how societal hostility affects local organizational development. The city is one of the main strongholds of radical left, autonomous and anarchist activism in Germany. Leipzig is also the city where the NPD set up its first district associations in Saxony in the 1990s, which evolved into one of the largest and most active district associations in the region. In 2008 the NPD opened an office in Odermannstraße 8, in Lindenau, which became a meeting place for the entire extreme right scene in Saxony, hosting various events and activities. In subsequent years, the brick-and-mortar presence of the NPD became a focal point for antifascist activity, from a combination of political, institutional and social actors. Local politicians from leftist parties, the social democratic mayor of the city and an alliance of antifascist groups systematically protested the presence of the NPD office. "Every time they had an event, a concert by a neo-Nazi band or a lecture by a *Wehrmacht* survivor, there were demonstrations against it. They always had resistance. Their events were never accepted without voicing opposition."[32] In 2014 the party had to abandon its office stating, among other reasons, that the NPD found itself in "a situation of siege." Like the GD, the NPD also claims that a major reason for its exit from Leipzig was financial, since after its electoral defeat in the Saxony elections in 2014, it

---

[31] Interview with two members of the group *Leipzig nimmt Platz*, October 2017.
[32] Interview with antifascist activist of *Chronikle*, Leipzig, October 2017.

had to streamline its operations and in 2015 it merged the Leipzig city branch with that of the broader Leipzig district. "Because of left-wing activities in Leipzig, after some time, it became impossible to stay there. We decided to merge the two districts and move outside the city."[33] The eventual shut down of one of the strongest Saxon branches of the NPD was partly due to internal party feuds, especially between the district and the regional party. As mentioned earlier, though, these troubles were not unrelated to the tactical dilemmas the party confronted due to the significant societal opposition to its presence in Leipzig. Like elsewhere in Germany, the NPD had to decide how to respond to antifascist activity, especially to violent confrontations with antifascists. As in Greece, such confrontations were more prevalent in localities where the NPD was most active and negatively affected its attempt to present a more moderate profile.

Societal pressure not only complicated the evolution of local party structures, as shown by the analysis of the Leipzig case, but it also affected the form and geographical focus of NPD activism. In large urban settings such as Hamburg, with a strong autonomous and anarchist scene, the regional party had trouble organizing outdoor activities. Its infrequent information booths, which usually involved a handful of activists, are known to attract considerable and sometimes violent reactions from antifascist groups. In Berlin, societal pressure had a different effect on NPD activism. Following the example of various nationalist networks, such as the Identitarian Movement, the Berlin NPD started flirting with the idea of having flash mobs – public actions that take place instantaneously, without prior warning, after which the activists quickly disperse, before the police or opponents get a chance to react. Moreover, like some of the GD branches, the Berlin NPD concentrated its activism outside major urban centers, where antifascist pressure is strongest.[34] Even in Saxony, which is thought to be an NPD stronghold, the party claims to face antifascist mobilization "in 95 percent of the events organized by the party. If we do something in Leipzig or other major cities, there is always a lot of reaction. We hence do a lot of political work in smaller cities or villages. There is no problem there."[35]

In Slovakia, responses to extremist right-wing parties are much more contained than in Greece or Germany, thereby presenting an opportunity

[33] Interview with two NPD functionaries in Saxony, Riesa, October 2017.
[34] Interview with Berlin functionary of the NPD, November 2016.
[35] Interview with a member of the NPD board, July 2015.

to examine how this difference in the societal environment affects organizational outcomes. Antifascist actors are rarer in Slovakia, with considerably fewer resources at their disposal and a much narrower range of tactics. Antifascism in Slovakia is a relatively new phenomenon. It gained traction in the 2010s when a number of civic associations defending human, social or civic rights started identifying right-wing radicalization as a major threat to their cause. The electoral ascendance of the LSNS and the broader appeal of its ideas pushed various civic networks and associations to turn their attention to countering right-wing extremism. Their organizational efforts became more visible after the 2013 success of the party in Banská Bystrica. The electoral victory of LSNS brought together activists involved in various civic advocacy projects to counter the presence and rise of extremist right-wing groups. These groups are primarily organized in Bratislava. For example, the Uprising Continues is a loose network of antifascist organizers founded in 2015 to counter the LSNS and various other extremist right-wing groups associated with the party or propagating similar ideas.[36] Bratislava Without Nazis is another initiative that seeks to organize antifascist activities mostly to counter those of the LSNS. Outside Bratislava, antifascist activity is very limited with the exception of Banská Bystrica, where the success of the LSNS led to the founding of the civic platform Not in Our Town to counter the activities of the party and its leader, who served as governor of the region from 2013 to 2017.[37]

The resources the various Slovak antifascist groups have at their disposal vary substantially from those available in Greece or Germany. In the absence of a strong radical left party in Slovakia, political pressure on Slovak authorities to counter extremism is considerably more limited than in other countries.[38] Lacking a radical left party to fully embrace their cause, antifascists rely on convincing individual MPs to agree to a cordon sanitaire against the party by refusing to accept or discuss any of its parliamentary proposals. By 2018, 21 out of the 136 MPs from nearly all other parliamentary parties had signed up to a declaration posted by the Stop Fascism initiative to counter all parliamentary motions of the LSNS and to refuse to take part in any media panels in which LSNS members are invited.[39] The organizational resources of the relatively few Slovak

---

[36] Interview with organizer of the Uprising Continues, March 2018.
[37] Interview with two organizers of Not in Our Town, March 2018.
[38] To the extent that social pressure is associated with institutional pressure, the relative weaknesses of the societal resistance to right-wing extremism might go some way to account for a less hostile institutional environment.
[39] http://stopfasizmu.sk/

antifascist groups vary considerably. Some groups, such as the Uprising Continues, rely on the organizational involvement of its key organizers in previous civic initiatives in the 1990s and 2000s. Previous participation in civic initiatives helped provide the necessary experience for organizing both conventional and contentious political action. As in Germany or Greece, for many Slovak groups countering right-wing extremism, the organizational resources at their disposal stop short of formal organizational structures. For example, the Uprising Continues is a non-registered ad hoc network of activists without a formal structure or hierarchy.[40] The platform Not in Our Town is also a civic initiative without a formal legal status. But the platform is much more institutionalized, as it relies on the organizational, financial and human resources of the Center for Community Organizing – an NGO founded in 1990s to promote various forms of citizen initiatives. With funding from national and international public and private sources, the Center has permanent staff involved in different aspects of antifascism, such as education, mobilization and aid to vulnerable communities. The link with the Center grants the platform access to other important social actors with intellectual resources, such as university departments and cultural centers.[41]

In terms of tactics, the few antifascist groups in Slovakia are primarily involved in conventional forms of political activism against the LSNS. At the institutional level, antifascist groups seek to exercise pressure on Slovak national and local authorities to take action against the party. Part of the pressure is on the Prosecutor General to initiate a legal process to outlaw the party. Another part is on municipal and regional authorities to publicly come out against the LSNS and, using their discretionary authority, to prevent the use of public spaces for party activities. In the social sphere, antifascist groups are active in the organization of events highlighting the ideological lineage of the LSNS and educational seminars aiming at youth de-radicalization. For example, the Not in Our Town platform initiated a de-radicalization program in various schools of Banská Bystrica utilizing the experiences of victims of discrimination. The most evident activities of the antifascist groups involve the mobilization of hundreds and, occasionally, thousands of people in demonstrations or protests against the LSNS. Street activism is primarily undertaken by various groups in Bratislava, which mobilize against demonstrations or commemorations organized by the LSNS or other extremist right-wing groups. In recent years, antifascists

---

[40] Interview with organizer of the Uprising Continues, March 2018.
[41] Interview with two organizers of Not in Our Town, March 2018.

demonstrate every March against the commemoration of the interwar Slovak state. There have also been demonstrations against anti-immigration or anti-Islam events organized by the LSNS in Bratislava, attracting a few hundred, and more rarely a few thousand, people. Interestingly, the controversial marches and protests of LSNS activists in densely populated Roma areas outside the main urban centers do not usually confront organized social opposition. Moreover, unlike in Greece or Germany, the action repertoire of Slovak antifascists does not involve the use of violence. In the absence of anarchist and autonomist groups that are usually associated with more violent tactics against extremist right-wing parties, Slovak antifascism occasionally leads to militant but not violent confrontations with opponents.

The absence of a strong and widely spread antifascist movement has a number of consequences for the organizational development of the LSNS. Without facing similar societal reaction as in Germany or Greece, the organizational expansion and evolution of the LSNS is largely unrelated to antifascist mobilization against it. The emphasis the party places on setting up subnational party structures and mobilizing its activists outside major urban centers means that LSNS is mostly left unchallenged by antifascists. Apart from a few high-profile events organized in Bratislava, much of the street activism of the party takes place in settings without organized antifascism. Marches, demonstrations and patrols in localities with a high density of Roma inhabitants do not face systematic, structured or substantial resistance by local societies, which tend to be apathetic or tolerant to the presence of the LSNS. Just like police officers and train personnel, passengers do not even raise their eyebrows to the uniformed presence of party activists on board – a type of activism that would probably be met with stiff social resistance in Germany or Greece.[42] Moreover, throughout most of the country, there is no critical mass of antifascists to counter the local party demonstrations, protests and petitions. As the head of a district association in the Prešov region notes, "I have not seen any members of antifa groups in the three years I have been involved in LSNS activism. In the cities of Prešov and Kosice there are some, very few. But, given their size, they cannot do much."[43] In the absence of strong societal reactions to its presence, the party has managed to avoid the social stigmatization that complicated the organizational development of similar parties in Germany

---

[42] Interviews with two members of the party executive, July 2017. Observation of four train patrols in the eastern Prešov region in July 2017.
[43] Interview with head of district association in the Prešov region, July 2017.

and Greece. Although there is some evidence of local organizational failure, this is mostly due to factors other rather than social pressure. Moreover, in the absence of militant or violent protest to its local development, the party has been able to not only continue but also institutionalize some of its controversial forms of activism, such as the train patrols, by paying some of the activists involved. An indirect effect of the relatively weaker societal hostility the LSNS faces relates to the institutional environment. Absent a strong antifascist movement, institutional actors in Slovakia seem to face less pressure to respond to extremist right-wing mobilization.

Conclusion

This chapter has analyzed the local organizational development of the NPD and the LSNS to probe the generalizability of the analytical framework developed and tested in the previous chapters. Like the GD, the two parties place a lot of emphasis on infiltrating local societies and dominating street politics by setting up dozens of local organizations and undertaking hundreds of local activities. A large number of these activities are contentious, involving aggressive marches, militant demonstrations and controversial commemorations. Others, such as political speeches or street canvassing, are reminiscent of the local activism undertaken by most political parties. This repertoire of conventional and contentious activity reinforces the hybrid nature of extremist right-wing parties – they operate on the frontier separating parties from movements. The analysis of their organizational lives reveals similarities with the organizational development of the GD: it is relatively unpredictable, uncertain and unstable. Organizational breakdown is as common in Germany and Slovakia as it is in Greece. Some local branches shut down or became empty shells without much activity to justify their presence in local communities. Others display notable organizational persistence, even in adverse environments.

In line with the analytical framework developed in Chapter 3, the notable variation in local organizational outcomes can be traced to the interplay of endogenous and environmental factors. The emphasis the NPD and the LSNS place on both conventional and contentious forms of political involvement and their charismatic nature complicate their organizational development and can go some way to account for the varied trajectories of their subnational units. The presence of a significant portion of militant activists is necessary for street action but generates friction with more moderate party functionaries. In the absence of well-institutionalized mechanisms for resolving feuds and distributing resources, this friction can partly account for the instability observed in the local trajectories of subnational party units. The friction between militants and moderates was most evident in the NPD, which changed leadership a number of times, amid feuds between the more moderate way advocated by its electorally successful regions and the more militant national party. The local organizations of the LSNS displayed similar albeit less pronounced instability than those of the NPD, changing their local heads several times in the short time span of their existence.

In both Germany and Slovakia, right-wing extremists displayed a notable difficulty in adjusting to changing environmental – particularly electoral – conditions, even when these conditions were increasingly more favorable. This difficulty was more evident in the case of the NPD than the LSNS, perhaps because the German party faced smaller electoral incentives for organizational adaptation and a more uncertain institutional and social environment. Regional electoral breakthroughs did not bring about a marked change in the emphasis the NPD placed on local street militancy. Nor did its near electoral demise in recent years coincide with street withdrawal. Similarly, rather than changing tactics, the LSNS remained committed to militant activism after its national electoral breakthrough. The newly acquired access to institutional politics did not alter its commitment to non-institutional politics through involvement in controversial local activism. The limited association between electoral change and organizational development can be observed not only at the level of the national party but also at the level of individual party subunits. The analysis of the association between local electoral results and local organizational outcomes yielded negative results similar to those recorded in Greece. Electoral logic, measured here as votes, cannot adequately account for local organizational development.

As in Greece, the organizational development of extremist right-wing parties in Germany and Slovakia generated institutional hostility, which took a toll on the local organizational efforts of the NPD and the LSNS. Institutional efforts to ban the two parties added to the broader environmental uncertainty they faced and curbed their organizational expansion. In Germany, where these efforts were more pronounced, the long judicial process to ban the NPD coincided with discontinuity in dozens of its local structures and the shrinking of its local branch network. In Slovakia, institutional pressure on the LSNS was weaker than in Germany. But the motion to ban the party stopped its rapid organizational expansion and complicated efforts to stabilize existing local structures. Although institutional pressure has a similar effect on the local organizations of extremist right-wing parties, it does not uniformly affect the capacity of such parties to mobilize their supporters. After the attempt to ban the LSNS, there was a statistically significant drop in local party activism – a pattern similar to that observed in Greece. But in Germany, the refugee crisis opened a window for increased NPD mobilization, even during the protracted period of litigation against the party. Lacking the institutional access enjoyed by their counterparts in Greece and Slovakia and facing a much less favorable electoral environment, German right-wing extremists increasingly resorted to Saxon streets to mobilize support for their cause. The spike in the mobilization of the Saxon NPD during the refugee crisis indicates that the hybrid nature of such parties is as much a liability as it is an asset. It is a liability because it generates organizational instability and an asset because it makes the party more resilient to environmental hostility.

Attempts by the NPD and the LSNS to grow roots in local societies have generated varied societal responses from a wide array of antifascist actors employing distinct tactics and with different resources at their disposal. Based on the qualitative evidence presented in this chapter and the qualitative and quantitative evidence from the Greek case, it is clear that antifascist mobilization is almost exclusively an urban phenomenon. It is takes different forms and it is distinctively more frequent, systematic but also more radical in Germany than in Slovakia. The important differences between German and Slovak antifascism are due to the number and size of antifascist groups and to the different resources they have at their disposal. These differences suggest that societal pressure against right-wing extremism is considerably weaker in Slovakia than in Germany. Whereas in Germany antifascist groups have managed to curb the organizational development of the NPD even in some of its strongholds, in Slovakia, the evolution of the LSNS does not seem to be affected by societal pressure. The relative weakness of antifascism in Slovakia might perhaps explain why institutional actors are far less hostile in Slovakia than in Germany or Greece. Absent a strong antifascist movement, Slovak authorities seem less compelled to deal decisively with extremism.

CHAPTER 11

Conclusions

From Washington to Warsaw and from Charlottesville to Chemnitz democracies are facing challenges from political actors who display little or no commitment to democratic institutions and practices. The growing political relevance of such actors adds to overall concerns that democracy is in trouble. The democratic optimism of the early 1990s is now being replaced by discussions of democratic backsliding, recession and decline (e.g., Diamond 2015; Plattner 2015; Bermeo 2016; Bernhard and O' Neill 2018). Parties such as the ones examined in this book bring to the surface some of the biggest challenges facing European democracies and add to scholarly anxiety about possible democratic retrenchment. Their ideologies, histories and practices are rooted in an epoch of destructive democratic collapse. Their contentious and, often, violent involvement in politics pushes modern democracy to its limits.

This book adds, then, important new dimensions to discussions about the fate of democracy by systematically tracing how three of the most extreme political parties in Europe seek to grow roots in local societies and examining the varied responses of institutional and societal actors to extremism. The challenges posed by such parties are not solely discursive but also organizational. Extremist right-wing parties challenge democracy not only with what they say but also with what they do. Moreover, these challenges are felt not only at the national political level but also in cities and neighborhoods, where these parties seek to establish their organizational presence before propelling themselves into the national political spotlight. Turning organization into a dependent rather than an independent variable and focusing on the subnational rather than the national level, this book took a rare look "inside" hundreds of local party organizations and thousands of their subnational activities to understand the factors affecting the capacity of extremist right-wing parties to establish strongholds in diverse political settings. Developing and testing an analytical framework to analyze the local organizational development of extremist

236

right-wing parties, the book showed how party evolution relates to the interplay of endogenous and environmental factors. To some extent, the organizational fate of these parties is sealed by their own decisions and, more importantly, by their internal organizational contradictions. Parties, though, that seek to challenge in such fundamental ways their external environment cannot easily develop in isolation from this environment. By breaking down this environment into its component parts, the book has shown how electoral, institutional and societal factors help shape the local organizational trajectories of such parties.

Parties like the ones studied in this book pose a different set of challenges to democracy than other parties studied in the now sizable literature on European far right parties. To better appreciate these challenges, Chapter 2 has undertaken a classification exercise to assess the conceptual proximity and distance between extremist and radical right-wing parties. Parties such as the Golden Dawn (GD), the National Democratic Party of Germany (NPD) and the Kotleba – People's Party Our Slovakia (LSNS) share with radical right-wing parties the ideological attachment to nationalism and programmatic opposition to immigration. Beyond these similarities, though, they tend to differ from radical right-wing parties by adopting an explicitly biological version of nationalism, reminiscent of interwar ideologies. Moreover, through their rhetoric and practices these parties associate themselves with interwar regimes and ideas. Furthermore, most extremist right-wing parties are marginalized even by radical right-wing parties and have their own international fora. More importantly, extremist right-wing parties tend to differ in their political *praxis* – the way they practice politics in the streets – by systematically adopting repertoires of contentious politics mostly associated with social movements. Some of these parties are relatively recent and electorally successful and others existed for decades on the margins of political life before becoming politically relevant.

The ideological emphasis extremist right-wing parties place on street dominance (Mann 2004) and their lack of financial and communicative resources encourages them to develop multiple subnational organizations. Local party branches are at the forefront of their efforts to grow organizational roots across the country, dominate city streets and village squares and build a capacity for contentious political action. The hundreds of party branches of the GD, NPD and LSNS are relatively small in size, relying on the voluntary work and modest financial backing of, at most, a few dozen supporters who usually organize a small number of noteworthy activities per year. The thousands of branch activities analyzed in Chapters 4 and 10 provide a rare glimpse of the "life" of local party organizations in Greece, Germany and Slovakia. The local organizational life of these parties bears some similarities to that of mainstream parties: they lecture on current affairs, present their candidates and canvass their localities. But they are also different from mainstream parties in that they systematically organize contentious forms of political action, mobilizing their activists to participate in controversial protests, demonstrations, petitions and commemorations. Marching through Roma villages and motorcading in leftist strongholds, local activists of extremist right-wing parties seek to signal dominance and instill fear to their opponents, propagate their ideas and recruit new zealots for their cause. In this sense, their political praxis is part of their political message, hence necessitating an approach that takes into account but also goes beyond the discursive level of politics.

By systematically tracing the local organizational evolution of extremist right-wing parties, this book has documented the important variation in developmental outcomes. The findings were similar in all three cases, demonstrating the utility of going below the national level to understand party evolution. In some settings, local organizations managed to grow local roots and become loci of routinized party activism, while in others they simply shut down or became empty shells that barely organized more than their inaugural event. The coding of all branch listings and activities publicized by the GD across a decade documented the divergent organizational trajectories of its local organizations. The analysis of the entire universe of local organizations in Chapter 5 showed how some outlived internal and external challenges sustaining high levels of routinized activism across a long stretch of time. It also brought to the surface a significant number of organizational fatalities – branches that shut down amid internal and external trouble. The examination of the local organizational development of the NPD and the LSNS identified similar levels of volatility in local party life. As Chapter 10 showed, NPD district structures closed down quite frequently, even in settings such as Saxony, where the party has had a notable presence in local councils. The local structures of the LSNS displayed high levels of personnel changes and considerable differences in their activism patterns.

This book sought to account for variation in local organizational outcomes by examining how different factors affect local organizational development. A notable tradition in the general literature on political parties, going back to Michels (1915) and Duverger (1954) attributes their organizational development to endogenous factors. Looking "inside" parties for clues related to their development, this strain of the literature tends to attribute organizational evolution to such factors as party origins and leadership decisions (Bolleyer 2013). The local organizational development of extremist right-wing parties confirms some of these scholarly findings. Variation in local organizational development is partly due to the organizational DNA of extremist right-wing parties. Chapter 6 analyzed how two features of these parties shape local organizational outcomes. First, the parties analyzed here are movement parties (Kitschelt 2006; della Porta et al. 2017) simultaneously involved in conventional and contentious politics. Their emphasis on street dominance makes these parties reliant on the recruitment of militant activists who, where dominant, they form relatively closed networks blocking the opening of the party to moderates. Second, extremist right-wing parties are charismatic organizations (Panebianco 1988) lacking the institutional infrastructure that characterizes Duvergerian mass parties (1954). They hence lack the institutional mechanisms to distribute selective incentives and manage the conflicts associated with this distribution. The combination of these two characteristics makes the local organizational development of such parties highly unstable. As Chapters 6 and 10 have shown, the local organizations of the GD, NPD and LSNS display high levels of organizational volatility, evident in their frequent shut downs or personnel changes. The detailed analysis of *each* GD branch in Chapter 6 presented strong evidence showing that organizational volatility is significantly lower in organizational structures in which the inherent tension between militants and moderates is lower. In a party like the GD, these tend to be branches dominated by militants, with strong experiential ties to the party leadership. Branches founded before the electoral breakthrough of the party, with older organizational roots and violent profile, were hence more likely to be organizationally resilient than the rest. In Germany, the significant presence of militants in the party similarly complicated its organizational development after its mid-2000s breakthroughs and left the NPD torn between its militant and more moderate wings. In Slovakia, the presence of a militant core similarly complicated efforts to stabilize its local structures, generating friction with newcomers to the party, who did not share its appetite for militancy.

The way local party structures evolve is not only subject to internal party dynamics and choices but it is also due to environmental factors. The electoral environment is one of the most important of such factors. A significant strain of literature on political parties in general (Kitschelt 1994; Grzymala-Busse 2002; Levitsky 2003; Samuels 2004; Tavits 2013) and far right parties in particular (Kitschelt and McGann 1995; Carter

2005; Art 2008) has focused on how organizational factors affect electoral outcomes but has overlooked the effect of electoral results on party organizational development. While confirming the emphasis the literature places on the positive effects of organizational presence on electoral outcomes, this book went beyond the existing literature by examining how electoral outcomes affect local organizational development. The meticulously collected data on local party organizations showed how changes in the electoral environment can shape local organizational outcomes. Electoral breakthroughs provide incentives for local organizational expansion but this expansion does not necessarily conform to electoral logic. The organizational evolution of such parties as the GD, the NPD and the LSNS is only partly driven by electoral inducements. The three parties chose to set up new branches in settings with low electoral potential and remained absent in settings with high electoral promise. More importantly, the subsequent development of these branches was unrelated to the local electoral votes the party won. Even after major breakthroughs, highly centralized extremist right-wing parties cannot easily adjust to the changed environment and transform themselves into highly efficient electoral machines.

The local organizational development of extremist right-wing parties is affected not only by the relative attractiveness of electoral "carrots" but also by the institutional and societal "sticks" these parties tend to confront. As in the interwar past (Loewenstein 1937a; 1937b; Capoccia 2005), contemporary democracies devise a broad range of institutional responses to defend themselves from those seeking to harm them. Due to the relative threat they pose to modern democratic orders, extremist right-wing parties tend to generate militant institutional responses against them. Chapters 8 and 10 documented the range of militant democracy measures used in Greece, Germany and Slovakia to curb extremism and then gauged how these measures affected their organizational evolution. In all three cases, institutional intervention contained the organizational development of the parties. The effects of militant democracy were mostly evident in the evolution of local party structures. After the measures taken against the extremist right-wing parties, the local organizational presence froze or shrank. The intervention of the state, especially the judicial process, also scared away more moderate party activists, who deserted local branches in fear of the consequences of being associated with these parties. Although state intervention undermined the organizational capacity of local party structures, the party militants who stayed behind managed to sustain considerable levels local activism. Their activism had to be adjusted to the changing institutional environment and, in Greece and Slovakia, it witnessed a significant contraction. State intervention contained but did not deal a fatal blow to right-wing extremism.

The local organizational development of extremist right-wing parties is affected by changes not only in the electoral and institutional, but also in the societal environment. Due to their very nature, extremist right-wing parties often generate varying degrees of societal opposition. This opposition is mostly exercised at the local level, in the cities, localities and neighborhoods where these parties seek to grow roots. This book examined the multitude of social actors involved in antifascist activity, the range of resources they have at their disposal and the different tactics they employ to confront extremist right-wing parties. Chapter 9 systematically analyzed thousands of activities organized by hundreds of antifascist actors in Greece. It traced the temporal and spatial evolution of antifascism and demonstrated its strong association with extremist right-wing mobilization. The stronger were the attempts of the GD to infiltrate localities through its activism, the stronger was the intensity and consistency of antifascist efforts to stop it. The qualitative analysis of a few micro-cases highlighted the factors associated with the relative success or failure of antifascist efforts to curb the organizational growth of the GD. Some of these factors were also identified in the analysis of German antifascism, undertaken in Chapter 10. As in Patra or Ioannina, antifascist activity in Saxony was more effective in settings such as Leipzig where the antifascists managed to build alliances with institutional actors. Unlike in Greece or Germany, antifascism in Slovakia is considerably weaker – there are fewer actors, with scarcer resources and a narrower range of tactics. In the absence of strong antifascist pressure, the institutional pressure against the LSNS is also weaker.

Party Organizational Development

The analysis of organizational development has focused on the evolution of extremist right-wing parties but the findings have implications for the broader study of political parties as well. By tracing the evolution of hundreds of subnational party structures in the three countries, this book has turned attention to the local dimension of party development. This dimension has been neglected in the broader literature on political parties because parties rely a lot less on their local bases than they once did. Local party branches and cells, once hailed by Duverger as one of the most notable characteristics of mass parties, seem no longer as critical for party organizations, which increasingly rely on centrally allocated financial and communicative resources to build electoral support (Katz and Mair 1995; Farrell and Webb 2000; Norris 2004). The evidence presented in this book shows that even in a socially transformed environment with shrinking party memberships and eroding social linkages (Dalton 2000; Scarrow 2000; Wattenberg 2000; Mair and van Biezen 2001; Poguntke 2006; van Biezen et al. 2012), some parties continue to invest on building strong local organizations. This investment has significant pay-offs: even the most extreme of parties do better in settings where they manage to establish local organizations. In line with the findings of the extant literature on far right parties, this work shows how internal party supply matters (Kitschelt and McGann 1995; Mudde 2007) – in this case, the "local supply" of party organizational infrastructure. The evidence on the relative importance of local party organizations is also consistent with findings of the broader party literature, which shows the electoral dividends paid by local party presence (Tavits 2013). It is also in line with evidence showing the importance of local party activism on party performance (Huckfeldt and Sprague 1992; Whiteley and Seyd 1994; Pattie et al. 1995; Gerber and Green 2000; Denver et al. 2004; Fisher et al. 2006; 2016). The findings of this book and the strong evidence in the broader literature on the importance of subnational organizational infrastructure suggest that the neglect of local party organizations might come at a significant cost for other parties. Without strong local organizations, mainstream parties might leave an organizational void for potential competitors to fill. Future research might help cast more light on how the local organizational life of mainstream parties might facilitate or hinder the organizational penetration of new parties in local societies.

The rare examination of the local organizational life of extremist right-wing parties has also brought to the surface the notable variation in organizational outcomes. Even in some of the most highly centralized *Führerparteien*, as far right parties are often unflatteringly called, there are remarkable differences in the evolution of their local organizations. Some local party units have been around for many years routinizing their local presence through the organization of relatively frequent local events. Others became empty shells without much political activity to justify their existence or subsequently withdrew from the local societies in which they sought to establish an organizational presence. The divergent trajectories of local party organizations are partly due to factors endogenous to the parties. The ideological origins of extremist right-wing parties make street dominance a key element of their organizational evolution and grant such parties considerable autonomy from their environments. As known from the broader literature on political parties, party origins matter (Duverger 1954; Panebianco 1988) and they determine the subsequent development of party organizations. The detailed analysis of local organizations reaffirms the emphasis on the organizational DNA of political parties. Local organizations rooted in the years of party ideological purity, with organizational legacy, experience and, even, militancy, proved to be much more resilient than those founded during the period of electoral ascendance (Chapter 6). This might be seem surprising, as militancy is directly or indirectly associated with organizational failure (Art 2011). The resilience of local organizations dominated by militants is less surprising, once one takes into account the ideological and experiential assets that, unlike moderates, militants share. As Panebianco notes, whereas party "believers" share the party identity and goals, the "careerists," with their eagerness to gain selective incentives, are a constant source of party factionalism (1988: 26–29).

The dominance of militants in extremist right-wing parties enhances their autonomy from their external environment but it also exacerbates the environmental uncertainty these parties face and complicates attempts to institutionalize party structures and processes. Despite the relative autonomy local party organizations get to enjoy from external environments, extremist right-wing parties cannot easily institutionalize their local structures and activities. The detailed analysis of local party organizations shows that, even when routinized, the local life of extremist right-wing parties remains highly unstable. Lacking in institutional density, these parties are much more likely to experience internal turmoil, especially in the face of major changes in their external environment. This book analyzed three sources of change. First, a change in the electoral environment might alter the structure of incentives and exacerbate internal conflicts regarding the distribution of selective rewards, especially parliamentary seats. Incumbency was shown to enhance the capacity for mobilization but to also exacerbate intra-party feuds. Second, a change in the institutional environment – in the cases studied here, institutional hostility – might increase the cost of sustaining local organizations and accentuate the tactical dilemmas such parties face. The intervention by the state increases the cost of party membership and the probability of member defection. At the same time, the dilemma between moderating and sustaining contentious forms of activism intensifies internal conflict. Third, a change in the societal pressure these parties face affects the relative autonomy local organizations have to determine their own fates. Local societal resistance to efforts for local party dominance increases the cost of being a member in an extremist organization, exacerbating internal dilemmas about tactical choices and, ultimately, tensions. Societal pressure can also indirectly affect the way institutional actors deal with extremism. All three environmental factors can seriously undermine the autonomy of local party organizations by increasing the uncertainty they face for survival and by generating internal processes that extremist right-wing parties cannot easily manage. In this sense, the purported choice party leaders have to institutionalize (Kitschelt 2006; Bolleyer 2013) is not entirely theirs but also subject to the degree of environmental uncertainty generated by external conditions. The higher the degree of uncertainty a party faces for survival, the less likely it is to adapt to its changing environment and institutionalize.

The Dynamics of Extremist Right-Wing Contention

By looking "inside" three of the most extreme parties in Europe, this book has brought to the surface a dimension of party life that is often neglected in the analysis of party development but is common in analyses of social movements (Caiani et al. 2012). Rather than solely looking at party structures, membership and finances, this book has examined thousands of local party events organized across time in Greece, Germany and Slovakia. The analysis of these events has highlighted the emphasis these parties place on a dual track of conventional and contentious politics and documented their relatively large repertoire of political action. Through their controversial marches, demonstrations, patrols, motorcades, commemorations or petitions, extremist right-wing parties send ideological cues, programmatic signals and historical hints to their potential supporters. Motorcades in communist strongholds in Piraeus, train patrols of routes used by the Roma in the Prešov region and marches in the alternative Connewitz district of Leipzig help communicate street dominance and aim to scare political opponents and targets – practices reminiscent of interwar fascist mobilization (Mann 2004). The street politics of extremist right-wing parties seek to bolster their anti-system profile and reinforce the sense that they are not embedded within the established political order. Their social activism, most prevalent in Greece and Slovakia, seeks to legitimize their presence in the local communities and to challenge the normative dominance of the Left in this type of activity. In this sense, "repertoires of actions are not just instruments of protest, but also reflect activists' values" (della Porta and Diani 2006: 192).

The systematic analysis of local party activism shows that the dynamics of extremist right-wing mobilization are similar to those observed across the entire social movement spectrum (Tarrow 1994; della Porta 1995; McAdam et al. 2001; Snow et al. 2004). First, the involvement of these parties in contentious action varies significantly across time. Extremist right-wing action is much more intense in some periods than in others, approximating the analogy of a cycle (della Porta and Diani 2006) or wave (Koopmans 2004). Episodes of intense extreme right mobilization tend to be associated with the opening of political opportunity structures (Kitschelt 1986; Tarrow 1994) and with broader disequilibrium in the web of socioeconomic relations in a given polity (Koopmans 2004). The economic crisis in Greece in the 2010s; the welfare crisis in Germany in the 2000s and the refugee crisis in the mid-2010s; and recent spurts of criminal activity in Slovakia differ significantly in nature but similarly influence the capacity of the extremist right-wing actors to have an impact on their environment (Kriesi 2004). Once these episodes in political life dissipate in importance, the levels of extremist right-wing mobilization are likely to subside. The decline in contentious activism, though, is not necessarily a tactical choice of extremist right-wing actors. It is often the result of institutional and societal reactions to extremism and the effect of counter-mobilization on the internal workings of extremist right-wing parties. Institutional hostility increases the cost of sustaining contentious activism as it confronts parties with the prospect of repression. Societal reactions compel parties to give up some localities, change their street tactics and concentrate their organizational resources in settings where they can best resist societal pressures. Even in favorable electoral settings, extremist right-wing parties might be unable to sustain for long their dual track of conventional and contentious politics.

Second, the patterns of contentious politics vary not only across time but also across space. Spatial variation is associated with the complex web of interactions between extremist right-wing actors and their opponents. The local development of extremist right-wing parties and their capacity to influence their environment cannot be viewed in isolation from the responses and mobilization of other actors in the political system (Koopmans 2004). For reasons analyzed in Chapters 2 and 3, extremist right-wing mobilization generates institutional and societal responses that affect developmental outcomes. The interaction with state authorities on the one hand and with antifascist groups on the other triggers internal processes that shape the subsequent development of extremist right-wing parties. The outcomes of these interactions cannot easily be generalized even across a centralized national context, like the one in Greece. In some settings, extremist right-wing activists were able to sustain significant levels of local activism even in the face of institutional and societal hostility. In other settings, they had to desert their organizational efforts and go home. This book has shown that, although national political culture can help account for broader reactions to extremism (Art 2005; 2011), there is significant subnational variation to merit distinct attention and to account for different outcomes.

Third, the systematic analysis of variation in organizational outcomes has helped highlight factors affecting local party resilience and failure. The variation in local developmental outcomes can largely be associated with the resources available to the different actors involved. The local organizations of extremist right-wing parties are more likely to survive in settings where they can rely on central organizational resources or sizable networks of people (della Porta and Diani 2006) with biographical profiles and experiences that allow the continuity of political contention (McAdam 1986). They are less likely to sustain their local presence in settings where they are grossly outnumbered or where their opponents have forged alliances with institutional actors who can use their authority against them. The tactical choices of the actors involved also matter. The use of violence is a double-edged sword for both the extremists and their opponents. Militancy can help establish local street dominance but can scare away wider segments of society and the political legitimacy associated with larger numbers of participants. Regardless of the resources the different actors can bring to bear in their confrontations, they cannot match those of the state. Hence, the attempt by the actors to influence the behavior of the institutional players.

Militant Democracy and Movement Parties

The analysis of three extreme parties has helped trace the effects of militant institutional responses on their organizational development. Going beyond normative defenses of democratic militancy (Kirshner 2014), this book has systematically analyzed how institutional hostility to extremism trickles down the targeted organizations and affects their evolution. The analysis has yielded a number of observations. First, institutional hostility compelled the extremist right-wing parties to freeze or reverse their local organizational expansion but did not deal them a fatal blow. In all three cases, the judicial processes against the parties took a toll on their local organizational structures. But all three parties sustained varying levels of local activism even in the face of institutional hostility. The fewer local branches and activists of the parties had to make adjustments to their tactics but did not easily give up their involvement in contentious politics. In this sense, there are important limits to the effectiveness of militant democratic responses to extremism (Minkenberg 2006). Modern democratic states can stall or reverse the organizational growth of extremist right-wing parties but, for as long as these parties remain legal, powerful institutional actors *alone* cannot easily eliminate their capacity to mobilize their devotees into action.

This outcome might seem puzzling because institutional actors are considerably more powerful than their challengers. Why cannot this relative asymmetry of power yield more decisive organizational outcomes? The analysis here has highlighted a number of possible reasons for this outcome. First, in both unitary and federal democratic states institutional mechanisms of repression cannot be expected to be uniformly enforced across space and time. The analysis here has shown that even in relatively centralized institutional settings, there is some scope for administrative agency, which might help explain variation in local outcomes (della Porta and Reiter 1998; Earl 2006). In settings where institutional structures are relatively open to political influence, there is also scope for the challengers and their opponents to influence the way administrative agency becomes exercised. The second reason relates to the characteristics of challengers. The hybrid nature of the targeted organizations grants them considerable organizational flexibility that most social movements or political parties lack. The legal protection and relative legitimacy political parties enjoy in democratic polities grants extremists a wider range of organizational tactics to challenge democracy – ranging from contentious and violent mobilization to institutional politics. When faced with institutional repression, extremist right-wing parties are likely to utilize their hybrid nature to deflect the institutional pressure – often by seeking refuge in the legally protected status of the party.

The propensity of democracy challengers to seek refuge to their party status when faced with institutional hostility does not necessarily mean that they make a turn toward conventional politics, as often observed in social movement studies (della Porta 1995; Koopmans 2004; Kriesi 2004; della Porta and Diani 2006). The hybrid nature of the party grants organizational flexibility but does not help resolve the dilemma such parties face between institutionalization and radicalization. Although none of the parties examined here underwent further

radicalization, they did not take a decisive step toward institutionalization either. Even when faced with a favorable electoral environment,
which provided institutionalized access, extremist right-wing parties
imperfectly adjusted to the electoral opportunities and did not fully
embrace the institutional mechanisms now available for expressing their
grievances. The three parties remained committed to their street tactics,
in some cases modifying their repertoire to match the more hostile
institutional and societal environment. During their criminal trial, GD
members continued to organize street activism, avoiding violent confrontation with antifascists and remaining active in non-urban centers
where antifascism tends to be relatively weaker. After the initiation of
the second party ban process, the NPD increased its street presence, not
only during the electoral campaign in Saxony, but also during the
refugee crisis, opting for smaller and more frequent events in suburban
areas, and avoiding large outdoor events, which constitute a pole of
attraction for antifascists. The motion by the state to ban the LSNS did
not deter the party from continuing its controversial train patrols,
primarily in rural areas, where antifascism is non-existent.

The imperfect institutionalization of the parties can be traced back to
their ideological roots. The emphasis they place on inducing fear in their
opponents through their street dominance is intrinsic to their rejection of
liberal democratic institutions and norms. The lack of institutionalization
can also be associated with their experiences: having gained electoral
traction while radicalized, the parties cannot easily move away from tactics
they associate with their electoral success. Dozens of interviews with
leaders and functionaries of the three parties highlighted their conviction
that their contentious practices work.

The relative continuity in party organizational behavior, though, is as
much a matter of choice as it is a matter of necessity. Confronted with a
hostile political environment, extremist right-wing parties cannot fully
abandon contentious politics. Institutional and societal hostility compels
extremist actors to sustain their links to militant networks and their
involvement in militant activism – as a means of organizational hedging.
Faced with the possibility of being blocked from institutional politics,
extremist right-wing parties stay on the frontier between conventional and
contentious politics for relatively long periods of time. This might explain
why these parties stick around for much longer than their institutional and
societal opponents would hope. It might also explain, though, why,
instead of further radicalization or de-radicalization, some of these parties
go through a period of organizational stagnation.

Future Research

This book has sought to contribute to the extant literature on the far right and the broader literature on political parties, social movements and militant democracies by systematically examining the local organizational lives of three of the most extreme parties in Europe. A key theme in the preceding chapters was the way in which such parties deal with different sources and degrees of environmental uncertainty. Future research can further examine the link between environmental uncertainty and organizational development. In the same way that environmental uncertainty might lead to organizational stagnation, parties can be expected to evolve differently in environments with less uncertainty. One source of further insights regarding the link between environmental uncertainty and organizational development can come from the analysis of the evolution of parties that have made a transition to less extreme forms of political involvement. The departure of parties such as the French National Front, the Sweden Democrats or the Hungarian Jobbik from contentious or, even, violence-prone forms of politics can provide more clues into how distinct electoral, institutional and social environments facilitate or hinder de-radicalization. For example, it is plausible that stronger electoral results – say, over 10 percent of the national vote – are better facilitators of party institutionalization than results below this threshold. It is also possible that less hostile institutional or social environments reduce the pragmatic need for local organizational infrastructure that, in really hostile environments, ensures organizational viability.

Another theme of this book that requires more attention revolves around societal responses to extremist right-wing mobilization. The examination of societal responses has largely focused on the mobilization of hundreds of organized groups, with different resources and distinct tactics. The mobilization of social actors is sometimes enough to drive extremists away and it can often compel institutional actors to use the means at their disposal to counter extremist right-wing actors. The emphasis on antifascist mobilization helped bring into the picture the importance of various societal groups in dealing with extremism and highlight the analytical utility of viewing these actors through the lens of the social movement literature. But in emphasizing antifascist mobilization, this book has left considerable room for future inquiry into less visible or less organized forms of societal resistance to extremism. Individuals who refuse to rent their empty offices to far right parties, corporations who refuse to take their business or teachers who seek to counter extremism in their classrooms

(Miller-Idriss 2005) are also part of the social nexus seeking to oppose the advent of far right parties and merit more systematic attention. These actors are not necessarily out in the streets protesting against the far right but their actions might be just as consequential as those of antifascist mobilizers.

Future research can also further problematize the institutional environment extremists face. One source of further insights might come from the consideration of a wider range of institutional responses to extremism. Although the emphasis in the book was on the relative hostility of the institutional environment, the way states choose to administer extremism (Shoshan 2016) varies substantially and, in some settings, it includes policies to integrate members of extremist groups. The relative effectiveness of such policies on the capacity of extremist actors to radicalize local youths or societies merits more attention. Another source of further insights might come from further investigation of the link between institutional and societal opposition extremism. Institutional hostility is often the result of mounting societal opposition to extremism. But institutional hostility can also signal to societal actors the need for, and permissibility of, action. The processes linking the two sources of opposition and the relative autonomy each enjoys from the other are likely to vary across time and space, in ways that seem to provide a promising venue for more scholarly exploration.

Based on the findings of this book, strong institutional and societal responses to extremism do not guarantee its demise. In some settings, anti-democrats will be able to withstand pressure from institutional and societal actors and remain rooted in local societies. In other settings, though, they will succumb to the pressure, shut down their local branches and give up. The variation in local organizational outcomes shows that even highly centralized democratic states and vibrant civil societies cannot easily and fully marginalize opponents of democracy. Even after decades spent on the margins of political life, extremists are known to achieve major comebacks, stunning their opponents. Their success is less likely, though, in settings where institutional and social actors, both national and local, cooperate and remain vigilant.

Bibliography

Albertazzi, D., & McDonnell, D. (2005). The Lega Nord in the second Berlusconi government: In a league of its own. *West European Politics*, *28*(5), 952–972.

Aldrich, H. (2008). *Organizations and environments*. Stanford University Press.

Aldrich, J. H. (1995). *Why parties? The origin and transformation of party politics in America*. University of Chicago Press.

Allen, T. J. (2015). All in the party family? Comparing far right voters in Western and post-communist Europe. *Party Politics*, 1354068815593457.

Almeida, P. (2010). Social movement partyism: Collective action and oppositional political parties. In Van Dyke, N., & McCammon, H. J. (Eds.). *Strategic alliances: Coalition building and social movements*. University of Minnesota Press, 170–196.

Andronikidou, A., & Kovras, I. (2012). Cultures of rioting and anti-systemic politics in Southern Europe. *West European Politics*, *35*(4), 707–725.

Anthopoulos, C. (2015). Political parties and democracy: Evidence for reinterpretation of Article 29:1 of the Constitution. *Journal of Administrative Law*, 2, 157–172 [in Greek].

Art, D. (2004). The wild, wild east – why the DVU doesn't matter and why the NPD does. *German Politics & Society*, *22*(4), 122–133.

(2005). *The politics of the Nazi past in Germany and Austria*. Cambridge University Press.

(2007). Reacting to the radical right: Lessons from Germany and Austria. *Party Politics*, *13*(3), 331–349.

(2008). The organizational origins of the contemporary radical right: The case of Belgium. *Comparative Politics*, *40*(4), 421–440.

(2011). *Inside the radical right: The development of anti-immigrant parties in Western Europe*. Cambridge University Press.

Arter, D. (2010). The breakthrough of another West European populist radical right party? The case of the True Finns. *Government and Opposition*, *45*(4), 484–504.

(2016). When new party X has the "X factor": On resilient entrepreneurial parties. *Party Politics*, *22*(1), 15–26.

Arzheimer, K. (2009). Contextual factors and the extreme right vote in Western Europe, 1980–2002. *American Journal of Political Science*, *53*(2), 259–275.

(2015). The AfD: Finally a successful right-wing populist Eurosceptic party for Germany? *West European Politics*, *38*(3), 535–556.

Aslanidis, P. (2015). Is populism an ideology? A refutation and a new perspective. *Political Studies*. doi: 10.1111/1467-9248.12224

Auers, D., & Kasekamp, A. (2015). The impact of radical right parties in the Baltic states. In Minkenberg, M. (Ed.). *Transforming the transformation?: The East European radical right in the political process*. Routledge, 137–153.

Backes, U. (2006). The electoral victory of the NPD in Saxony and the prospects for future extreme-right success in German elections. *Patterns of Prejudice*, *40*(2), 129–141.

(2018). The radical Right in Germany, Austria, and Switzerland. In Rydgren J. (Ed.). *The Oxford Handbook of the Radical Right*. Oxford University Press, 452–477.

Backes, U., & Mudde, C. (2000). Germany: Extremism without successful parties. *Parliamentary Affairs*, *53*(3), 457–468.

Bale, T. (2007). Are bans on political parties bound to turn out badly? A comparative investigation of three "intolerant" democracies: Turkey, Spain, and Belgium. *Comparative European Politics*, *5*(2), 141–157.

Barnes, S. H., & Kaase, M. (1979). *Political action: mass participation in five western democracies*. Sage.

Beck, P. A., & Heidemann, E. D. (2014). Changing strategies in grassroots canvassing: 1956–2012. *Party Politics*, *20*(2), 261–274.

Beissinger, M. R. (2002). *Nationalist mobilization and the collapse of the Soviet State*. Cambridge University Press.

Berman, S. (1997). The life of the party. *Comparative Politics*, *30*(1), 101–122.

(2008). Taming extremist parties: Lessons from Europe. *Journal of Democracy*, *19*(1), 5–18.

Bermeo, N. (1992). Democracy and the lessons of dictatorship. *Comparative Politics*, *24*(3), 273–291.

(2016). On democratic backsliding. *Journal of Democracy*, *27*(1), 5–19.

Bernhard, M., & O'Neill, D. (2018). The persistence of authoritarianism. *Perspectives on Politics*, *16*(3), 595–598.

Betz, H. G. (1998). Introduction. In Betz, H. G., & Immerfall, S. (Eds.). *The new politics of the right: Neo-populist parties and movements in established democracies*. Macmillan, 1–10.

Betz, H. G., & Immerfall, S. (1998). *The new politics of the right: Neo-populist parties and movements in established democracies*. Macmillan.

Birchall, S. (2010). *Beating the fascists: The untold story of anti-Fascist action*. Freedom Press.

Birenbaum, G. (1992). *Le Front National en politique*. Éditions Balland.

Birnbaum, P. (1988). *States and collective action: The European experience*. Cambridge University Press.

Bluhm, W. T. (1973). *Building an Austrian nation: The political integration of a Western state*. Yale University Press.

Bodnárová, B., & Vicenová, R. (2013). *Anti-extremist strategies of political parties in Slovakia: Political parties and anti-extremism policy in Slovakia.* Center for European and North Atlantic Affairs.

Bolleyer, N. (2013). *New parties in old party systems: persistence and decline in seventeen democracies.* Oxford University Press.

Bolleyer, N., Correa, P., & Katz, G. (2018). Political party mortality in established party systems: A hierarchical competing risks approach. *Comparative Political Studies,* 0010414018758764.

Bornschier, S. (2010). *Cleavage politics and the populist right: The new cultural conflict in Western Europe.* Temple University Press.

Bourne, A. K. (2012). Democratization and the illegalization of political parties in Europe. *Democratization, 19*(6), 1065–1085.

Brandstetter, M. (2013). *Die NPD under Udo Voigt. Organisation, Ideologie, Strategie.* Nomos.

Brems, E. (2006). Belgium: The Vlaams Blok political party convicted indirectly of racism. *International Journal of Constitutional Law, 4*(4), 702–711.

Bustikova, L. (2014). Revenge of the radical right. *Comparative Political Studies,* 0010414013516069.

(2015). The democratization of hostility. In Minkenberg, M. (Ed.). *Transforming the transformation?: The East European radical right in the political process.* Routledge, 59–79.

Caciagli, M. (1988). The Movimento sociale Italiano-Destra Nazionale and neo-fascism in Italy. *West European Politics, 11*(2), 19–33.

Caiani, M., Della Porta, D., & Wagemann, C. (2012). *Mobilizing on the extreme right: Germany, Italy, and the United States.* Oxford University Press.

Cain, B. E., Ferejohn, J. A., & Fiorina, M. P. (1984). The constituency service basis of the personal vote for US representatives and British members of parliament. *American Political Science Review, 78*(1), 110–125.

Capoccia, G. (2005). *Defending democracy: Reactions to extremism in interwar Europe.* Johns Hopkins University Press.

(2013). Militant democracy: The institutional bases of democratic self-preservation. *Annual Review of Law and Social Science, 9,* 207–226.

Carter, E. (2005). *The extreme right in Western Europe: Success or failure?.* Manchester University Press.

Christopoulos, D. (2014). *The "deep" state in contemporary Greece and the extreme right.* Rosa Luxemburg Stiftung [in Greek].

Clark, A. (2004). The continued relevance of local parties in representative democracies. *Politics, 24*(1), 35–45.

Copsey, N. (2004). *Contemporary British fascism: The British National Party and the quest for respectability.* Palgrave.

(2011). From direct action to community action: The changing dynamics of anti-fascist opposition. In Copsey, N. & Macklin, G. D. (Eds.). *British National Party: Contemporary perspectives.* Routledge, 123–141.

Crotty, W. J. (1968). The party organization and its activities. In Crotty, W. J. (Ed.). *Approaches to the Study of Party Organization.* Allyn and Bacon, 247–306.

Dalton, R. J. (1984). Cognitive mobilization and partisan dealignment in advanced industrial democracies. *The Journal of Politics*, *46*(01), 264–284.

(2000). The decline of party identification. In Dalton, R. J., & Wattenberg, M. P. (Eds.). *Parties without partisans: Political change in advanced industrial democracies*. Oxford University Press, 19–36.

(2006). *Citizen politics: Public opinion and political parties in advanced industrial democracies*. 4th ed. CQ Press.

Dalton, R. J., & Wattenberg, M. P. (Eds.). (2000). *Parties without partisans: Political change in advanced industrial democracies*. Oxford University Press.

Dalton, R. J., McAllister, I., & Wattenberg, M. (2000). The consequences of partisan dealignment. In Dalton, R. J. & Wattenberg, M. (Eds.). *Parties without partisans*. Oxford University Press, 37–63.

Davenport, C. (2005). Repression and mobilization: Insights from political science and sociology. In Davenport C., Johnston, H. and Mueller C. (Eds.) *Repression and mobilization*. University of Minnesota Press, vii–xli.

(2009). *Media bias, perspective, and state repression: The Black Panther Party*. Cambridge University Press.

Davies, P. (1999). *The National Front in France: Ideology, discourse and power*. Routledge.

Decker, F., & Miliopoulos, L. (2009). From a five to a six-party system? Prospects of the right-wing extremist NPD. *German Politics & Society*, *27*(2), 92–107.

DeClair, E. G. (1999). *Politics on the fringe: the people, policies, and organization of the French National Front*. Duke University Press.

De Lange, S. L. (2007). A new winning formula? The programmatic appeal of the radical right. *Party Politics*, *13*(4), 411–435.

De Lange, S. L., & Art, D. (2011). Fortuyn versus Wilders: An agency-based approach to radical right party building. *West European Politics*, *34*(6), 1229–1249.

De Witte, H., & Klandermans, B. (2000). Political racism in Flanders and the Netherlands: Explaining differences in the electoral success of extreme right-wing parties. *Journal of Ethnic and Migration Studies*, *26*(4), 699–717.

Della Porta, D. (1995). *Social movements, political violence, and the state: A comparative analysis of Italy and Germany*. Cambridge University Press.

Della Porta, D., & Diani, M. (2006). *Social movements: An introduction*. Blackwell.

Della Porta, D., & Reiter, H. R. (Eds.). (1998). *Policing protest: The control of mass demonstrations in Western democracies*. University of Minnesota Press.

Della Porta, D., Fernandez, J., Kouki, H., & Mosca, L. (2017). *Movement parties against austerity*. John Wiley & Sons.

Denver, D., Hands, G., & MacAllister, I. (2004). The electoral impact of constituency campaigning in Britain, 1992–2001. *Political Studies*, *52*(2), 289–306.

Deschouwer, K. (2006). Political parties as multi-level organizations. In Katz, R. S., & Crotty, W. J. (Eds.). *Handbook of Party Politics*. Sage, 291–300.

Diamond, L. (2015). Facing up to the democratic recession. *Journal of Democracy*, *26*(1), 141–155.

Dinas, E., Georgiadou, V., Konstantinidis, I., & Rori, L. (2013). From dusk to dawn: Local party organization and party success of right-wing extremism. *Party Politics*, 1354068813511381.

Dolný, B., & Malová, D. (2016). Organizational structures of political parties in Slovakia: Parties not for members. In W. K. Sobolewska-Myślik, B. Kosowska-Gąstoł, P. Borowiec (Eds.). *Organizational Structures of Political Parties in Central and Eastern European Countries*. Jagiellonian University Press, 391–418.

Downs, A. (1957). *An economic theory of democracy*. Addison Wesley.

Downs, W. M. (2012). *Political extremism in democracies: Combating intolerance*. Palgrave Macmillan.

Dunning, T. (2012). *Natural experiments in the social sciences: A design-based approach*. Cambridge University Press.

Duverger, M. (1959). *Political parties: Their organization and activity in the modern state*. Methuen.

Earl, J. (2006). Introduction: Repression and the social control of protest. *Mobilization: An International Quarterly*, *11*(2), 129–143.

Eatwell, R. (2000). The rebirth of the "Extreme Right" in Western Europe. *Parliamentary Affairs*, *53*(3): 407–425.

(2006). The concept and theory of charismatic leadership. *Totalitarian movements and political religions*, *7*(2), 141–156.

Ellinas, A. A. (2007). Phased out: Far right parties in Western Europe. *Comparative Politics*, *39*(3), 353–371.

(2010). *The media and the far right in Western Europe: Playing the nationalist card*. Cambridge University Press.

(2013). The rise of Golden Dawn: The new face of the far right in Greece. *South European Society and Politics*, *18*(4), 543–565.

(2015). Neo-Nazism in an established democracy: The persistence of Golden Dawn in Greece. *South European Society and Politics*, *20*(1), 1–20.

Ellinas, A. A., & Katsourides, Y. (2013). Organisational continuity and electoral endurance: The communist party of Cyprus. *West European Politics*, *36*(4), 859–882.

Ellinas, A. A., & Lamprianou, I. (2017). How far right local party organizations develop: The organizational buildup of the Greek Golden Dawn. *Party Politics*, *23*(6), 804–820.

(2018). Far right activism and electoral outcomes. *Party Politics*, 1354068817728213.

Ennser, L. (2012). The homogeneity of West European party families: The radical right in comparative perspective. *Party Politics*, *18*(2), 151–171.

Erk, J. (2005). From Vlaams Blok to Vlaams Belang: The Belgian far-right renames itself. *West European Politics*, *28*(3), 493–502.

Farrell, D. M., & Webb, P. (2000). Political parties as campaign organizations. In R. J. Dalton & M. P. Wattenberg (Eds.). *Parties without partisans: Political change in advanced industrial democracies*. Oxford University Press, 102–128.

Farrell, D. M. (2006). Political parties in a changing campaign environment. In Katz, R. S., & Crotty, W. J. (Eds.). *Handbook of party politics*. Sage, 122–133.

Fennema, M. (1997). Some conceptual issues and problems in the comparison of anti-immigrant parties in Western Europe. *Party Politics*, 3(4), 473–492.

(2000). Legal repression of extreme-right parties and racial discrimination. In Koopmans, R., & Statham, P. (Eds.). *Challenging immigration and ethnic relations politics*. Oxford University Press, 119–144.

Fisher, J., Denver, D., & Hands, G. (2006). The relative electoral impact of central party co-ordination and size of party membership at constituency level. *Electoral Studies*, 25(4), 664–676.

Fisher, J., Fieldhouse, E., Johnston, R., Pattie, C., & Cutts, D. (2016). Is all campaigning equally positive? The impact of district level campaigning on voter turnout at the 2010 British general election. *Party Politics*, 22(2), 215–226.

Flanagan, S. C., & Dalton, R. J. (1984). Parties under stress: Realignment and dealignment in advanced industrial societies. *West European Politics*, 7(1), 7–23.

Ford, R., & Goodwin, M. J. (2010). Angry white men: Individual and contextual predictors of support for the British National Party. *Political Studies*, 58(1), 1–25.

Fragoudaki, A. (2013). *Nationalism and the rise of the extreme right*. Alexandria [in Greek].

Froio, C., & Gattinara, P. C. (2015). Neo-fascist mobilization in contemporary Italy. Ideology and repertoire of action of CasaPound Italia. *Journal for Deradicalization*, (2), 86–118.

Gaspard, F. (1995). *A small city in France*. Harvard University Press.

Gattinara, P. C., Froio, C., & Albanese, M. (2013). The appeal of neo-fascism in times of crisis: The experience of CasaPound Italia. *Fascism*, 2(2), 234–258.

Georgiadou, V. (2013). Right-wing populism and extremism: The rapid rise of "Golden Dawn" in crisis-ridden Greece. In R. Melzer & S. Sebastian (Eds.). *Right-wing Extremism in Europe*. Friedrich Ebert Stiftung, 75–101.

Gerber, A. S., & Green, D. P. (2000). The effects of canvassing, telephone calls, and direct mail on voter turnout: A field experiment. *American Political Science Review*, 94(3), 653–663.

Geser, H. (1999). The local party as an object of interdisciplinary comparative study: Some steps toward theoretical integration. In Saiz, M., & Geser, H. (Eds.). *Local parties in political and organizational perspective*. Westview Press, 3–43.

Gibson, E. L. (2005). Boundary control: Subnational authoritarianism in democratic countries. *World Politics*, 58(01), 101–132.

Givens, T. E. (2004). The radical right gender gap. *Comparative Political Studies*, 37(1), 30–54.

Gnad, O. (2005). Nationaldemokratische Partei Deutschlands: Mitgliedschaft und Sozialstruktur. In Gnad, O., Gniss, D., Hausmann, M., & Reibel, C.-W. (Eds.). *Handbuch zur Statistik der Parlamente und Parteien in den westlichen Besatzungszonen und in der Bundesrepublik Deutschland*. Droste Verlag, 595–681.

Golder, M. (2003). Explaining variation in the success of extreme right parties in Western Europe. *Comparative Political Studies, 36*(4), 432–466.

(2016). Far right parties in Europe. *Annual Review of Political Science, 19*, 477–497.

Goodwin, M. J. (2010). Activism in contemporary extreme right parties: The case of the British National Party (BNP). *Journal of Elections, Public Opinion and Parties, 20*(1), 31–54.

(2011). *New British fascism: Rise of the British National Party.* Routledge.

Goodwin, M., Ford, R., & Cutts, D. (2013). Extreme right foot soldiers, legacy effects and deprivation: A contextual analysis of the leaked British National Party (BNP) membership list. *Party Politics, 19*(6), 887–906.

Grzymala-Busse, A. M. (2002). *Redeeming the communist past: The regeneration of communist parties in East Central Europe.* Cambridge University Press.

Gyárfášová, O., & Mesežnikov, G. (2015). Actors, agenda, and appeal of the radical nationalist right in Slovakia. In Minkenberg, M. (Ed.). *Transforming the transformation?: The East European radical right in the political process.* Routledge, 224–248.

Hagelund, A. (2003). A matter of decency? The Progress Party in Norwegian immigration politics. *Journal of Ethnic and Migration Studies, 29*(1), 47–65.

Hainsworth, P. (2000). *The politics of the extreme right: From the margins to the mainstream.* Pinter.

Harmel, R., & Svåsand, L. (1993). Party leadership and party institutionalisation: Three phases of development. *West European Politics, 16*(2), 67–88.

Harteveld, E., Van Der Brug, W., Dahlberg, S., & Kokkonen, A. (2015). The gender gap in populist radical-right voting: Examining the demand side in Western and Eastern Europe. *Patterns of Prejudice, 49*(1–2), 103–134.

Hasapopoulos, N. (2013). *Golden Dawn: History, personalities and the truth.* Livanis [in Greek].

Heaney, M. T., & Rojas, F. (2015). *Party in the street: The antiwar movement and the democratic party after 9/11.* Cambridge University Press.

Heinisch, R., & Mazzoleni, O. (2016). *Understanding populist party organisation.* Palgrave Macmillan.

Hicken, A., & Kuhonta, E. (2011). Reexamining party system institutionalization through Asian lenses. *Comparative Political Studies, 44*(5), 572–597.

Hix, S., Noury, A. G., & Roland, G. (2007). *Democratic politics in the European Parliament.* Cambridge University Press.

Hopkin, J., & Paolucci, C. (1999). The business firm model of party organisation: Cases from Spain and Italy. *European Journal of Political Research, 35* (3), 307–339.

Huckfeldt, R., & Sprague, J. (1992). Political parties and electoral mobilization: Political structure, social structure, and the party canvass. *American Political Science Review, 86*(1), 70–86.

Husbands, C. (1982). Combating the extreme right with the instruments of the constitutional state: Lessons from experiences in Western Europe. *Journal of Conflict and Violence Research, 4*(1), 52–73.

Husbands, C. T. (2002). How to tame the dragon, or, what goes around comes around. In Schain, M., Zolberg, A., & Hossay, P. (Eds.). *Shadows over Europe: The development and impact of the extreme right in Western Europe.* Palgrave. 39–59.

Ignazi, P. (1992). The silent counter-revolution: Hypotheses on the emergence of extreme right-wing parties in Europe. *European Journal of Political Research*, 22(1), 3–34.

(1997). New challenges: Postmaterialism and the extreme right. In Rhodes, M., Heywood, P. & Wright V. (Eds.). *Developments in West European Politics.* St. Martin's Press, 300–319.

(2003). *Extreme right parties in Western Europe.* Oxford University Press.

(2005). Legitimation and evolution on the Italian right wing: Social and ideological repositioning of Alleanza Nazionale and the Lega Nord. *South European Society & Politics*, 10(2), 333–349.

Inglehart, R. (1990). From class-based to value-based politics. In Mair, P. (Ed.). *The West European Party System.* Oxford University Press, 266–284.

Ishiyama, J. T. (1997). The sickle or the rose? Previous regime types and the evolution of the ex-communist parties in post-communist politics. *Comparative Political Studies*, 30(3), 299–330.

(2001). Party organization and the political success of the communist successor parties. *Social Science Quarterly*, 82(4), 844–864.

Issacharoff, S. (2006). Fragile democracies. *Harvard Law Review*, 120, 1405–1466.

Ivarsflaten, E. (2005). The vulnerable populist right parties: No economic realignment fuelling their electoral success. *European Journal of Political Research*, 44 (3), 465–492.

(2008). What unites right-wing populists in Western Europe? Re-examining grievance mobilization models in seven successful cases. *Comparative Political Studies*, 41(1), 3–23.

Jackman, R. W., & Volpert, K. (1996). Conditions favouring parties of the extreme right in Western Europe. *British Journal of Political Science*, 26, 501–522.

Janda, K. (1983). Cross-national measures of party organizations and organizational theory. *European Journal of Political Research*, 11(3), 319–332.

Jelinek, Y. (1971). Storm-troopers in Slovakia: The Rodobrana and the Hlinka Guard. *Journal of Contemporary History*, 6(3), 97–119.

Jenkins, J. C. (1995). *The politics of social protest: Comparative perspectives on states and social movements.* University of Minnesota Press.

Jupskås, A. R. (2016). The taming of the shrew: How the Progress Party (almost) became part of the mainstream. In Akkerman, T., de Lange, S. L. & Rooduijn, M. (Eds.). *Radical right-wing populist parties in Western Europe.* Routledge, 187–210.

Kalyvas, S. (2015). *Modern Greece: What everyone needs to know.* Oxford University Press.

Karácsony, G., & Róna, D. (2011). The secret of Jobbik: Reasons behind the rise of the Hungarian radical right. *Journal of East European and Asian Studies*, 2 (1), 61–92.

Karp, J. A., Banducci, S. A., & Bowler, S. (2008). Getting out the vote: Party mobilization in a comparative perspective. *British Journal of Political Science, 38*(1), 91–112.

Katsourides, Y. (2013). Determinants of extreme right reappearance in Cyprus: The National Popular Front (ELAM), Golden Dawn's sister party. *South European Society and Politics, 18*(4), 567–589.

(2016). *Radical left parties in government: The cases of SYRIZA and AKEL.* Springer.

Katz, R. S., & Mair, P. (1993). The evolution of party organizations in Europe: The three faces of party organization. *American Review of Politics, 14*(4), 593–617.

(1995). Changing models of party organization and party democracy: The emergence of the cartel party. *Party Politics, 1*(1), 5–28.

(2009). The cartel party thesis: A restatement. *Perspectives on Politics, 7*(04), 753–766.

Katzenstein, P. J. (1976). *Disjoined partners: Austria and Germany since 1815.* University of California Press.

Kelemen, R. D. (2015). Europe's Other Democratic Deficit. Paper presented at International Conference of Europeanists. Paris, 1–19.

Kirchheimer, O. (1957). The waning of opposition in parliamentary regimes. *Social Research,* 127–156.

(1966). The transformation of the Western European party systems. In Weiner, M. & LaPalombara, J. (Eds.). *Political parties and political development.* Princeton University Press, 177–200.

Kirshner, A. S. (2014). *A theory of militant democracy: The ethics of combatting political extremism.* Yale University Press.

Kitschelt, H. (1986). Political opportunity structures and political protest: Antinuclear movements in four democracies. *British Journal of Political Science, 16*(1), 57–85.

(1989). *The logics of party formation: Ecological politics in Belgium and West Germany.* Cornell University Press.

(1994). *The transformation of European social democracy.* Cambridge University Press.

(2006). Movement parties. In Katz, R. S., & Crotty, W. J. (Eds.). *Handbook of party politics.* Sage, 278–290.

Kitschelt, H., & McGann, A. J. (1995). *The radical right in Western Europe: A comparative analysis.* University of Michigan Press.

Klandermans, B., & Mayer, N. (2006). *Extreme right activists in Europe: Through the magnifying glass.* Routledge.

Kluknavská, A. (2015). A right-wing extremist or people's protector? Media coverage of extreme right leader Marian Kotleba in 2013 regional elections in Slovakia. *Intersections. East European Journal of Society and Politics, 1*(1), 147–165.

Kluknavská, A., & Smolík, J. (2016). We hate them all? Issue adaptation of extreme right parties in Slovakia 1993–2016. *Communist and Post-Communist Studies, 49*(4), 335–344.

Knechtle, J. C. (2008). Holocaust denial and the concept of dignity in the European Union. *Florida State University Law Review, 36*(1) 41–65.

Knigge, P. (1998). The ecological correlates of right-wing extremism in Western Europe. *European Journal of Political Research*, *34*(2), 249–279.

Koelble, T. A. (1992). Recasting social democracy in Europe: A nested games explanation of strategic adjustment in political parties. *Politics & Society*, *20*(1), 51–70.

Koopmans, R. (2004). Protest in time and space: The evolution of waves of contention. In Snow, D. A., Soule, S. A., & Kriesi, H. (Eds.). *The Blackwell companion to social movements*. Blackwell, 19–46.

Kopecký, P. (1995). Developing party organizations in east-central Europe: What type of party is likely to emerge? *Party Politics*, *1*(4), 515–534.

Kriesi, H. (1995). The political opportunity structure of new social movements: Its impact on their mobilization. In Jenkins, J. C. (Ed.). *The politics of social protest: Comparative perspectives on states and social movements*. University of Minnesota Press, 167–198.

(2004). Political context and opportunity. In Snow, D. A., Soule, S. A., & Kriesi, H. (Eds.). *The Blackwell companion to social movements*. Blackwell, 67–90.

(2015). Party systems, electoral systems, and social movements. *The Oxford handbook of social movements*. Oxford University Press, 667–680.

Kriesi, H., Grande, E., Lachat, R., Dolezal, M., Bornschier, S., & Frey, T. (2008). *West European politics in the age of globalization*. Cambridge University Press.

Krouwel, A. (2006). Party models. In Katz, R. S., & Crotty, W. J. (Eds.). *Handbook of Party Politics*. Sage, 249–269.

Kuhonta, E. (2011). *The institutional imperative: The politics of equitable development in Southeast Asia*. Stanford University Press.

Lamprianou, I., & Ellinas, A. A. (2017a). Institutional grievances and right-wing extremism: Voting for Golden Dawn in Greece. *South European Society and Politics*, *22*(1), 43–60.

(2017b). Why Greeks rebel: Re-examining conventional and radical political action. *Acta Politica*, *52*(1), 85–109.

Lawson, K., & Merkl, P. (1988). *When parties fail: Emerging alternative organizations*. Princeton University Press.

LeBas, A. (2011). *From protest to parties: Party-building and democratization in Africa*. Oxford University Press.

Levitsky, S. (1998). Institutionalization and Peronism: The concept, the case and the case for unpacking the concept. *Party Politics*, *4*(1), 77–92.

(2001). An "organised disorganisation": Informal organisation and the persistence of local party structures in Argentine Peronism. *Journal of Latin American Studies*, *33*(01), 29–65.

(2003). *Transforming labor-based parties in Latin America: Argentine Peronism in comparative perspective*. Cambridge University Press.

Lijphart, A. (1975). The comparable-cases strategy in comparative research. *Comparative Political Studies*, *8*(2), 158–177.

Linden, A., & Klandermans, B. (2006). Stigmatization and repression of extreme-right activism in the Netherlands. *Mobilization: An International Quarterly*, *11*(2), 213–228.

Lipset, S. M. (1962). Introduction to Robert Michels. In Michels, R. *Political parties: A sociological study of the oligarchical tendencies of modern democracy.* University of California Press, 15–39.

Lipset, S. M., & Rokkan, S. (1967). Cleavage structures, party systems, and voter alignments: An introduction. In Lipset, S. M., & Rokkan, S., *Party systems and voter alignments: Cross-national perspectives.* Free Press.

Loewenstein, K. (1937a). Militant democracy and fundamental rights, I. *American Political Science Review, 31*(3), 417–432.

(1937b). Militant democracy and fundamental rights, II. *American Political Science Review, 31*(4), 638–658.

Loudos, N. (2014). The resistible rise of Golden Dawn. *Irish Marxist Review, 3* (9), 17–26.

Lubbers, M., & Scheepers, P. (2000). Individual and contextual characteristics of the German extreme right-wing vote in the 1990s: A test of complementary theories. *European Journal of Political Research, 38*(1), 63–94.

Lubbers, M., Gijsberts, M., & Scheepers, P. (2002). Extreme right-wing voting in Western Europe. *European Journal of Political Research, 41*(3), 345–378.

Lundell, K. (2004). Determinants of candidate selection the degree of centralization in comparative perspective. *Party Politics, 10*(1), 25–47.

Luther, K. R. (2000). Austria: A democracy under threat from the Freedom Party? *Parliamentary Affairs, 53*(3), 426–442.

Mainwaring, S. (1998). Party systems in the third wave. *Journal of Democracy, 9* (3), 67–81.

Mair, P. (Ed.). (1990). *The west European party system.* Oxford University Press.

Mair, P., & Mudde, C. (1998). The party family and its study. *Annual Review of Political Science, 1*(1), 211–229.

Mair, P., & Van Biezen, I. (2001). Party membership in twenty European democracies, 1980–2000. *Party Politics, 7*(1), 5–21.

Mammone, A. (2015). *Transnational Neofascism in France and Italy.* Cambridge University Press.

Mann, M. (2004). *Fascists.* Cambridge University Press.

March, L. (2011). *Radical left parties in Europe.* Routledge.

Marcus, J. (1995). *The National Front in French politics.* Macmillan.

Mareš, M. (2011). Czech extreme right parties: An unsuccessful story. *Communist and Post-Communist Studies, 44*(4), 283–298.

(2012). Czech militant democracy in action: Dissolution of the Workers' Party and the wider context of this act. *East European Politics and Societies, 26*(1), 33–55.

Marien, S., Hooghe, M., & Quintelier, E. (2010). Inequalities in non-institutionalised forms of political participation: A multi-level analysis of 25 countries. *Political Studies, 58*(1), 187–213.

Mayer, N. (1998). The French National Front. In Betz, H.-G. & Immerfall S. (Eds.). *The new politics of the right: Neo-populist parties and movements in established democracies,* 11–25.

Mazzoleni, O., & Skenderovic, D. (2007). The rise and impact of the Swiss People's Party: Challenging the rules of governance in Switzerland. In Delwit, P. & Poirier, P. (Eds.). *The extreme right parties and power in Europe.* Editions de l'Université de Bruxelles, 85–116.

Mazzoleni, O., & Voerman, G. (2016). Memberless parties: Beyond the business-firm party model? *Party Politics,* 1354068815627398.

McAdam, D. (1986). Recruitment to high-risk activism: The case of Freedom Summer. *American Journal of Sociology, 92*(1), 64–90.

McAdam, D., & Tarrow, S. (2010). Ballots and barricades: On the reciprocal relationship between elections and social movements. *Perspectives on Politics, 8*(2), 529–542.

McAdam, D., Tarrow, S., & Tilly, C. (2001). *Dynamics of contention.* Cambridge University Press.

McPhail, C., & McCarthy, J. D. (2005). Protest mobilization, protest repression, and their interaction. In Davenport C., Johnston, H., & Mueller C. (Eds.). *Repression and Mobilization.* University of Minnesota Press, 3–32.

Meguid, B. M. (2005). Competition between unequals: The role of mainstream party strategy in niche party success. *American Political Science Review, 99*(3), 347–359.

Michels, R. (1915). *Political parties: A sociological study of the oligarchical tendencies of modern democracy.* Free Press.

Mikušovič, D. (2007). Slovenská pospolitosť včera a dnes. *Rexter, 6*(1), 1–52.

   (2009). Militantná demokracia na Slovensku? Teoretické a praktické problémy aplikácie v slovenskom prostredí. Dissertation. Masaryk University at Brno.

Milesi, P., Chirumbolo, A., & Catellani, P. (2006). Italy: the offspring of Fascism. In Klandermans, B., & Mayer, N. (Eds). *Extreme right activists in Europe: through the magnifying glass.* Routledge, 67–92.

Miller-Idriss, C. (2005). Citizenship education and political extremism in Germany: An ethnographic analysis. In Wilde, S. (Ed.). *Political and Citizenship Education: International perspectives.* Symposium Books, 101–122.

Minkenberg, M. (1992). The new right in Germany. *European Journal of Political Research, 22*(1), 55–81.

   (2000). The renewal of the radical right: Between modernity and anti-modernity. *Government and Opposition, 35*(02), 170–188.

   (2006). Repression and reaction: Militant democracy and the radical right in Germany and France. *Patterns of Prejudice, 40*(1), 25–44.

   (2009). Leninist beneficiaries? Pre-1989 legacies and the radical right in post-1989 Central and Eastern Europe: Some introductory observations. *Communist and Post-Communist Studies, 42*(4), 445–458.

   (2013). The European radical right and xenophobia in west and east: Trends, patterns and challenges. In Melzer, R. & Serafin, S. (Eds.). *Right-wing extremism in Europe: Country-analyses, counter-strategies and labor-market oriented exit strategies.* Friedrich Ebert Stiftung, 9–34.

   (Ed.). (2015). *Transforming the transformation?: The radical right in the political process in Central and Eastern Europe.* Routledge.

Montuori, L. A. (2000). Organizational longevity: Integrating systems thinking, learning and conceptual complexity. *Journal of Organizational Change Management, 13*(1), 61–73.

Mudde, C. (1995). One against all, all against one!: A portrait of the Vlaams Blok *Patterns of Prejudice, 29*(1), 5–28.

(2000). *The ideology of the extreme right*. Manchester University Press.

(2004). The populist zeitgeist. *Government and Opposition, 39*(4), 542–563.

(2007). *Populist radical right parties in Europe*. Cambridge University Press.

(2010). The Geert Wilders Enigma. *Open Democracy*.

Muller, E. N. (1979). *Aggressive political participation*. Princeton University Press.

Müller, J. W. (2016). Protecting popular self-government from the people? New normative perspectives on militant democracy. *Annual Review of Political Science, 19*, 249–265.

Nagle, J. D. (1970). *The National Democratic Party: Right radicalism in the Federal Republic of Germany*. University of California Press.

Nociar, T. (2012). Right-wing extremism in Slovakia. In Melzer R. & Serafin S. (Eds.). *Right-wing extremism in Europe*. Friedrich Ebert Stiftung.

Norris, P. (2002). *Democratic phoenix: Reinventing political activism*. Cambridge University Press.

(2004). The evolution of election campaigns: Eroding political engagement. Conference paper.

(2005). *Radical right: Voters and parties in the electoral market*. Cambridge University Press.

Ostrogorski, M. (1902). *Democracy and the organization of political parties*. Macmillan.

Panebianco, A. (1988). *Political parties: Organization and power*. Cambridge University Press.

Papanicolaou, G., & Papageorgiou, I. (2016). The police and the far right in Greece: A case study of police voting behaviour in Athens. *Crime, Law and Social Change, 66*(4), 397–419.

Papapantoleon, C. (2014). Justice. In Christopoulos D. (Ed.). *The "deep" state in contemporary Greece and the extreme right*. Rosa Luxemburg Stiftung, 151–226 [in Greek].

Pappas, T. S. (2016). The specter haunting Europe: Distinguishing liberal democracy's challengers. *Journal of Democracy, 27*(4), 22–36.

Pattie, C. J., Johnston, R. J., & Fieldhouse, E. A. (1995). Winning the local vote: The effectiveness of constituency campaign spending in Great Britain, 1983–1992. *American Political Science Review, 89*(4), 969–983.

Pedahzur, A. (2004). The defending democracy and the extreme right. In Eatwell, R., & Mudde, C. (Eds.). *Western democracies and the new extreme right challenge*. Routledge, 108–132.

Pedersen, K., Bille, L., Buch, R., Elklit, J., Hansen, B., & Nielsen, H. J. (2004). Sleeping or active partners?: Danish party members at the turn of the millennium. *Party Politics, 10*(4), 367–383.

Pedersen, M. N. (1982). Towards a new typology of party lifespans and minor parties. *Scandinavian Political Studies*, *5*(1), 1–16.

Perrineau, P. (1996). Les étapes d'une implantation électorale (1972–1988). In Mayer, N. & Perrineau P. (Eds.). *Le Front National à découvert*, Presses de la Fondation Nationale des Sciences Politiques, 37–62.

Plattner, M. F. (2015). Is democracy in decline? *Journal of Democracy*, 26(1), 5–10.

Poguntke, T. (2006). Political parties and other organizations. In Katz, R. S., & Crotty, W. J. (Eds.). *Handbook of party politics*. Sage, 396–405.

Pop-Eleches, G. (2008). A party for all seasons: Electoral adaptation of Romanian Communist successor parties. *Communist and Post-Communist Studies*, *41*(4), 465–479.

(2010). Throwing out the bums: Protest voting and unorthodox parties after communism. *World Politics*, *62*(2), 221–260.

Przeworski, A., & Sprague, J. D. (1988). *Paper stones: A history of electoral socialism*. University of Chicago Press.

Psarras, D. (2012). *The black bible of Golden Dawn*. Polis [in Greek].

(2014). *The Golden Dawn before justice*. Rosa Luxemburg Stiftung [in Greek].

Rensmann, L. (2006). From high hopes to on-going defeat: The new extreme right's political mobilization and its national electoral failure in Germany. *German Politics & Society*, *24*(1), 67–92.

Rensmann, T. (2003). Procedural fairness in a militant democracy: The 'uprising of the decent' fails before the federal constitutional court. *German Law Journal*, *4*(11), 1117–1136.

Riedlsperger, M. E. (1978). *The lingering shadow of Nazism: the Austrian Independent Party movement since 1945*. East European Monographs.

Rokkan, S. (1970). *Citizens, elections, parties: Approaches to the comparative study of political development*. Universitetsforlaget.

Rosenfeld, M. (2002). Hate speech in constitutional jurisprudence: a comparative analysis. *Cardozo Law Review*, *24*, 1523–1567.

Rüdig, W., & Karyotis, G. (2014). Who protests in Greece? Mass opposition to austerity. *British Journal of Political Science*, *44*(3), 487–513.

Rummens, S., & Abts, K. (2010). Defending democracy: The concentric containment of political extremism. *Political Studies*, *58*(4), 649–665.

Rydgren, J. (2005). Is extreme right-wing populism contagious? Explaining the emergence of a new party family. *European Journal of Political Research*, *44*(3), 413–437.

(2006). *From tax populism to ethnic nationalism: Radical right-wing populism in Sweden*. Berghahn.

(2008). Immigration sceptics, xenophobes or racists? Radical right-wing voting in six west European countries. *European Journal of Political Research*, *47*(6), 737–765.

(Ed.). (2018). *The Oxford handbook of the radical right*. Oxford University Press.

Samuels, D. (2004). From socialism to social democracy: Party organization and the transformation of the Workers' Party in Brazil. *Comparative Political Studies, 37*(9), 999–1024.

Sartori, G. (2005). *Parties and party systems: A framework for analysis.* Cambridge University Press.

Scarrow, S. E. (1993). Does local party organisation make a difference? Political parties and local government elections in Germany. *German Politics, 2*(3), 377–392.

(1994). The "paradox of enrollment": Assessing the costs and benefits of party memberships. *European Journal of Political Research, 25*(1), 41–60.

(1996). *Parties and their members: Organizing for victory in Britain and Germany.* Clarendon Press.

(2000). Parties without members?: Party organization in a changing electoral environment. In Dalton, R. J., & Wattenberg, M. P. (Eds.). *Parties without partisans: Political change in advanced industrial democracies.* Oxford University Press, 64–76.

Scott, J. C. (1985). *Weapons of the weak: Everyday forms of peasant resistance.* Yale University Press.

Scott, W. R. (2008). *Institutions and organizations: Ideas and interests.* Sage.

Seyd, P., & Whiteley, P. (1992). *Labour's grass roots: The politics of party membership.* Oxford University Press.

(2002). *New Labour's grassroots: The transformation of the Labour Party membership.* Springer.

Shefter, M. (1977). Party and patronage: Germany, England, and Italy. *Politics & Society, 4*, 403–451.

(1994). *Political parties and the state: The American historical experience.* Princeton University Press.

Shields, J. (2013). Marine Le Pen and the "New" FN: A change of style or of substance? *Parliamentary Affairs, 66*(1), 179–196.

Shoshan, N. (2016). *The management of hate: Nation, affect, and the governance of right-wing extremism in Germany.* Princeton University Press.

Skenderovic, D. (2009). *The radical right in Switzerland: Continuity and change, 1945–2000.* Berghahn Books.

Snow, D. A., Soule, S. A., & Kriesi, H. (2004). Mapping the terrain. In Snow, D. A., Soule, S. A., & Kriesi, H. (Eds.). *The Blackwell companion to social movements.* Blackwell, 3–16.

Snyder, R. (1999). After neoliberalism: The politics of reregulation in Mexico. *World Politics, 51*(02), 173–204.

(2001). Scaling down: The subnational comparative method. *Studies in Comparative International Development, 36*(1), 93–110.

Sotiropoulos, D. A. (2004). Southern European public bureaucracies in comparative perspective. *West European Politics, 27*(3), 405–422.

Spáč, P., & Voda, P. (2014). Slovak extreme right and its support based on local Roma incidence. Paper presented at ECPR General Conference, Glasgow.

Spourdalakis, M. (2013). Left strategy in the Greek cauldron: Explaining Syriza's success. *Socialist Register, 49*, 98–119.

Stadelmann, M. (2013). The rise of the extreme right: The Movement for a Better Hungary (Jobbik). *National Social Science Journal, 39*, 97–103.

Stöss, R. (1991). *Politics against democracy*. Berg.

Stolle, D., & Hooghe, M. (2011). Shifting inequalities: Patterns of exclusion and inclusion in emerging forms of political participation. *European Societies, 13*(1), 119–142.

Swyngedouw, M., & Ivaldi, G. (2001). The extreme right utopia in Belgium and France: The ideology of the Flemish Vlaams Blok and the French Front National. *West European Politics, 24*(3), 1–22.

Szczerbiak, A. (1999). Testing party models in east-central Europe local party organization in postcommunist Poland. *Party Politics, 5*(4), 525–537.

(2001). *Poles together?: The emergence and development of political parties in postcommunist Poland*. Central European University Press.

Szôcs, L. (1998). A tale of the unexpected: The extreme right vis-à-vis democracy in post-communist Hungary. *Ethnic and Racial Studies, 21*(6), 1096–1115.

Taggart, P. (1996). *The new populism and the new politics: New protest parties in Sweden in a comparative perspective*. Palgrave Macmillan.

Tarrow, S. (1994; 2011). *Power in movement: Social movements, collective action and mass politics in the modern state*. Cambridge University Press.

Tavits, M. (2013). *Post-communist democracies and party organization*. Cambridge University Press.

Taylor, S. (1982). *The National Front in English Politics*. Palgrave Macmillan.

Teorell, J., Torcal, M., & Montero, J. R. (2007). Political participation: Mapping the terrain. In van Deth, J. W., Montero, J. R., & Westholm A. (Eds.). *Citizenship and involvement in European democracies: A comparative perspective*. Routledge, 334–357.

Thiel, M. (2009). *The militant democracy principle in modern democracies*. Ashgate.

Tilly, C. (1978). *From mobilization to revolution*. Addison-Wesley.

(2005). Repression, mobilization and explanation. In Davenport C., Johnston, H. and Mueller C. (Eds.). *Repression and mobilization*. University of Minnesota Press, 211–226.

Tsakatika, M., & Eleftheriou, C. (2013). The radical left's turn towards civil society in Greece: One strategy, two paths. *South European Society and Politics, 18*(1), 81–99.

Tsakatika, M., & Lisi, M. (2013). "Zippin' up my boots, goin' back to my roots": Radical left parties in Southern Europe. *South European Society and Politics, 18*(1), 1–19.

Tyulkina, S. (2015). *Militant democracy: Undemocratic political parties and beyond*. Routledge.

Van Biezen, I. (2000). On the internal balance of party power: party organizations in new democracies. *Party Politics, 6*(4), 395–417.

(2003). *Political parties in new democracies*. Macmillan.

(2004). Political parties as public utilities. *Party Politics, 10*(6), 701–722.

(2005). On the theory and practice of party formation and adaptation in new democracies. *European Journal of Political Research, 44*(1), 147–174.

Van Biezen, I. V., & Kopecký, P. (2014). The cartel party and the state: Party–state linkages in European democracies. *Party Politics, 20*(2), 170–182.

Van Biezen, I., Mair, P., & Poguntke, T. (2012). Going, going, . . . gone?: The decline of party membership in contemporary Europe. *European Journal of Political Research, 51*(1), 24–56.

Van der Brug, W., & Fennema, M. (2003). Protest or mainstream?: How the European anti-immigrant parties have developed into two separate groups by 1999. *European Journal of Political Research, 42*(1), 55–76.

Van der Brug, W., & Mughan, A. (2007). Charisma, leader effects and support for right-wing populist parties. *Party Politics, 13*(1), 29–51.

Van der Brug, W., Fennema, M., & Tillie, J. (2000). Anti-immigrant parties in Europe: Ideological or protest vote? *European Journal of Political Research, 37* (1), 77–102.

(2005). Why some anti-immigrant parties fail and others succeed: A two-step model of aggregate electoral support. *Comparative Political Studies, 38*(5), 537–573.

Van Dyke, N., & D. Meyer (2016). *Understanding the tea party movement.* Routledge.

Van Haute, E., & Pauwels, T. (2016). The Vlaams Belang: Party Organization and Party Dynamics. In Heinisch, R., & Mazzoleni, O. (Eds.). *Understanding Populist Party Organisation.* Palgrave, 49–77.

Van Spanje, J., & De Vreese, C. (2015). The good, the bad and the voter: The impact of hate speech prosecution of a politician on electoral support for his party. *Party Politics, 21*(1), 115–130.

Van Spanje, J., & Van Der Brug, W. (2007). The party as pariah: The exclusion of anti-immigration parties and its effect on their ideological positions. *West European Politics, 30*(5), 1022–1040.

Varga, M. (2014). Hungary's "anti-capitalist" far-right: Jobbik and the Hungarian Guard. *Nationalities Papers, 42*(5), 791–807.

Vasilopoulou, S., & Halikiopoulou, D. (2015). *The Golden Dawn's "nationalist solution": Explaining the rise of the far right in Greece.* Palgrave.

Vernardakis, C. (2011). Political parties, elections and the party system: The transformations of political representation 1990–2010. Sakkoulas [in Greek].

Vossen, K. (2011). Classifying Wilders: the ideological development of Geert Wilders and his Party for Freedom. *Politics, 31*(3), 179–189.

Wattenberg, M. P. (2000). The decline of party mobilization. In Dalton, R. J., & Wattenberg, M. P. (Eds.). *Parties without partisans: Political change in advanced industrial democracies.* Oxford University Press, 64–76.

Webb, P. D. (1994). Party organizational change in Britain: The iron law of centralization? In Katz, R. S., & Mair, P. (Eds.). *How parties organize: Change and adaptation in party organizations in western democracies.* Sage, 109–133.

Webb, P. (2002). Introduction. In Webb, P., Farrell, D., & Holliday, I. (Eds.). *Political parties in advanced industrial democracies*. Oxford University Press, 1–15.

Webb, P., Farrell, D., & Holliday, I. (Eds.). (2002). *Political parties in advanced industrial democracies*. Oxford University Press.

Welch, D. (2004). Nazi propaganda and the Volksgemeinschaft: Constructing a people's community. *Journal of Contemporary History*, *39*(2), 213–238.

Whiteley, P. F. (2011). Is the party over?: The decline of party activism and membership across the democratic world. *Party Politics*, *17*(1), 21–44.

Whiteley, P., & Seyd, P. (1992). Labour's vote and local activism: The impact of local constituency campaigns. *Parliamentary Affairs*, *45*(4), 582–595.

Whiteley, P. F., & Seyd, P. (1994). Local party campaigning and electoral mobilization in Britain. *Journal of Politics*, *56*(1), 242–252.

(1998). The dynamics of party activism in Britain: A spiral of demobilization?. *British Journal of Political Science*, *28*(1), 113–137.

Widfeldt, A. (2014). *Extreme right parties in Scandinavia*. Routledge.

Zald, M. N., & McCarthy, J. D. (1979). *The dynamics of social movements: Resource mobilization, social control, and tactics*. Little Brown & Co.

Party and Other Material

Amnesty International (2014). Impunity, excessive force and links to extremist Golden Dawn blight Greek police.

Council Framework Decision 2008/913/JHA (2008). Combating certain forms and expressions of racism and xenophobia by means of criminal law. Official Journal of the European Union L 328/55.

CFR-CDF [E.U. Network of Independent Experts on Fundamental Rights] (2005). Report on the Situation of Fundamental Human Rights in the European Union.

Danish People's Party (2002). Program of the Danish People's Party [downloaded on April 4, 2016, from http://tinyurl.com/jawzomw]

European Court of Human Rights (2013). Hungarian authorities' dissolution of association involved in anti-Roma rallies and paramilitary parading was not disproportionate [downloaded on May 5, 2015, from https://goo.gl/fV6dKk]

Golden Dawn (2012a). Ideology [downloaded on April 4, 2016, from https://goo.gl/wFHrZa]

(2012b). Identity [downloaded on April 4, 2016, from https://goo.gl/R9BRfb]

(2012c). Political Positions [downloaded on April 4, 2016, from https://goo.gl/Rgg3HK]

(2012d). Statutes of the political party with the name "Popular Association – Golden Dawn."

(2016). "A modern and dynamic ideological movement." Ideological pamphlet prepared for the 8th congress. Athens.

Human Rights Watch (2012). Hate on the streets: xenophobic violence in Greece.

Jobbik (2003). Manifesto [downloaded on April 4, 2016, from https://goo.gl/XdJf4F]

    (2010). "Radical change: A guide to Jobbik's parliamentary electoral manifesto for national self-determination and social justice."

LSNS (2016). Kotleba – Ľudová strana Naše Slovensko: Volebný program politickej strany [https://goo.gl/SX94m6]

NPD (2013). NPD Bundeswahltagsprogram 2013 [downloaded from https://goo.gl/1VCEfd].

Venice Commission (2000). Guidelines on the prohibition of political parties and analogous measures.

United Kingdom Independence Party (2015). Believe in Britain: UKIP manifesto.

Index